THE CAMBRIDGE COMPANION TO
PASCAL

Each volume in this series of companions to major philosophers contains specially commissioned essays by an international team of scholars, together with a substantial
bibliography, and will serve as a reference work for students
and non-specialists. One aim of the series is to dispel the in-
timidation such readers often feel when faced with the work
of a difficult and challenging thinker.

Blaise Pascal (1623–62) occupies a position of pivotal
importance in many domains: philosophy, mathematics,
physics, religious polemics and apologetics. In this volume a
team of leading scholars presents the full range of Pascal's
achievement and surveys the intellectual background of
his thought and the reception of his work. In addition to
chapters on Pascal's life and intellectual legacy, topics include his work on probability, decision theory, physics,
philosophy of science, theory of knowledge, philosophical
method, polemics, biblical interpretation, grace and religious
belief, the social world, and the art of persuasion.

New readers and non-specialists will find this the most
convenient and accessible guide to Pascal currently available. Advanced students and specialists will find a conspec-
tus of recent developments in the interpretation of Pascal.

NICHOLAS HAMMOND is Senior Lecturer in the Depart-
ment of French, Cambridge University, and Director of
Studies in Modern Languages at Gonville and Caius College,
Cambridge.

T0381599

NEWTON   *Edited by* I. BERNARD COHEN *and*
  GEORGE E. SMITH
NIETZSCHE   *Edited by* BERND MAGNUS *and*
  KATHLEEN HIGGINS
OCKHAM   *Edited by* PAUL VINCENT SPADE
PLATO   *Edited by* RICHARD KRAUT
PLOTINUS   *Edited by* LLOYD P. GERSON
ROUSSEAU   *Edited by* PATRICK RILEY
SARTRE   *Edited by* CHRISTINA HOWELLS
SCHOPENHAUER   *Edited by* CHRISTOPHER JANAWAY
THE SCOTTISH ENLIGHTENMENT   *Edited by*
  ALEXANDER BROADIE
SPINOZA   *Edited by* DON GARRETT
WITTGENSTEIN   *Edited by* HANS SLUGA *and*
  DAVID STERN

The Cambridge Companion to
PASCAL

Edited by

Nicholas Hammond
University of Cambridge

CAMBRIDGE
UNIVERSITY PRESS

University Printing House, Cambridge CB2 8BS, United Kingdom

Cambridge University Press is part of the University of Cambridge.

It furthers the University's mission by disseminating knowledge in the pursuit of education, learning and research at the highest international levels of excellence.

www.cambridge.org
Information on this title: www.cambridge.org/9780521006118

© Cambridge University Press 2003

First published 2003

A catalogue record for this publication is available from the British Library

ISBN 978-0-521-80924-5 Hardback
ISBN 978-0-521-00611-8 Paperback

CONTENTS

FIGURES

ACKNOWLEDGEMENTS

I am very grateful to all the contributors for their knowledge and helpfulness. Emma Gilby assisted me enormously both by writing a translation of one of the chapters and by reading parts of the volume. Bradley Stephens provided help with the bibliography. Alexei Kudrin has been a constant source of support and strength. Some of the work on this book was done while I was on sabbatical leave from Gonville and Caius College and the Department of French at Cambridge University, and I would like to thank them for allowing me this opportunity. Hilary Hammond's exemplary work as copy-editor and Jackie Warren of Cambridge University Press made my task much easier. My warmest thanks go to Hilary Gaskin, my editor at Cambridge University Press; she has been unfailingly good-humoured, supportive and efficient.

CONTRIBUTORS

HÉLÈNE BOUCHILLOUX is Professor of Philosophy at the Université de Nancy 2. She is the author of *Apologétique et raison dans les pensées de Pascal* (1995) and the editor of Locke, *Que la religion chrétienne est très-raisonnable* (1999).

DESMOND CLARKE is Professor of Philosophy at University College, Cork. His publications include *Descartes' Philosophy of Science* (1982), *Occult Powers and Hypotheses* (1989), translations of La Barre – *Equality of the Sexes* (1990) – and La Forge – *Treatise on the Human Mind* (1997) – and a two-volume Penguin edition of Descartes (1998, 1999).

A. W. F. EDWARDS is Professor of Biometry at the University of Cambridge and author of *Pascal's Arithmetical Triangle* (1987 and 2002). His other books include *Likelihood* (1972 and 1992) and *Foundations of Mathematical Genetics* (1977 and 2000).

JON ELSTER is Professor of Political Science and Philosophy at Columbia University, New York. Among his recent works are *Alchemies of the Mind* (1999) and *Ulysses Unbound* (2000).

PIERRE FORCE is Nell and Herbert M. Singer Professor of Contemporary Civilization and Chairman of the French Department at Columbia University. He is the author of *Le Problème herméneutique chez Pascal* (1989), *Molière ou le prix des choses* (1994) and editor of *De la morale à l'économie politique* (1996).

DANIEL C. FOUKE is Associate Professor of Philosophy at the University of Dayton and author of *The Enthusiastical Concerns of*

Dr Henry More (1996) as well as various articles on early modern philosophy and theology.

NICHOLAS HAMMOND is Senior Lecturer in French at Cambridge University and Director of Studies in Modern Languages at Gonville and Caius College, Cambridge. He is editor of the Duckworth New Readings series and also the author of *Playing with Truth: Language and the Human Condition in Pascal's Pensées* (1994) and *Creative Tensions: An Introduction to Seventeenth-century French Literature* (1997) as well as an edition and various articles on French theatre and thought.

JEAN KHALFA is Newton Trust Lecturer in French at Trinity College, Cambridge. He is editor of the Routledge French Thought and Religion series and his publications include editing *What is Intelligence?* (1994), *The Dialogue Between Painting and Poetry. Livres d'artistes in France, 1874–1999* (2001) and *An Introduction to the Complete Philosophical Work of Gilles Deleuze* (forthcoming). He has also published on Francophone writing, poetry, modern philosophy and cinema.

ANTONY MCKENNA is Professor in French Literature at the University of Saint-Etienne and author of *De Pascal à Voltaire. Le rôle des Pensées de Pascal dans l'histoire des idées entre 1670 et 1734* (1990).

MICHAEL MORIARTY is Professor of French Literature and Thought at Queen Mary, University of London. He is the author of *Taste and Ideology in Seventeenth-century France* (1988) and *Roland Barthes* (1991).

RICHARD PARISH is Professor of French at the University of Oxford and a Fellow of St Catherine's College. He is the author of *Pascal's Lettres provinciales: A Study in Polemic* (1989) and *Racine: The Limits of Tragedy* (1993) as well as a range of briefer studies, editions and articles.

HENRY PHILLIPS is Professor of French at the University of Manchester and is the author of *The Theatre and its Critics in Seventeenth-century France* (1980), *Racine: Language and Theatre* (1994) and *Church and Culture in Seventeenth-century France* (1997).

BEN ROGERS is a senior research fellow at the Institute for Public Policy Research. He is also the author of *Blaise Pascal: In Praise of Vanity* (1998), *A. J. Ayer, a Life* (1999), and *'Beef and Liberty': Roast Beef and English Identity* (2003).

DAVID WETSEL is Professor of French Literature at Arizona State University. He is the author of *Pascal and Disbelief: Catechesis and Conversion in the Pensées* (1995) and *L'Ecriture et le reste: The Pensées of Pascal in the Exegetical Tradition of Port-Royal* (1982) and editor of the six-volume *Actes de tempe: hommage à Jean Mesnard* (2002).

CHRONOLOGY

1651–4   Frequents worldly circles and works on mathematics
1653   Pope Innocent X condemns the 'five propositions'
         believed to be found in Jansen's *Augustinus*
1654   Writes his *Traité du triangle arithmétique*. On 23
         November has a mystical experience known as his
         'night of fire', recorded in the *Mémorial*
1655   Goes on retreat to Port-Royal des Champs. His
         conversation with one of the spiritual directors, Sacy,
         is recorded by Sacy's secretary Fontaine. Possible date
         of composition of *De L'Esprit géométrique*. Possible
         date of composition of *Ecrits sur la grâce*
1656   Start of his *Lettres provinciales*, defending Antoine
         Arnauld and then attacking the Jesuits
1657   Final of his *Lettres provinciales*
1658   Works on the cycloid. Presents plan of his apologetic
         project at Port-Royal des Champs
1659   Falls ill
1660   Writes *Trois discours sur la condition des grands*
1661   Nuns at Port-Royal, including Jacqueline, forced
         to sign anti-Jansenist formulary. Jacqueline dies
         4 October
1662   First omnibus service instituted by Pascal in Paris.
         Falls ill in the spring and dies on 19 August
1670   Posthumous publication by Port-Royal of Pascal's
         Pensées

ABBREVIATIONS

Throughout this book references to Pascal's works are made in parentheses in the main body of the text. References to the Complete Works (*Oeuvres complètes*) will be from the two-volume Pléiade edition by Michel Le Guern (Paris: Gallimard, 1998–2000), by volume and page number, e.g. *OC* 1, 235. All references to the *Pensées* will give the Lafuma and Sellier numberings, e.g. L 177/S 208.

NICHOLAS HAMMOND

Introduction

> The principles of pleasure are not firm and steadfast. They
> are different for everyone, and vary in each particular, with
> such diversity that there is no one more unlike another
> than themselves at different periods.
>
> (De l'esprit géométrique, OC II, 174)

Pascal is a name familiar to students and scholars in an astonishingly wide range of disciplines. Mathematicians recognise him through Pascal's Triangle or Pascal's calculating machine (which itself gave its name to a computer language). Physicists and historians of science (as well as those in technological fields) acknowledge his pioneering work on the vacuum. The word *jesuitical* owes its pejorative sense exclusively to Pascal's blistering satirical attack on the Society of Jesus in his *Provincial Letters*. Students of philosophy and theology know him through Pascal's famous Wager, which itself forms part of one of the most renowned pieces of religious apologetics, the *Pensées*. Even early forms of train-spotter (or, rather, coach-spotter) have cause to be grateful to him for helping to set up the first public transport system in Paris. It is a sobering thought that he achieved all this, having suffered from years of ill health, before the age of 39, when he died.

In our age of increasing specialisation, perhaps unsurprisingly, very few books have been able to reflect adequately the diversity of Pascal's achievements. Moreover, all too often studies of Pascal can be uncritical of his work, sometimes amounting simply to hagiographies of the man. It is hoped that this *Companion* to Pascal will go some way not only toward weaving together the many strands of his thought and influence, but also to offer a balanced view of his work.

I

Although each of the chapters can be read separately, various links between the chapters will enable the reader to make connections between the different areas of Pascal's output.

Pascal lived at a time of political and religious upheaval, which is reflected in much of his writing. In chapter 1 Ben Rogers examines Pascal's life within the context of seventeenth-century France, and ponders the paradox of how much and yet how little we know of Pascal the man. In order to understand more fully the influence exerted by Pascal on subsequent generations of writers, it is essential to explore those thinkers who influenced him. Many names will reappear over the course of this book, but none more so than two major writers. In chapter 2 Henry Phillips considers Montaigne (whose *Essais* Pascal knew well) and Descartes (whom Pascal met on two occasions), both of whom shaped Pascal's thought as much as he reacted against them.

Pascal's achievements in the field of mathematics are discussed in chapters 3 and 4. A. W. F. Edwards considers briefly Pascal's work on mathematics as a whole before analysing in detail Pascal's treatise on the Arithmetical Triangle (chapter 3). In the following chapter Jon Elster explores decision theory from many angles of Pascal's output, comparing Pascal's conception of human behaviour with elements of modern decision theory and focusing particularly on the Wager.

The great contribution Pascal made to scientific research forms the basis of the next two chapters. Daniel Fouke's study of Pascal's physics (chapter 5) takes into account the major part played by experimentation in his investigation of the vacuum and the statics of fluids. Given the importance of experimental evidence in Pascal's scientific thought, Desmond Clarke examines in a chapter on Pascal's philosophy of science (chapter 6) the implications of such experiments and the concept of scientific knowledge, which Pascal formulated. Jean Khalfa develops this concept in chapter 7, in his piece on Pascal's theory of knowledge, extending his analysis to Pascal's religious thought.

Pascal's spiritual writing is marked by a particular conception of grace formulated by various thinkers who named themselves 'disciples of St Augustine'. Michael Moriarty demonstrates in his chapter on grace and religious belief (chapter 8) the role played by faith in Pascal's work, explaining also the background to seventeenth-century debates on grace that so dominate his *Writings on Grace*. It is to be expected, then, that biblical texts form an essential part of Pascal's opus. In 'Pascal and holy writ' (chapter 9) David Wetsel considers how biblical exegesis in Pascal's time differs greatly from modern biblical interpretation, at the same time showing how Pascal's rendering of aspects such as biblical chronology remain key to his apologetic writing.

The *Provincial Letters* are justly celebrated for the way in which Pascal makes what might have seemed like an obscure theological debate accessible to a wider readership. In Richard Parish's piece (chapter 10), Pascal's brilliance as polemicist and parodist is convincingly brought to the fore.

The remaining chapters of this book deal primarily with the *Pensées* and a number of related shorter texts. Pascal's contribution to social and political thought is shown by Hélène Bouchilloux in chapter 11 to form a coherent part of his wider persuasive aims. In chapter 12 Pierre Force considers the role of philosophical method, a term more often associated with Descartes. He refers to the part played by what he calls 'the business of persuasion' in Pascal's writing, and it is precisely this aspect which forms the focus of my discussion in chapter 13.

The final chapter, by Antony McKenna, is devoted to the extraordinary afterlife of the *Pensées* in the seventeenth and eighteenth centuries, dominated as it was by the influential readings of the original Port-Royal edition by such prominent thinkers as Malebranche and Bayle.

In the *Pensées* Pascal often states his abhorrence for indifference: for example, in L 427/S 681 he argues that 'the immortality of the soul is something which is of such importance to us and which touches us so profoundly that we must have lost all sense to be in a state of indifference as to what it is all about'. It would be safe to conclude that the many furious debates which his mathematical, scientific, philosophical and religious thought inspired both during his lifetime and in subsequent centuries convincingly prove his success in avoiding indifference in his reader. To provoke a reaction, whether positive or negative, represents for Pascal an important step in the search for truth.

It is hoped that this volume will lead readers back to Pascal's own writing, always so rich and provocative. As he would say, 'Vous êtes embarqué [You have embarked]'.

1 Pascal's life and times

We know little about Pascal. We also know a great deal about Pascal. We know little in the sense that Pascal never wrote about himself or his life in any detail, while contemporaries who did write about him offered something close to hagiography.[1] We know a great deal about him in the sense that his writings on science and human nature, society and salvation, tell us much about his view of the world and the developments of his day. We know or can confidently infer, to take a few random examples, how he perceived birth and death, royalty and papacy, Epictetus and Descartes, hare coursing and theatre-going, the execution of Charles I and the Peace of the Pyrenees.[2] Indeed, to the extent that his perceptions were always fresh and insightful – and that taken together they offer an almost unfathomably original and subtle philosophical vision – it is easy to feel that we know him intimately.

CHILDHOOD

France of the 1620s and 1630s, the France in which Pascal was raised, was one of Europe's major powers, the centre of a vibrant movement of Catholic renewal and of an increasingly educated and refined ruling class. But it was also a place of seething conflict and chronic political instability. The Wars of Religion, which very nearly led to the permanent break-up of France, had come to an end in 1594, when Henri IV took Paris, but civil war – identified by Pascal as 'the worst of evils' – remained a very real peril (L 94/S 128). Henri himself was assassinated in 1610 by a Catholic zealot who disapproved of his tolerant treatment of French Protestants ('Huguenots'), leaving the country in the hands of his 9-year-old son, Louis XIII. This brought renewed instability. True, Louis XIII eventually secured an outstanding first minister, Cardinal Richelieu, who, during a tenure of almost two decades (1624–42), succeeded in imposing a measure of order and political continuity on France. He demolished the few remaining French Protestant strongholds, most notably La Rochelle; pursued an aggressive foreign policy that took France into the Thirty Years' War; introduced new taxes, extended old ones, and imposed, where necessary, brutal measures to extract them; and clamped down on aristocratic lawlessness. The state he left behind was stronger and more centralised than the one he had inherited. But his policies provoked widespread unrest among a hungry and over-taxed populace and a resentful, much abused aristocracy. France's Protestants – some 5 per cent of the population – while cowed, were far from reconciled to their situation. And the Catholic Church itself harboured deep, perhaps growing, divisions between a cosmopolitan, 'high church' wing, represented at the extreme by the Jesuits, founded by Loyola in 1534 and closely connected to Rome, and a more rigorous, puritanical wing that felt a special loyalty to the French Catholic Church. The Pascal family identified closely with the latter.[3]

Pascal's parents, Antoinette Begon and Etienne Pascal, had married in 1616, when she was around 20 and he 28. Three of their children survived infancy: a daughter, Gilberte (b. 1620), Pascal (b. 1623) and another daughter, Jacqueline (b. 1625). In 1626, however, Antoinette died – Pascal would have had only the haziest memories of her. In her absence a governess, Louise Delfault, helped bring up Pascal and the two girls, but it was their father who exercised by far the greatest influence on them.

Etienne was a prominent member of the class of lawyers and government officials, the *noblesse de robe*, who had traditionally manned the upper echelons of the French state – his father had been one of the highest ranking officials in the Auvergne under Henri III. Trained as a lawyer himself, Etienne served as a tax assessor, then a senior financial magistrate (Président à la Cour des Aides), in the small administrative centre of Clermont, now Clermont-Ferrand, Auvergne's capital and the meeting place for one of France's twelve provincial tax courts.

But Etienne was much more than a civil servant: an accomplished humanist with fluent Greek and Latin, he was also one of the leading mathematicians of his age. In 1631, five years after Antoinette's death, he resigned from his legal duties, sold his position and moved with his family to Paris, in order to concentrate on his studies. There he became an important figure in the circle of natural philosophers gathered around the Minim friar Père Mersenne, a circle which included such leading mathematicians as Roberval, Desargues and Fermat and which maintained close links with Europe's scholarly elite, including Gassendi, Hobbes and Descartes (then resident in Holland). The Mersenne circle had already made their break with Aristotelian philosophy, which still dominated the universities, and must have viewed Rome's prosecution of Galileo, renewed in 1633, with horror.

Etienne attached great importance to schooling and, free of any official responsibilities, undertook to educate his children himself. Employing what was, even by today's standards, an exceptionally liberal or 'child-centred' approach, he favoured experimentation and discovery over rote learning. The children were encouraged to teach one another, were given household responsibilities and were involved in adult concerns and debates. Pascal showed his genius early on, producing, if his sister is to be believed, a little treatise on sound at the age of 11 and discovering Pythagoras' Theorem by himself at 12. This made him the talk of Paris. Etienne had not originally intended to introduce Pascal to mathemathics, the queen of sciences, until 15 or 16, but, seeing his aptitude and enthusiasm, he began to coach him. It was not long before Pascal was contributing on equal terms to the discussions within the Mersenne circle (*La Vie de M. Pascal par Mme Périer*, *OC* 1, 63–6). It is interesting to note that in 1634 Pascal's father had been appointed by Richelieu to an inquiry into the claims of the astrologer Jean-Baptiste Morin, professor of Mathemathics at the Collège Royal, to have discovered a way of establishing longitudes, so putting maritime navigation on to a scientific footing. The method did not prove sound (Morin refused to accept the earth's mobility), but Etienne's work on this problem seems to have stimulated Pascal, whose *Pensées* often use images of disorientation – of drifting, lost at sea – to evoke the predicament of man without God: 'Just as I do not know from where I come, so I do not know where I am going... Such is my state, full of weakness and uncertainty' (L 427/S 681).[4]

Whatever credit Pascal's father gained for his work on this inquiry was jeopardised a year later. Having sold his Clermont presidency in 1634, Etienne had invested heavily in government bonds. When in 1638 the French state, its finances stretched to breaking point by its entry into the Thirty Years' War, defaulted on these, Etienne took a leading part in the protests. Threatened with the Bastille, he fled to the Auvergne, where he would have had to remain in disgrace had it not been for Jacqueline. Educated, like Pascal, into an appreciation of good writing, she had developed into a talented poet and actress – Blaise was not the only Pascal talked about in the *salons*. After appearing in 1639 in a private performance laid on for Richelieu, she introduced herself to the cardinal, charmed him and made representation on behalf of her father, who was forgiven. The episode reminds us that the Pascals were connected not just to Paris's leading scientific circles, but also to its social ones – Jacqueline, at least, was a not infrequent visitor to the royal court. But it also reminds us that even a good loyalist like Etienne could find himself on the wrong side of the state. Pascal's life would illustrate the point again and again.

ROUEN

Richelieu, in fact, did more than forgive Etienne. No sooner had he returned to Paris than the cardinal gave him the post of chief tax officer to Rouen, Normandy's capital city, then in the throes of violent unrest provoked by bad harvests, high taxes and an outbreak of the plague. It was a position of great responsibility and Etienne appears to have executed his duties diligently, refusing to enrich himself at the tax-payer's expense. The three Pascal children, who were extremely close to their father, accompanied him to Rouen, where Pascal spent the early years of his adult life. This was the third place in which the young Blaise lived, and it is tempting to suggest that each added a layer to his imagination. If the *Pensées'* frequent evocations of vertiginous drops and dangerous abysses can be traced to the steep hills and volcanic peaks of Pascal's native Auvergne, and that work's many images of urban life to Paris, then perhaps Rouen, an important trading centre on the Seine, represents another source for his recurrent resort to watery and maritime metaphors. Perhaps it was a source, too, for some of Pascal's more graphic evocations of violence; though the worst of the unrest was put down before Blaise's arrival, its embers occasionally burst into flame.

Notwithstanding the presence of Pierre Corneille, whom the Pascals befriended, intellectual life was necessarily more constricted in Rouen than it was in Paris. It was here, however, that Pascal began to establish an international reputation as a mathematician and experimenter. In 1639 Mersenne had written to Descartes telling him about work that Etienne's young son was doing on conic sections. In 1640 he published a short treatise on projective geometry, *Essai pour les coniques*. In 1642 he produced a plan for a calculating machine capable of adding, subtracting, dividing and multiplying sums up to six figures long. Pascal was heavily involved in his father's tax work; the *machine d'arithmétique* was invented, he explained, to help with the tedious calculations it involved, though he also hoped that it could be of help to the public more generally (*Lettre Dédicatoire, OC* 1, 331). Over the next few years Pascal worked with an anonymous local craftsman to produce over fifty models of different construction and made from different materials, before arriving at the efficient and hard-wearing model he patented (*OC* 1, 340). The device was costly and Pascal's efforts to market it met with little success, but at least six survive, most of which are in good working order. They provide lasting physical testimony to Pascal's skill as a mathematician and an engineer.

Soon after putting the finishing touches to his adding machine, Pascal heard of the controversy caused by experiments conducted by the Florentine, Torricelli, a disciple of Galileo. When a tube filled with mercury was turned upside down in a basin of the same substance, an apparently empty space appeared at the end of the tube. What was in it? More modern-minded scientists, including Torricelli, contended that space was indeed empty, but orthodox scholastic thinkers taught, as a mainstay of scholastic science, to believe that 'nature abhors a vacuum', disagreed. With the aid of his father and a family friend, Pierre Petit, Richelieu's chief military and naval engineer, Pascal decided to repeat these experiments for himself. This marked the beginning of a series of extraordinarily elaborate and rigorous investigations stretching over four years, by which Pascal attempted to discredit, for once and for all, the scholastic doctrine, while also establishing the fact of atmospheric pressure. Pascal, who advocated the still novel view that scientific disputes should be resolved by appeal to the senses and reason rather than to ancient authority, made a point of involving neutral observers in his experiments, and reporting his findings in as clear and objective a manner as possible.[5] This helped make his arguments all the more conclusive.

The controversy provoked by these experiments brought Pascal for the first time into open conflict with the Jesuits in the person of Père Noel, rector of the Jesuit Collège de Clermont in Paris and a dedicated upholder of scientific tradition. The two men exchanged a series of letters, Pascal treating the holy father's argument for 'a refined air' that entered the test tube through 'tiny pores' in the glass with an exaggerated respect bordering on mockery, and the Jesuit in turn, twisting and turning in an attempt to find answers to Pascal's objections. By this stage, however, Pascal had other reasons for quarrelling with the Society of Jesus.

When, early in 1646, Etienne Pascal had fallen and broken a leg, two local gentlemen who were expert bone-setters, the Deschamps brothers, moved in to take care of him. These two men turned out to be disciples of Jean Duvergier de Hauranne, the abbé de Saint-Cyran, who, until his death in 1643, had been spiritual director to the nuns of Port-Royal.

There is no need here to go into the history of Port-Royal in detail. It is enough to highlight two turning points. First, in the early years of the seventeenth century, under its formidable abbess, La Mère Angélique, the ancient Cistercian convent had moved from its old premises outside Paris – Port-Royal des Champs – to a large site within the city, gaining a reputation for rigour and extreme devotion in the process. (From 1648 they occupied both sites.) Second, in the course of the 1630s and early 1640s, under Saint-Cyran's direction, Port-Royal had ceased to be merely a convent and had become a centre of the French Augustinian movement, attracting influential friends and supporters. The Princesse de Guémené and the Marquise de Sablé, for instance, both leading society figures, took lodgings there. At the same time, a number of young, high-born male *solitaires* gathered first around Port-Royal de Paris and then in some buildings adjacent to the old Port-Royal des Champs, where they passed their time in penance, in worship and (much more unconventionally) in manual labour. The Augustinians of Port-Royal defined themselves as much against the optimistic views of the Jesuits as they did against the opposite extreme of the Protestants, and in accordance with what they took to be the teachings of

St Augustine, emphasised man's corruption and feebleness and his need to find salvation in a self-abnegating love of God. When Pascal wrote

> Without Christ man can only be vicious and wretched. With Christ man is free from vice and wretchedness.
>
> In him is all our virtue and all our happiness.
>
> Apart from him there is only vice, wretchedness, error, darkness, death, despair (L 416/S 1)

he was giving expression to characteristically Augustinian sentiments.

At first, under the leadership of Saint-Cyran, Port-Royal was known for the particularly rigorous forms of penitence and devotion it encouraged and for the good works it promoted, including, famously, the establishment of pioneering children's classes, the *petites écoles de Port-Royal*.[6] But, from the mid-1640s the convent became embroiled in the quarrel caused by its refusal to condemn a book, the *Augustinus*, by the Flemish theologian Jansenius, who argued that Augustine himself had taught that all human virtue was false virtue and that an individual's salvation lay entirely in the hands of God.

It would be quite wrong to suggest that the Pascal family were, even prior to the encounter with the Deschamps brothers, in any way religiously sceptical. Etienne was probably a good modern-minded Catholic, who, somewhat in the tradition of Montaigne, combined a devotion to the Bible and the ancient fathers with a strong allergy to speculative theology, especially the scholastic variant. Gilberte reported that he subscribed to the principle that 'anything that was a matter of faith, could not be a matter for reason' (*OC* 1, 68). His children would have been instructed in the Bible, the ancient fathers and the history of the church.

The Deschamps brothers, nevertheless, had a profound effect on the Pascal family. Giving Blaise works of spiritual guidance by Saint-Cyran, Jansenius and Antoine Arnauld – Saint-Cyran's successor as leader of the Augustinian movement, a gifted theologian with close family ties to Port-Royal – they converted first him and then, through him, the rest of the family to a more demanding form of Christian devotion. Jacqueline, perhaps the most bowled over of all, decided that she wanted to join the nuns of Port-Royal, but was restrained from doing so by Etienne, who though himself 'converted' by the Rouen encounter, did not want to lose a daughter.

RETURN TO PARIS

In the summer of 1647 Pascal moved back to Paris, accompanied by Jacqueline. Suffering from an illness that has never been identified, he had for some months been paralysed from the waist down, was irritable and impatient and could only take nourishment in the form of warm liquid, swallowed drop by drop. Against his doctor's advice, he continued his scientific work and was visited by Descartes – the two men, who disagreed about the vacuum, among other things, did not become friends. He also began to visit Port-Royal, taking the monastery's side in the bitter debate then developing about Jansen's doctrines as defended by Antoine Arnauld, and a powerful theologian in his own right. But ties between Pascal and Port-Royal were not yet close, Pascal writing to Gilberte that his spiritual advisor there, M. de Rebours, was wary of his (Pascal's) confidence in his mental powers and that Pascal, in turn, did not feel able to submit to his spiritual guidance (OC 11, 4–7).

In the early 1640s, when the Pascals were in Rouen, Richelieu and Louis XIII died, exposing France yet again to the dangers of a royal minority – the king's heir, Louis XIV, was only 4 years of age. At first the political scene, artfully managed by Richelieu's Italian successor, Cardinal Mazarin, remained relatively calm. In 1648, however, at the end of eighteen years of expensive warfare, matters came to a head. The government's desperate attempt to squeeze yet more money out of the owners of France's royal officers, and the hasty U-turn that followed on the first signs of resistance, unleashed a series of violent countrywide uprisings known as the Fronde. Pascal came from the officer class that led the first stage of the revolt, the *Fronde parlementaire*, and must have felt a certain sympathy with the parliamentarians' complaints that the government had mishandled the country's finances and abused its tax-raising powers. But he was convinced that insubordination would only make matters worse – that ultimately it was the poor who would suffer – and hence opposed active opposition (L 60/S 94; L 85/S 119).

The Pascals, fleeing Paris, went to stay with the oldest Pascal daughter, Gilberte, and her husband, Florin Pèrier, in Clermont. Not perhaps quite as accomplished as Pascal or Jacqueline, Gilberte and her family were nevertheless important figures in Pascal's life. Florin had conducted a famous experiment for him on Auvergne's highest summit, the puy-de-Dôme; Pascal sent carefully written letters of spiritual guidance to Gilberte; she in turn looked after him in illness and would, after his death, produce an artfully constructed, beautifully vivid, not always reliable biography – one which offered his life as an exemplary progression from worldly engagement, through conversions, to devotion and good works.[7]

The Pascals returned to Paris a year or so later. In September 1651, the same month as Louis XIV came of age, Pascal's father died, eliciting a letter of great grace and beauty to Gilberte that reflected, in characteristically abstract terms, on death. The pagan philosophers had nothing helpful to say about death because they saw it as natural to man, when in fact it was a product of sin. When undergone by a true Christian, death marks the point at which the soul rids itself of the last traces of sin and enters into union with Christ (OC 11, 19). 'We must search for consolation for our afflictions [maux] not in ourselves, not in other people, not in creation, but in God' (OC 11, 15). Within a few months Jacqueline had fulfilled her ambition and entered Port-Royal as a nun, leaving Pascal to live by himself.

Pascal was now 28, one of the most distinguished natural philosophers of his day, and financially independent, albeit in a modest way, for the first time in his life. He took advantage of his new situation, spending more time than ever before in the company of what passed, by the austere standards of Port-Royal, for corrupt, worldly circles.

In the summer of June 1652 he sent Queen Christina of Sweden, known for her enlightened patronage of writers and philosophers, one of his adding machines, along with a dedicatory letter (Lettre á la sérénisme reine de Suède) in which he heaped praise on the queen for combining the great and admirable attribute of temporal authority with the still greater and more admirable one of intellectual accomplishment. The religious perspective that dominated his letter to Gilberte on his father's death and that would later, in the Pensées, frame his treatment of the relation between political power and intellectual achievement is here not even hinted at (L 58/S 91 and 92).

WORLDLY PERIOD

In the course of the next few years Pascal became very close to his childhood friend, the duc de Roannez, one the highest-born noblemen in France, who was destined for a great future as a statesman – the two men shared a deep interest in maths and physics. Roannez, in turn, introduced Pascal to two older gentlemen, the chevalier de Méré and Damien Mitton. (Mitton appears as a worldly interlocutor in several of the *Pensées'* fragments.) These aristocratic, sensuous, free-thinking and well-read connoisseurs had worked the gentlemanly code of *honnêteté* or good breeding into something like a full-blown, philosophical ethic – one that attached an extreme value to a rounded versatile sociability, defined in opposition to all forms of selfishness, small-mindedness and pedantry. Pascal would later repudiate this as being based, at bottom, on nothing but pride and vanity: 'The self is hateful. You cover it up, Mitton, but that does not mean that you take it away. So you are still hateful' (L 597/S 494). But his connection with men like Méré and Mitton gave him a formidable value system to argue against, and, paradoxically, greatly enriched his understanding of a good Christian life. Pascal admired the *honnête* ideal of a finely tuned sensitivity to other people's needs, believing that it offered a standard that Christians, and Christians alone, could hope to meet (L 647/S 532, L 778/S 643). Prompted by Méré, a keen gambler, Pascal, still scientifically active, began to work on a method for determining an equitable distribution of stakes between participants in a game terminated before its conclusion. The result, formulated in letters to the Toulouse mathematician Fermat and in some unpublished papers, laid the ground for modern probability theory.

For a long time biographers saw this period after his father's death as marking a new 'worldly phase' in Pascal's life, but this is now generally conceded to have been much overdone. Pascal certainly seems to have gone somewhat adrift during these years. He quarrelled with Jacqueline, who wanted to donate all of her wealth to Port-Royal, and doubtless missed her presence in his life. He threw himself into a social round at once beguiling and disappointing – as all *divertissements*, Pascal believed, were destined to be (L 135/S 168, L 620/S 513, etc.). And he found himself dwelling, perhaps a little too much, on his scientific reputation – on what Jacqueline, who came, at this time, to fear for his soul, called 'l'estime et la mémoire des hommes' (*OC* 1, 24). Yet Pascal was never tempted by religious scepticism or sensual indulgence. There was never a Pascal *libertin*.[8]

CONVERSION

We know, moreover, from the letters Jacqueline wrote to Gilberte, that even at the height of his social engagement, and while pursuing his mathematical and scientific inquiries, Pascal felt hollow and unfulfilled, and that he began, in the course of 1654, to seek frequent spiritual counsel with Jacqueline at Port-Royal.[9] Then, quite suddenly, on the night of 23 November between about 10.30 and 12.30, Pascal underwent an extraordinary spiritual conversion, in which, his pride finally humbled, he felt the presence of God – an experience he immediately recorded on a piece of parchment that he then carried with him, sewn into his jacket, for the rest of his life. The 'Memorial', with its simple juxtapositions of words, phrases and biblical quotations, and its explicit repudiation of the 'God of the philosophers' in favour of the 'God of Abraham, God of Isaac, God of Jacob', gave powerful expression to the fervent, Bible-centred spirituality of Port-Royal.

It would be quite wrong to suggest that Pascal had now reached an end to his spiritual journey. The Augustinians recognised no such end for any but saints and angels; ordinary men would always be prey to temptations, distractions and doubts. But this second conversion was decisive in the sense that Pascal now became much more single-minded in his devotion, put himself under the spiritual direction of Antoine Singlin, the head of Port-Royal, and remained closely allied to the convent and its cause for the rest of his life.

In January 1655 Pascal went to Port-Royal des Champs to join the *solitaires*. It was probably during this stay that he had the conversation with the nuns' confessor, Isaac de Saci (recorded in the *Conversation avec M. de Saci*), in which, in an early version of the *pour au contre* method he would adopt in the *Pensées*, he used the sceptical Montaigne to disqualify the Stoic, Epictetus, and Epictetus to disqualify Montaigne, so as to clear the way for a Christian resolution of problems that both philosophers had highlighted. It was a dazzling performance – a little too dazzling perhaps for the devout de Sacy. It was also during this time or soon afterwards that Pascal is believed to have produced some of his best-known spiritual writing, including *Ecrit sur la conversion de pécheur*, *Le Mystère de Jésus* and the 'Infini-rien' passage – the famous wager – later to be included in the *Pensées*.

An important backdrop to Pascal's conversion and subsequent association with Port-Royal is provided by the gradual intensification of the battle over Jansenius' *Augustinus*. Although the Augustinians of Port-Royal had the support of many French priests, including some prominent reforming bishops, France's leaders – Richelieu, Mazarin and Louis XIV – disapproved of the tone of Port-Royal's Christianity. They feared its desperate emphasis on human corruption and its steadfast renunciation of all worldly values would undermine the social order, weaken faith and play into the hands of the Protestants. In 1653 a papal bull, *Cum occasione*, had condemned five propositions relating to grace, which it was claimed Jansenius had advanced. In the same year Mazarin began the long processes to ensure that the French church formally accepted the bull. Meanwhile, early in 1655 the duc de Liancourt, an old friend of Port-Royal, was refused the sacrament at the church of Saint-Sulpice, in Paris, for his Jansenist sympathies. Antoine Arnauld responded with two open 'letters' – in fact thick tomes – in which he attacked his opponents, denied that the five propositions were to be found in Jansenius and reiterated unequivocally determinist, Augustianian views on grace. His enemies succeeded in having him arraigned before Paris's Faculty of Theology (the 'Sorbonne') and censured.

THE *LETTRES PROVINCIALES*

By this time the Augustinians had turned to Pascal for help. He responded with a series of best-selling pseudonymous 'letters', the *Provinciales*, produced with the help of Arnauld and his colleague, Nicole, in the utmost secrecy. (Had their role been identified, they would have faced imprisonment or worse.) Adopting the persona of a concerned but bemused outsider, who sets out to explain to a friend in the provinces (hence the 'Provincial Letters') what is really going on in the Sorbonne, Pascal's first letters had attempted to demonstrate that opposition to Arnauld was of an entirely opportunistic kind; the Thomists' and Jesuits' agreement on empty terms hid a deep disagreement on matters of substance. When Arnauld was expelled from the Sorbonne, Pascal necessarily changed tack. The next seven letters mock the Jesuit's practical ethical doctrines – their teaching on sin and penance. Pascal's chief point here was to demonstrate, by citing published Jesuit texts, that in their eagerness to win allies and converts, the company, rather than adhering to more exacting supernatural standards of properly Christian ethics, permitted things – lying, murder, adultery – which were forbidden by natural law. Letters 11 to 17 represent a second change in tactics, as their author addresses himself directly to the Jesuits, defending his earlier accusations against them and answering their attacks on him. Irony has been replaced by anger and indignation. Indeed, by this stage Pascal had dropped his persona, if not his anonymity.[10] The letters address real people and the voice is Pascal's own.

It is easy for us, drenched in newspapers and television reporting and living in a society where public opinion and consumer preference are recognised as the last authority in almost everything, to underestimate the *Provinciales'* novelty and force. Pascal took an intensely important but obscure conflict, hitherto the preserve of trained theologians and casuists, and, by artfully combining the letter form with reportage and dialogue, made it the subject of a gripping drama. The achievement is all the more stunning when it is recalled that the *Provinciales* represent a new departure for Pascal: previously he had written only on scientific and spiritual topics.

We do not know why, after two final letters pillorying Louis XIV's Jesuit confessor, Father Annat, the *Provinciales* stop abruptly – perhaps it was simply too dangerous to go on with them, perhaps Pascal worried that they were merely calling further persecution on Port-Royal. This, however, was not the end of Pascal's involvement in religious polemic. The battle was over, but the war continued. Pascal had a hand in Antoine le Maître's *Lettre d'un avocat au parlement* (1657), which attempted to dissuade the Paris *Parlement*, semi-successfully, from registering *Cum occasione*, and wrote several 'letters' (*Ecrits des curés de Paris*) supporting a successful campaign to have a new Jesuit text, *Apologie pour les casuites*, condemned by the Parisian authorities.

But these, the final years of Pascal's activities, saw him pursuing a host of other projects too. Soon after his own second conversion, Pascal had succeeded in converting his good friend, the duc de Roannez, so deterring him from a profitable marriage. Now, while in the midst of the *Provinciales* campaign, Pascal embarked on a long and moving correspondence with the duc's younger sister, Charlotte de Roannez, who was wrestling with the decision of whether to join the nuns of Port-Royal. The letters, or the portions of them that survive, though impersonal, are intimate in tone. They show a Pascal whom we do not quite see anywhere else: a man happy to offer advice on Christian duty, penance and devotion; one who feels confident that he is on the right path, even if he cannot be sure of getting to his destination. In 1658 Pascal, encouraged by the duc de Roannez, who saw a chance of winning Port-Royal further intellectual credibility, launched an international competition, inviting solutions to the problem of the 'roulette' or cycloid – the problem of tracing the path of a point on the circumference of a wheel moving along a straight line. Pascal, who had first become interested in the matter while trying to distract himself from a crippling bout of toothache, had already identified a solution; declaring that none of the entries submitted to him was adequate or correct, he produced a series of papers and letters that helped lay the basis of infinitesimal calculus.[11]

THE *PENSÉES*

One project, above all, however, dominated these years – or at least our perspective on them. In March 1656, between the fifth and sixth *Provinciale*, Pascal's niece Marguerite Périer was cured of a long-standing eye abscess after touching a relic of the Holy Thorn – supposedly part of the Crown of Thorns that Christ hard worn on the cross – kept at Port-Royal. Pascal, like other Port-Royalists, interpreted this as a sign of divine favour, and began work on a treatise on the theory and history of Judeo-Christian miracles. This project slowly evolved into a broader, more ambitious work, aimed at converting the open-minded, worldly sceptic – a Méré or a Mitton – to Christianity. In the summer or perhaps the autumn of 1658, more than two years after the Miracle of the Holy Thorn, Pascal gave a talk at Port-Royal, laying out his basic approach.

We will never know whether, had Pascal had the time, he would have completed this 'apology' for the Christian religion or what form it would have taken if he did.[12] Pascal, after all, left many unfinished works behind him (most notably the *Ecrits sur la grâce*, a rough series of 'letters' aimed at clarifying and defending Augustinian teachings on grace, written at the time of the *Provinciales*). As it was, he had got no further than producing a large body of notes towards the project, some of which he then ordered under provisional headings and which today constitute the first half of the *Pensées*, before falling seriously ill. Looking back, we can see that Pascal produced his greatest work – *Provinciales*, *Ecrits des curés de Paris*, his writings on grace, letters to the Roannez, the work on miracles and fragments of the apology – in the space of about five years in his mid-thirties (1655–8). It had been a remarkably productive flowering, but by the spring of 1659 he was not even able to respond to letters, let alone undertake any creative work.

This, however, was not quite the end of Pascal's life. Over a year later he was well enough to travel to Clermont to see the Périers and take the waters, returning to Paris late in 1660. To this time belongs the *Prière pour demander à Dieu le bon usage des maladies* (Prayer asking God to allow us to make good use of illness), a work that obviously grew from Pascal's own experience of illness, and the *Trois discours sur la Condition des Grands* (Three essays on nobility), an extraordinarily dense and stimulating reflection on the prerogatives and duties of a ruling class that, Pascal held, had no intrinsic claim to its privileged position. He also supported various charitable initiatives, helped out indigent families on a personal basis, and, towards the very end of his life, in a characteristic display of practical-mindedness, worked in partnership with the duc de Roannez to establish Paris's first system of public coaches, the *carrosses à cinq sols*. Profits from the service went to the poor.

Despite these achievements, there was much to distress him. In February 1661 the Assemblée du Clergé de Paris, encouraged by Louis XIV, passed an act obliging all clergy and nuns to put their signatures to a formulary stating unconditionally that the five propositions were heretical *and* that they were to be found in Jansen's *Augustinus*. At the same time the '*petites écoles*' were forcibly disbanded and Port-Royal forbidden to recruit new nuns. Following instructions of Arnauld and his colleagues, the nuns of Port-Royal signed the formulary, but unwillingly. The episode almost certainly contributed to Jacqueline's death later that year. As a layman, Pascal was not himself obliged to sign the formulary, but he disapproved of Port-Royal's doing so. During the summer of 1662 his illness worsened. Confined to bed, he was looked after by Gilberte in her house in the parish of

Sainte-Etienne-du-Mont, where, in August, he died. His last words were 'Que Dieu ne m'bandonne jamais!', 'May God never abandon me!'

NOTES

1. Pascal, in fact, thought that all autobiographical writing was inherently objectionable, describing Montaigne's attempt to capture himself in the *Essais* as 'stupid' (*sot*) (L 649/S 534; L 780/S 644).
2. For hare coursing see L 136/S 168 and for theatre-going see L 764/S 630 and L 628/S 521. For Charles I see L 62/S 96; for a possible oblique reference to the Peace of the Pyrenees of 1659 see L 60/S 94.
3. Briggs (1977) gives a good overview of the period.
4. See also *Trois Discours sur la condition des Grands*, which draws an analogy between the position of a man born into nobility and the victim of a shipwreck cast on to a foreign island (*OC* 11, 194).
5. For the distinction between reason and authority see *Préface sur le traité du vide, OC* 1.
6. These only lasted until 1660, but they taught Racine, among others, and through the publication of textbooks such as the *Grammaire* and the *Logique* had a lasting impact on French thought and education.
7. For a good discussion of Gilberte's biography see Philipe Sellier, 'Principes d'édition de *La Vie de M. Pascal*', in Pascal, *Pensées*, ed. P. Sellier (Paris: Garnier, 1991), pp. 136–45.
8. The best treatment of Pascal's so-called *période mondaine* is still to be found in Jean Mesnard, *Pascal*, revised 5th edn (Paris: Hatier, 1967), ch. 2, pp. 37–64.
9. See Jacqueline's letters to Gilberte dated 8.12.1654 and 25.1.1655, *OC* 1, 21–6.
10. Pascal was not identified as the author of the letters, which had been put on the papal index in 1657, until after his death.
11. See the works collected under 'Oeuvres mathématiques d'Amos Dettonville' in *OC* 11.
12. Pascal himself never used the word 'apology', which can have misleading implications if it encourages the view that he was aiming to 'prove' the truth in Christianity; Pascal believed that where religion was concerned, you had to believe it, to see it (L 7/S 41).

2 Pascal's reading and the inheritance of Montaigne and Descartes

The discernible traces of Montaigne's and Descartes' works in Pascal's writings, whether explicit or implicit, result from deliberate choices of reading, determined ultimately by Pascal's eventual vocation as an apologist for the Christian religion. Pascal's interest in Descartes was, in its early stages, associated with Pascal's own purely scientific and mathematical pursuits. However, his engagement with the *Discourse on Method*, the *Meditations* and the *Principles of Philosophy*, as more directly with his discovery of Montaigne, must be situated among other sorts of reading deriving from more purely religious preoccupations. Before embarking on the inheritance of Montaigne and Descartes in Pascal's writing, it is essential to explore briefly some of what we know more generally of Pascal's reading habits at crucial times of his life.[1]

Pascal's scientific culture was first developed through his father's contact with the circle of Father Marin Mersenne, who acted as one of the major disseminators of new scientific thinking and who was, in particular, responsible for obtaining critical views on Descartes' *Meditations*, including those of Antoine Arnauld, the major polemicist among the Port-Royal Solitaires. While Pascal did not receive during his own education the same sort of humanist education as Descartes at the Jesuit school of La Flèche, his letters on the question of the existence of the vacuum to Father Noël, rector of the Collège de Clermont and former teacher of Descartes, and his short works, *De l'esprit géométrique* and *L'Art de persuasion*, demonstrate an awareness of issues arising from Aristotelian concepts of the physical universe and modes of philosophical discourse used by ancient philosophers. However, Pascal's first conversion in 1646 led him, along with his father and sisters, to a study of theological works, especially those of Cornelius Jansen, also known as Jansenius, Duvergier de Hauranne, abbot of Saint-Cyran, and Arnauld. In addition, the influence of Jansen is to be found in Pascal's *Abrégé de la vie de Jesus-Christ* (A short life of Jesus Christ), and in his preface to a lost treatise on the vacuum.[2] It is important to note that, generally, Pascal's thinking on religious issues is dominated by the clear preference of his Jansenist spiritual directors for positive theology, which places emphasis on principles arising from interpretation of Scripture, the history of the early or 'primitive' church, and the works of the early church fathers, rather than for speculative theology, which, using scholastic philosophical principles, concentrates on the more abstract commentary of issues relating to doctrine and tradition.

From 1646 to 1662 Pascal's reading in the purely religious context was given over, on the one hand, to the Bible and a study of the liturgy. The two are connected in a particular way. According to his sister, Gilberte, Pascal regularly recited in part or in whole the Breviary, a work vital to the life and religious practice of the Christian in the Catholic Church, which contains prayers for the saints, prayers associated with divine office for each stage of the liturgical calendar, and includes, among other things, the Psalter, a collection from the Book of Psalms. From 1656 Pascal's works, especially the *Abrégé* and the *Mémorial*, a text sewn by Pascal into the lining of his clothes as a reminder of his personal relation to Christ, contain extensive reminiscences of the Breviary, particularly its Parisian version. The Psalms were important for Pascal in the ways in which they may be held to prophesy the life of Christ, a theme essential to the section of the *Pensées* devoted to figurative law (section IX and section XX in the Lafuma and Sellier editions respectively), and paraphrases of the Psalms appear in the *Prière à Dieu pour le bon usage de la maladie* (Prayer to God for the proper use of illness). As Philippe Sellier convincingly argues, however, Pascal's knowledge of biblical texts would largely have derived from their appearance in liturgical texts, to the extent that his devotion to liturgical reading constituted at the same time a directed reading of Scripture.[3]

On the other hand, Pascal immersed himself in the works of Saint Augustine, regarded by many as the most eminent of the church fathers. Very often filtered through what Pascal considered the authoritative interpretation of his Jansenist masters, these alone shaped the direction of his thinking and spiritual reflection. For his apologetic strategy, Pascal took from Augustine proofs rooted in the Bible and an insistence on the values of witness and prophecy.[4] In this sense, Pascal's intention was not to be innovative, but to offer an original understanding of Augustinian thought. His approach to Augustine's works ranged from the adoption of an Augustinian argument, using the same technical terms or images, to developing in extended form what was only suggestion in his theological master.[5] This, as I shall show, is not dissimilar to his use of Montaigne's *Essays*. Pascal also drew on existing models from other sources for his shorter works, while at the same time incorporating the influence of Saint Augustine. For example, the *Prière à Dieu pour le bon usage de la maladie*, based on a known model for special prayers, discards the very personal style of the autobiographical *Confessions* for a more general approach in line with the spirit of the latter.[6] It would, however, be wrong to believe that Pascal and the Jansenists were alone in their attachment to Augustine's writings, since the seventeenth century as a whole was marked by the revival of interest in the saint, which led eventually to a French edition of the complete works under the aegis of the Benedictine scholars of the Order of Saint-Maur, based at Saint-Germain des Prés. Pascal did, however, become associated with a particularly radical interpretation of Augustine which eventually placed the unity of the French church under considerable strain.

Two differing views exist concerning the acquisition from 1648 of Pascal's profound knowledge of Augustine's works. The first, expressed by Philippe Sellier, holds that Pascal had direct recourse either to the six in-folio volumes of the standard edition of Augustine's works published by the University of Louvain in 1566–7, or at least to another of the major editions produced by the Dutch Faculty of Theology.[7] The second view, that of Jean Mesnard, rests on Pascal's initial acquaintance as more probably founded on a well-known collection of quotations compiled by a Louvain theologian and published in 1648. Such collections, frequently used by theologians of the time, were known as *excerpta*. These anthologies would then have determined his reference to the works themselves. An in-depth knowledge of Augustine's works being beyond the capacity of a single individual, Pascal depended as much on his contemporaries' knowledge of Augustine as on his own.[8]

Pascal's acquaintance with important religious texts extended beyond Augustine and the Paris Breviary. Mesnard argues that the nature of Pascal's paraphrasing demonstrates his first-hand knowledge of the deliberations of the Council of Trent, which sat from 1548 to 1563, in order to clarify the true Catholic doctrine in the light of the Protestant Reformation. Pascal drew on them directly for his short *opuscule*, composed in 1657–8, *Sur la conversion du pécheur* (On the conversion of the sinner), and, in 1655–6, for his *Ecrits sur la grâce* (Writings on grace). It can be further demonstrated that, for the *Mémorial*, Pascal must have used various translations into French of the Bible dating from the sixteenth century, and published either in Switzerland or by the Louvain doctors.[9]

By contrast, with the exception of the mention and quotation of Pierre Corneille (L 413/S 32), Pascal is singularly indifferent to the profane culture of his day. His hostile reference to drama (L 764/S 630) is in fact a text of Madame de Sablé, which she submitted to Pascal for comment, and to which he made certain changes and additions. This indifference was undoubtedly due in part to the absence of such culture in his own education and the general attitude evident at Port-Royal towards the literature of the time. But, as Mesnard notes, that indifference tends to yield at points where elements of profane culture could be considered useful in a Christian context, and when they could serve the cause of the faith.[10] Before the *Pensées*, this emerges most eloquently in the *Entretien avec Monsieur de Sacy* (Conversation with Monsieur de Sacy). On this occasion, Pascal found himself confronted by an interlocutor who clearly preferred Augustine's authority to that of Montaigne and Epictetus.

Descartes was also referred to explicitly in this conversation, and it is to him and Montaigne that I shall now turn, beginning with the author of the *Essays*.

PASCAL AND MONTAIGNE

A number of dates have been proposed for Pascal's first encounter with Montaigne. While Michel Le Guern locates the high point of Montaigne's influence in the years 1657–8, Bernard Croquette identifies the period 1654–5 as the likely point of departure.[11] Certainly, Pascal was familiar with Montaigne by the time he presented the results of his reading to Sacy in 1655. Pascal, especially through the circle he frequented in the days before his retreat to Port-Royal des Champs in that same year, could not have failed to come into contact with Montaigne's work, since he was still widely read in the seventeenth century, especially by those whose views did not entirely coincide with Christian orthodoxy. The so-called 'libertines', widely believed to be the principal audience to which Pascal's *Pensées* were addressed, looked to Montaigne for confirmation of aspects of their hedonistic lifestyle or for their adoption of neo-stoic positions, that is to say, the ability of man, through his own strength of will, to withstand the vicissitudes of human existence. Montaigne was an obvious reference point, too, for the consideration of other moral issues and for the process of self-examination. The number of editions of Montaigne's *Essays* facilitated access to his writings: from 1600 until Pascal's death in 1662, some twenty editions were published in France. Evidence suggests that Pascal used the in-folio edition of 1652.[12]

Pascal's engagement with Montaigne can be identified as operating on four levels. First, Montaigne provided a compendium of information in respect of aspects of profane culture that Pascal lacked, especially concerning the philosophy of antiquity. In the conversation with Monsieur de Sacy, Pascal refers to Montaigne as the most illustrious defender of scepticism, with Epictetus, read in the translation of Dom Goulu, as representing stoicism. The second level represents an intellectual engagement, in terms of a mutual interest, with Montaigne's considerations on the major ethical and social themes illuminating the human condition, both as they affect the individual and humankind at large. Thirdly, Montaigne fulfils the purpose of offering familiar material accessibly in order for Pascal to reach his own readers more effectively. As Pascal notes himself, the style of the *Essays* is persuasive in '[consisting] entirely of thoughts deriving from everyday conversations' (L 745/S 618). Indeed, one of the originalities of Pascal's form of apologetics is a familiar and direct form of argument quite different from that of professional clerics. Finally, Pascal confronts Montaigne as an adversary of the way of thinking and way of life he finds embedded in the *Essays*, and which are contrary to the true Christian religion. Pascal's reading of Montaigne is, therefore, far from dispassionate. The coincidence of Pascal's own positions with those of Montaigne on individual points gives rise, therefore, to a complex engagement based on frequent similarity but essential difference. Equally, Pascal's conversation is not so much with Montaigne himself. Such an isolated exercise would serve no practical purpose for the Christian apologist. Rather, Pascal addresses himself to Montaigne's readers, who might be tempted to adopt Montaigne's overall perspective for themselves. Pascal, using Montaigne as a familiar starting point, provides simultaneously a basis for going beyond Montaigne.

The precise way in which Pascal worked with the text of the *Essays* is unclear. Jean Mesnard argues plausibly that Pascal adopted the method of his contemporaries, in working from a collection of quotations, or *excerpta*, the form, in fact, which many fragments of the *Pensées* themselves take (see, for example, L 507/S 675 and L 730/S 612).[13] The question remains how Pascal worked from there, and in particular whether, from his notes, he referred back to the original text in the edition of 1652. But it is certainly not just an issue of eye to page. In addition to the notes which Pascal made, his familiarity with Montaigne, especially with 'An Apology for Raymond Sebond', the most frequently quoted essay (II: 12), would, on the basis of repeated reading, have ranged from a general saturation in the moral and ethical orientation of the arguments to the memory of individual words or phrases that had impressed themselves upon his mind, and which he could easily have spontaneously reproduced.[14]

At one level, the *Pensées* reveal themselves as a sort of textual reflecting mirror for the *Essays*. This is evident in the copying, and sometimes listing, of Montaigne's Latin quotations (e.g. L 506/S 673–4 and L 507/S 675), which Pascal may have conceived as reminders for later developments. Pascal's form of note-taking, resuming a whole argument in Montaigne (II: 3, 396–7), is observable in L 123/S 156. In other cases, Pascal copies expressions or sentences almost literally, as in the case of the senses deceiving reason (L 45/S 78; II: 12, 673), sometimes modernising aspects of vocabulary, for example '*coutume*' (L 126/S 159) replacing '*accoustumance*' (III: 10). Individual phrases are considered appropriate for Pascal's purposes, such as Montaigne's reference to the life and death of beasts. This is especially notable when a phrase in the same sentence appears in a different context, '*la maniere de naistre*' (II: 12, 524–5) acting in this instance as a trigger to Pascal's own development (L 150/S 183). Pascal may take an expression of Montaigne, but situate it in a more precisely developed context: Pascal uses the example of the '*tintamarre*' ('din'), of Alcibiades' wife, and the buzzing of the fly (L 48/S 81; III: 13, 1228) in order to illustrate the '*puissances trompeuses* [powers of deception]'. Or, on the basis of Montaigne's initial argument, Pascal may push a phrase of Montaigne, 'you must accept a touch of madness' (III: 9, 1125) a little further, 'Men are so inevitably mad' (L 412/S 31).

The most important 'translations' from the *Essays* to the *Pensées* occur at the level of the themes Montaigne and Pascal share regarding the component features of the human condition. Montaigne's frequent references to the changeability of man, to his inconstancy and the contradictions inherent in his behaviour, to the diversity and variety in reason and experience manifest in the diversity of solutions among philosophers, all find textual echoes in the *Pensées* (L 54/S 87, L 55/S 88, L 65/S 99, L 127/S 160). Human weakness and moral corruption come together in the image of 'filth' (III: 2, 914) and in Pascal's celebrated description of man as a 'sink of doubt and error, glory and refuse of the universe' (L 131/S 164). At a more developed level, Pascal takes up in a number of fragments (e.g., L 60/S 94, L 280–1/S 312–13) Montaigne's disquisitions on man's error in assuming the origins of laws to be just (I: 23, 130–6; II: 12, 658; II: 17, 745), wrongly accusing Montaigne into the bargain of an error of understanding (L 525/S 454). This method of putting in a single series of arguments references from several essays is repeated with the subject of diversion, or '*divertissement*' (L 132–9/S 165–71), an integral part of Montaigne's own vision of a restless humanity (I: 41, 285; II: 12, 622; III: 4, 941; III: 8, 1051). Man must also recognise that what there is to know vastly outstrips his limited intellectual capacity (I: 31, 229; III: 6, 1028; L 199/S 230), and that the highest point of man's knowledge lies in the acknowledgement of his ignorance (e.g. II: 12, 560; III: 13, 1220; L 83/S 117).

What, then, drives Pascal's reading of Montaigne? What determines some things attracting Pascal's attention rather than others? Pascal's encounter with Montaigne took place between two periods of intense religious activity, bridging at one end his theological apprenticeship and at the other the preparation of his planned *Apology for the Christian Religion*, for which he had begun to collect material in the second half of the 1650s. Pascal's conversation with Monsieur de Sacy already indicates that Montaigne had become part of a *strategic* programme of reading in which he took his place as one pole of an argument, with Epictetus as the other, but in a process where both were transcended in the search for and discovery of the ultimate truth in God. Ranging widely over human behaviour and thinking, Montaigne's *Essays* constituted an invaluable source of illustrations to be incorporated into Pascal's plan for his apology along with the latter's *explanation*, on the basis of the Christian religion, of the moral and spiritual state of humankind. The evidence Montaigne provided thus took its place within a framework of Christian metaphysics. Montaigne's 'wretchedness', one of his terms for the state of humankind, now fits into a structure in which 'Wretchedness of man without God' is set against 'Happiness of man with God' (L 6/S 40). *'Bassesse'* ('vileness') and *'grandeur'* ('greatness') then form the two poles of human endeavour, within which, for example, pride and presumptuousness, two of Montaigne's targets, occupy specific positions in the duality of man, with despair as the counterpart of pride (L 352/S 384). Aspects of man's behaviour are subsequently apportioned to one side of the equation or the other.

While the concept of original sin is not absent from the *Essays*, it figures prominently and continuously at the centre of Montaigne's assessment of humankind only in the 'Apology for Raymond Sebond', the single most important indicator of Montaigne's religious belief and, significantly, the text most used by Pascal for the conversation with Monsieur de Sacy. For Pascal, it is the one principle on which the whole edifice of human behaviour and organisation rests. Whereas Montaigne argues that we are born to seek after truth and that only God possesses it (III: 8, 1051), a position reinforced by his presentation of the sceptical position, Pascal relates our desire for truth and our subsequent discovery only of uncertainty to a punishment which makes us aware of what we have fallen from (L 401/ S 20). Pascal not only proposes an explanation of the human condition, but also, as the necessary component of an apology, the remedy that removes us from the moral impasse of purely human solutions. The most important part of that solution is Christ, hardly ever mentioned by Montaigne, a redeemer who combines the human and the divine. It is essential to remember that, in the Pascalian system, greatness is inseparable from vileness since, if we concentrated on vileness alone, the area of most of the illustrations taken from Montaigne, man would despair of union with God, and would thereby deny his greatness, identifiable in his discernible aspiration to reach the state from which he has fallen (L 117/S 149). When Montaigne expresses his desire to force men to 'bow their heads and bite the dust', he omits to suggest that their heads should also be raised (II: 12, 501). The angel cannot be separated from the beast (L 353/S 385, L 358/S 390).

Montaigne's greatest usefulness lies in his descriptive anthropology. Indeed, Pascal imitates this, as in section VIII of the *Pensées* on diversion, and the discussion of imagination (L 44/S 78), where at no point, with the exception of the example of the preacher, does the mention of religion intrude. Montaigne thus serves Pascal's new form of apologetics, which does not begin with the traditional proofs of God. Rather, Pascal offers a portrait of the human condition that provokes questions whose answers will be found only in the Christian religion. Montaigne's observations, component parts of an anthropology that is validatory but certainly not explanatory, are thus transformed into arguments. It is from this perspective that Pascal reproaches Montaigne for failing to see the reason behind custom (L 577/S 480). Pascal seeks in the Christian religion the objective correlative insufficiently present in the *Essays*, which means that the relative positions of Montaigne as observer and Pascal as apologist are very different. Montaigne, in his own words, does not teach but simply recounts (III: 2, 909), writing 'an account of the assays of my life' (III: 13, 1224), refusing to contemplate telling people how to behave (I: 28, 216). Certainly Pascal concedes that Montaigne did not set out to be an apologist himself (L 680/S 480). But Montaigne, rooted in his humanity, serves no purpose as a witness, explicitly disregarding himself as an authority to be believed (I: 26, 167), Pascal aiming by contrast to convince of the 'marks of divinity within me' (L 149/S 182, S 274). Pascal has recourse to Montaigne for a purpose not designed by Montaigne.

This does not represent a rejection of Montaigne, who may indeed have inspired Pascal to adopt a view on writing about man, not in the close individual attention to the self, but in the difficulty of attaining a level of continuous and coherent discourse about an ever-changing and contradictory subject. For Montaigne, the instability inherent in man means that even sound authors are deceiving themselves into thinking that they can provide a 'one invariable and solid fabric' (II: 1, 374). Discontinuity of being excludes being able to link one action to another (III: 13, 1222). While Pascal finds an overriding principle in Christian metaphysics, the very nature of man leads to fragmentation in writing. But there is also an issue of reading. For Montaigne, it is the 'undiligent reader' who loses me 'when my pen and my mind both go a-roaming', and his material, that is his own self, can dispense with 'an intricate criss-cross of words, linking things and stitching them together' for the inattentive (III: 9, 1126). Of necessity, Pascal's fragments are, between them, without connectors. But, as Pascal points out, his own order, determined as it is by the apologetic framework, is not 'aimless confusion', and in any case the apparent disorder of his apology precisely reveals his purpose (L 532/S 457). Both writers require, therefore, active reading,[15] but, whereas Montaigne's reader is absorbed by a picture that is complex and rich in texture, which by its very nature must remain diffuse, Pascal's reader must construct for himself a convincing and convergent argument from the evidence Pascal provides. While indeed Pascal may seem to find some value in 'Montaigne's muddle', his lack of a 'rigid method', and his practice of 'jumping from one subject to another' (L 780/S 644), Pascal's own approach, while without order, is nonetheless directional.

Pascal famously accuses Montaigne of the 'foolish idea to paint his own portrait' and of '[talking] nonsense deliberately' (L 780/S 644). Montaigne himself writes of this 'thorny undertaking', founded as it is on the moving sands of humanity at large and of his own self (II: 6, 48–9). He anticipates objections such as Pascal's, arguing that he is not obliged to avoid writing 'daft things' as long as he does not deceive himself '[by] recognising them as such' (II: 17). That is natural in the process of the recording of the self. What one suspects as being at the origin of Pascal's critique of Montaigne's project is Montaigne's indulgence in the self, especially as it runs counter to St Augustine's rejection of man's 'self-love', dangerous in distracting him from the love of God which should be our primary purpose. Pascal echoes Augustine in advancing that 'The self is hateful' (L 597/S 494), or 'We must love God and hate ourselves alone' (L 373/S 405). Montaigne's self-deprecation at no point reaches the level of self-disgust.

Ultimately, it is another of Pascal's criticisms of Montaigne that marks their definitive difference, the latter's 'indifference regarding salvation'. Pascal deliberately makes Montaigne's living life 'lazily and leisurely' into 'dying a death of cowardly ease', '*lâchement*' having a completely different meaning in each text (III: 9, 1074–5; L 680/S 559). Certainly, Montaigne's attitude to life avoids the sort of combativeness associated with ambition or interventionist religious proselytism, although he does not refrain from firm expressions of belief or tirades against atheists and trouble-making reformers. But he prefers to go with the flow, that is to say, with 'this world's general law' (III: 13, 1217), and to serve life 'on its own terms' (III: 9, 1118). It is wrong to despise the self: rather we should derive enjoyment from it, and Montaigne's overriding ambition is to know how to live this life (III: 13, 1261): 'Oh what a soft and delightful pillow, and what a sane one on which to rest a well-schooled head, are ignorance and unconcern' (III: 13, 1218). This resigned view of life is simply a provocation for Pascal, for whom the questions that govern what happens to us after death are so urgent that all other human activity or reflection on life is of a second order. In what might stand as a reproof to Montaigne, in that he does nothing to suggest otherwise to his readers, Pascal writes: 'Nothing is so important to man as his state: nothing more fearful than eternity. Thus the fact that there exist men who are indifferent to the loss of their being and the peril of an eternity of wretchedness is against nature' (L 427/S 681). Montaigne, without Pascal's argumentative framework, is dangerous, not because Montaigne is irreligious, but precisely because he claims to profess Christian belief. Pascal therefore maintains a deliberate distance from Montaigne, despite their seeming convergence on many issues. The absence of 'Montaigne says that...' in the *Pensées* avoids presenting Montaigne as an authority. Montaigne in this sense is not a source, much less an influence, but evidence in Pascal's own cause. Whereas Montaigne offers the wisdom of a man at ease with himself, seeking a point of rest in an unstable world, Pascal is, in the words of Jacques Morel, a 'master of anxiety'.[16] For Pascal, there is no rest for the wicked, or for the good.

PASCAL AND DESCARTES

Descartes' place in the writings of Pascal cannot fail to be different from that of Montaigne, not least because the two men met in Paris in 1647 on 23 and 24 September, an event recorded in a letter of the 25th from Jacqueline Pascal to her sister, Gilberte (*OC* I, 14–15).

Their discussions addressed in part issues relating to the theory of the vacuum and to the experiments on atmospheric pressure Pascal had devised, which Descartes credited himself with suggesting to the young scientist.[17] The meeting was, according to some commentators, the ideal opportunity for Pascal to become better acquainted with the works of Descartes, especially since the French translations from the Latin of the *Meditations* and the *Principles of Philosophy* had just appeared. Le Guern claims that Descartes' philosophy in fact constituted Pascal's introduction to philosophy itself, his own education having centred more on concrete experience.[18] Relations between the two were polite but not entirely cordial, since Pascal did not appreciate Descartes' less than fulsome admiration for the treatise on conical sections. If it is correct to assume that by 1655 Pascal had a good knowledge of a range of Descartes' writings, how are we to define his engagement with these, especially in the light of the Chevalier de Méré's assertion that the former was a disciple of the latter, and Le Guern's claim that Pascal accepted *'en bloc'* Descartes' system, except where his own experience and personal reflection led him to reject certain of its parts?[19] Pascal and Descartes also shared the same scientific context. As with Pascal's approach to Montaigne, we can work from a position of similarity within a framework of significant difference.

Starting from textual similarities, one can identify in Pascal's writings images found, for example, in the *Discourse* and the *Principles*, including the watch (L 534/S 457), roads or ways (*Traité des ordres numériques*), the tree with its trunk and branches (L 535/S 457 and L 698/S 577) – Descartes conceived the relation of metaphysics to other areas of knowledge and thought in this way – and the image of the vessel to illustrate perceptions of movement and repose (L 699/S 577).[20] It is likely that these images were meant to act as triggers in reminding Pascal of an idea, or were perhaps to be incorporated at a later stage of the development of his apology. They may, on the other hand, simply have been reminiscences deriving from a concentrated reading of the texts. Borrowings of a more precise philosophical nature, like the origins of the self in L 135/S 167, are based on several sources: articles 8 and 14 of part 1 of the *Principles*, and *Meditation* 3. Descartes' reference to the need to correct errors learnt in childhood (article 18, part 2 of the *Principles*) is included in L 44/S 78, alongside significant borrowings from Montaigne. Literal borrowings may be found in the letter to Father Noël on the void (art. 22, part 2 of the *Principles*), and the phrase 'Axioms and common notions' (the *Second Replies to the Second Objections*) in the *Conversation with Monsieur de Sacy*. Very close resemblances occur between parts of Descartes' correspondence and L 660–3/S 544.[21]

In particular, aspects of Descartes' philosophy are alluded to without direct critical comment, such as the theory of animal machines expounded in the *Discourse*, part 5 (L 105/S 137, L 738/S 617, L 741/S 617). It can be argued that notions of the indivisibility and indefinite extension of matter, found in article 20, part 2 of the *Principles*, influenced Pascal in L 199/S 230, and Pascal alludes in the *Conversation* to a 'false and evil being' (the 'evil genius' of *Meditation* 1) (*OC* 11, 90).[22] Like Montaigne, Descartes also served the purpose of a source, in this instance for the theory of the circulation of the blood (*Discourse*, part 5; L 736/S 617). Perhaps the most celebrated reference to Descartes outside the *Pensées* occurs in *De l'esprit géométrique*, where Pascal mentions the recourse the French philosopher and Augustine have to the *cogito*, suggesting that Descartes generates a different meaning in a different context to the same words, a useful enough legitimation of Pascal's references to others in his own writings (*OC* 11, 179–80). In the *Conversation*, however, Pascal manages to confuse Montaigne and Descartes in the account of scepticism, where he credits the former with elements of the latter, thus attesting to the orientation given to his reading habits in the 1650s (*OC* 11, 89–90). Such textual reminiscences should not obscure the fact that Pascal firmly opposed Cartesian physics on the question of the void, and offered Descartes' opinions on matter and space as an example of a 'daydream approved on the basis of obstinacy' (L 1005). He also regarded Cartesian philosophy as a 'romance about nature' (L 1007), although these two accounts, attributed posthumously to Pascal, may be unreliable. Mesnard, however, points to the caricatural account in the *Conversation* of Descartes' presentation of the world in the *Principles*.[23]

Beyond purely textual references, Descartes is inevitably present in Pascal's works by virtue of his status as an important reference point in the elaboration of the new science of seventeenth-century Europe, which, it was felt by some, could advance only when enslavement to the authority of antiquity in scientific enquiry had been discarded. Both Descartes and Pascal adopted this point of view.

The former articulates his views on this inheritance in part 1 of the *Discourse*, and in his implicit criticisms of Aristotelianism in the *Meditations*. Pascal includes in L 199/S 230 a dismissive reference to Aristotle's 'substantial forms', that is to say, a view of things in the world as combining body and soul, a concept taken up by St Thomas Aquinas, whose synthesis of Christian and Aristotelian thought continued to exercise such a powerful influence in France, principally through the agency of Jesuit schools and the University of Paris. In the preface to his lost *Treatise on the Void* (1651) Pascal separates the properly unchanging authority of knowledge based on memory, such as theology, and knowledge subject to change through successive generations' reasoning on the knowledge of their predecessors, thus arguing that knowledge advances through time. Any similarity between the two thinkers, however, soon turns to difference. Pascal's position stands against Descartes' ahistorical concept of the status of knowledge, which is acquired and demonstrated once and for all according to the rigorous principles I shall examine briefly below, and highlights the difference between Descartes' metaphysical approach to scientific knowledge and an empirical approach based on constant experimentation. More crucially, Pascal contrasts in the preface the permanence of religious knowledge and knowledge of the divine with the impermanence of knowledge that is purely the product of the human mind (*OC* 11, 452–8).

Where Pascal and Descartes diverge most significantly and absolutely is in their respective positions as religious apologists. Apologetics were certainly not Descartes' prime concern, but he did claim to offer, as a philosopher, proofs of God's existence and of the immortality of the soul that would, by their clarity, convince the unbeliever. By means of the *cogito*, Descartes believed, on the one hand, that he had defeated the sceptics in discovering an idea resistant to doubt, since doubting is a form of thinking which, in the moment even of doubt, proves the existence of the thinking being, and on the other, that he had proved the immateriality of the soul, since it could not be confused with the extension of things in the physical world. A direct consequence of immateriality was immortality, an argument that seems to respond to Pascal's own thinking in L 108/S 140 and L 161/S 193. Descartes goes further in establishing the existence of God on the basis of the rigorous application of the principles of clearness and distinctness emerging from the *cogito*, which determine whether an idea is certain and true. All that can be known of God, he writes in his address to the Deans and Doctors of the Paris Faculty of Theology, can be shown by reasons drawn from nowhere but ourselves. Moreover, he makes the claim that philosophers are better at demonstrating matters of God and the soul than theologians.[24] One last point that will help to illuminate Pascal's attitude to Descartes is the latter's principal quest to find 'something firm and constant in the sciences'.[25] For Descartes, the clarity and incontrovertible nature of his idea of God stands as a guarantee of the truth of all ideas clearly and distinctly conceived. A clear idea of God is therefore accessible to the human mind and, while revealed truth stands as the ultimate authority, can be proved by human reason unaided by divine agency.

Pascal's response to such an overwhelmingly optimistic view of the capacities of the human mind is firm and uncompromising, especially in relation to Descartes' apologetic claims, to which the *Pensées* as a whole stand as a monumental objection. Reason as an instrument in understanding faith is acceptable (L 7/S 41), but faith in reason is not. An important theme of the *Pensées* is the failure of philosophy, resulting from the false pretension of reason to possess anything like the fixed point Descartes locates in the *cogito*. The fragment entitled 'Disproportion of Man' demonstrates the inherent incapacity of human reason ever to encompass what there is to know of the universe, and the incapacity of the finite to contain the idea of the infinite (L 199/S 230). Pascal uses Descartes' concept of the indivisiblity of matter as part of a moral lesson against the Cartesian assertion that, through the use of reason, man can reach constancy in the sciences. If man's mind is so limited, how can it come to an idea of the nature of God? Descartes bases his confidence in the certainty of human reason on the rigorous application of the right criteria to the construction of our knowledge. For Pascal, competing forces within the moral composition of man put many obstacles in its way: 'Reason never wholly overcomes imagination, while the contrary is quite common'; or, since imagination is the dominant faculty in man, it is the 'master of error and falsehood'. Hence, 'man has no exact principle of truth' (L 44/S 78). Pascal concludes the section 'Submission and Use of Reason' with his assertion that 'Reason's last step is the recognition that there are an infinite number of things which are beyond it. It is merely feeble if it does not go as far as to realise that.' Significantly, he adds, no doubt in an implicit reference to Descartes: 'If natural things are beyond it, what are we to say about supernatural things?' (L 188/S 220). Pascal thus denies the validity of what Descartes claims to know about God through the agency of human reason.

Although Descartes, in the address I quoted above, is not always positive about the merits of geometrical demonstration, he believes that the merits of his own method render doubt obsolete. Pascal, on the other hand, objects that proof by order does not of itself lead to truth. For example, if we are to prove by examples, we need to prove these by other examples (L 527/S 454). Pascal is sceptical that, at a human level, there are such things as true proofs: it is simply that 'it is not certain that everything is uncertain' (L 521/S 453). Whereas Descartes' principal aim has been to defeat, through the *cogito*, the sceptics' assertion of the impossibility of indubitable knowledge, the *Pensées* abound with thoughts on man's incapacity of proof beyond doubt (i.e., L 406/S 25). We are indeed 'incapable of certain knowledge or absolute ignorance', possessing no fixed point (L 199/S 230). Hence the impotence of the order of demonstration, this concept, according to Le Guern, constituting the most significant influence of Descartes on Pascal. While Pascal mentions in *L'Art de persuader* the need for method, without which proofs cannot be convincing, even to the extent, in his letter to Father Noël on the void, of adopting clearness and distinctness as a rule in judging a proposition to be positive or negative, these principles cannot apply to an apologetic framework where Pascal's subject, man, is incapable of order (L 532/S 457; *OC* II, 174 and 377). Descartes has simply confused the orders of philosophy and theology. Putting 'I know' for 'I believe' is a category mistake condemned by St Augustine. Moreover, in the domain of human knowledge, science or even the scholastic philosophy of St Thomas Aquinas have not always kept to the order they seemed to propose: 'Mathematics keeps it, but it goes so far as to be useless' (L 694/S 573). In *De l'esprit géométrique* Pascal asserts that we are naturally and immoveably incapable of dealing with any form of knowledge 'in an absolutely accomplished order' (*OC* II, 157–8). Pascal, in his onslaught on certainty and the illusory advantages of order, concludes that, despite the elements of truth in Descartes' construction of his science, his endeavours are ultimately 'pointless, uncertain and arduous' (L 84/S 118).

Other elements in Descartes' apologetic pretentions attract Pascal's critical attention, not least the nature and insufficiency, even danger for faith, of metaphysical proofs themselves. His rejection of them as arguments reaching out to unbelievers rests on their remoteness from human reasoning and their complexity, such that they make little impact or that their impact resides in the moment of demonstration, only subsequently to be forgotten (L 190/S 222-3). The greater danger, however, is that, taking metaphysical ideas as a starting point, faith becomes, as in traditional apologetics, an extension of reason, whereas, contrary to other religions, in Christianity faith is a gift of God and not of reason (L 588/S 487). This is a position adopted by Pascal in a celebrated dispute with the abbot Forton as early as 1647.[26] The effectiveness of proofs comes from reason, but also habit and inspiration (L 808/S 655). While Le Guern adduces as another possible source of influence a letter to the princess Elizabeth of 1645, in which Descartes mentions habit as a way of imprinting ideas in the mind,[27] Pascal's 'automaton' concerns the whole person, not just the mind, and with a view to a change of life (L 821/S 661). Metaphysical proofs are most harmful for what they omit. It is clear that Pascal considers Descartes' apologetic framework too close for comfort to the unauthoritative perspective of speculative theology, with its dependence on philosophical principles, and not enough to positive theology, which, looking to the sources of the faith, privileges the definition of man within religion as history. In L 190/S 661 Pascal adds to his critique of metaphysical proofs on grounds of lack of impact a quotation from St Augustine asserting that the gains of man's curiosity are lost through pride. This is what happens when knowledge of God is not accompanied by knowledge of Christ. The Christian God is not therefore the God of mathematical truths (for Descartes, God guarantees the truth and certainty of mathematics) but 'the God of Abraham, the God of Isaac, the God of Jacob' (L 449/S 690), Pascal repeating in similar terms this attachment to a God who intervenes through history in the *Mémorial* (L 913/S 742). Moreover, the utter clarity that Descartes claims to place at the heart of his metaphysical proofs runs completely counter to the notion of the Hidden God, that is to say a God who reveals himself only to those prepared to seek him (see L 427/S 681). This is why God wishes 'to move the will rather than the mind' (L 234/S 266). Cartesian, and traditional, apologetics satisfy only the mind, the danger being that the mind will consider that sufficient.

A major weakness that Pascal perceived in the Cartesian position is the association of apologetics with science and Descartes' proof of the idea of God as the foundation of certainty in human knowledge. Marguerite Périer reported Pascal's reproach that Descartes dispensed with God, once God had given a start to the world (L 1001), although in fact Descartes held to the notion of continuous creation, where God intervenes constantly to maintain the world in existence.[28] Whatever the authenticity of this attribution, it illustrates how Cartesian proofs could be held to lead away from rather than back to God. Science, as an autonomous activity legitimated once the idea of God has guaranteed the truth of properly conceived ideas, becomes a distraction to the true nature of considering man in relation to God. Just as Montaigne's philosophy of life failed to respond to the urgent questions posed by Pascal, Descartes' proofs too encourage us to ignore them. This is why Pascal affirms the 'Vanity of science', since 'Knowledge of physical science will not console me for ignorance of morality in time of affliction' (L 23/S 57). Pascal claims that the abstract sciences, inappropriate to man, had caused him to stray further from his true condition than those individuals who had no knowledge of them at all (L 687/S 566). In addition to Descartes' scientific construction being pointless and uncertain, the whole of philosophy is not worth 'an hour's effort' (L 84/S 118). It may be that Pascal's emphasis on man's thought as part of his greatness reminds us of the primacy of the thinking being in Descartes (L 135/S 167 and L 759/S 628). But the gift of thought is for raising consciousness in respect of our moral condition, not for the construction of ultimately useless philosophical and scientific systems. Hence the meaning of L 553/S 462: 'Write against those who probe science too deeply. Descartes.' As Henri Gouhier comments most aptly, the apologist must, for Pascal, never be seen outside the temple.[29]

CONCLUSION

Montaigne and Descartes represent for the author of the *Pensées* two important focal points in order better to situate his own aplogetics. The first offers the right evidence but not the right answers, while the second fails even to come up with the right evidence. Both, however, in their respective errors, offer encouragement of the wrong sort to others. Pascal engages, as well as with the authors themselves, with their potential followers. Another aspect of Pascal's conversation with the two writers highlights how Montaigne, despite Pascal's reservations, serves to act as a corrective to Descartes. The former's insistence that being convinced of certainty 'is certain evidence of madness and extreme unsureness' (II: 12, 607) could not fail to have had a bearing on his reading of the latter, especially Montaigne's assertion that 'Human reason goes astray... especially when she concerns herself with matters divine' (II: 12, 581). In addition, Montaigne's emphasis on the body, problematic for Pascal in terms of pleasure, serves to undermine the possibility of a pure life of the mind, from which would emerge the eternal certainty of its products. Even partial adherence to either Montaigne or Descartes represents too much of a compromise for a form of apologetics which is not so much a support for the Christian religion in terms of argument, but a product of exemplary faith. Mind and body are transcended at the point where Pascal envisages, perhaps, their fusion: 'It is the heart which perceives God' (L 424/S 680).

NOTES

1. The references to Montaigne represent first the book of the *Essays*, translated by Screech (1991), then chapter and page of the edition (e.g., II: 12, 673).
2. J. Mesnard (ed.), *Oeuvres complètes* (hereafter *OC*) (Paris: Desclée de Brouwer, 1964–92), III, 543–6 and Sellier 1966, pp. 78–9.
3. Sellier 1966, especially pp. 6–29 and pp. 52–4.
4. Sellier 1970, p. 54.
5. ibid., p. 6.
6. Mesnard, *OC*, IV, 978 and 985–6.
7. Sellier 1970, p. 7 and pp. 17–18.
8. Mesnard, *OC*, III, 551–7.
9. Mesnard, *OC*, III, 548; III, 52–3; and IV, 38.
10. Mesnard, *OC*, III, 116–17. See also Sellier 1970, p. 181.
11. Le Guern 1969, p. 98 and Croquette 1974, p. 114.
12. French editions of Montaigne's *Essais* are listed in Sayce, and Maskell 1983.
13. Mesnard, *OC*, III, 103.

14. Croquette 1974, p. 87.
15. Terence Cave refers to the 'active reader' in the context of Montaigne ('Problems of Reading in the *Essais*', in McFarlane, MacLean 1982, p. 159).
16. Morel 1986, p. 382.
17. See Mesnard, *OC*, II, 478–82.
18. Le Guern 1971, p. 90 and p. 125.
19. ibid., pp. 121–2 and p. 131.
20. These examples are enumerated by Le Guern 1969, pp. 43–9 and p. 84.
21. See Le Guern 1971, pp. 55–8 and 20 sq.
22. The parallel text of the *Conversation* and *Meditation* I (Le Guern 1971, pp. 21–3) includes a misquotation of Pascal, referring only to an '*Etre méchant*', thus testifying to another confusion.
23. Mesnard, *OC*, III, 127.
24. R. Descartes, *Oeuvres et lettres* ed. A. Bridoux (Paris: Gallimond, 1953), pp. 257–61.
25. R. Descartes, *Meditation* I, in *Discourse on Method and the Meditations*, trans. F. E. Sutcliffe (Harmondsworth: Penguin, 1971), p. 95.
26. For this dispute, see Gouhier 1974.
27. Le Guern 1971, p.144.
28. Descartes, *Meditation* I, trans. Sutcliffe 1971, p.128.
29. Gouhier 1986, p. 154.

3 Pascal's work on probability

Anceps fortuna aequitate rationis reprimitur

Before the time of Pascal there was no theory of probability, merely an understanding (itself incomplete) of how to compute 'chances' in gaming with dice and cards by counting equally probable outcomes. In addition, problems encountered in the enumeration of dice throws and the counting of arrangements and selections of things had led to an incipient mathematical theory of combinations and permutations, but the rules that appeared in the works of such authors as Tartaglia (1500–57) and Cardano (1501–76) still had the form of recipes rather than as parts of a coherent whole. It fell to Pascal to bring together the separate threads and weave them into a structure that enabled him to progress far beyond his predecessors by introducing entirely new mathematical techniques for the solution of problems that had hitherto resisted solution, techniques which became the foundation of the modern theory of probability.

Pascal's influence was not direct, for none of his writings on probability were published during his lifetime, but instead was transmitted via Huygens to James Bernoulli, where it appeared in the latter's influential *Ars conjectandi* of 1713, and via the *Essay d'analyse sur les jeux de hazard* of Montmort, first published in 1708. These two books, together with De Moivre's *The Doctrine of Chances* (1718), firmly established probability theory as a branch of mathematics. Later scholarship has confirmed the view that Pascal may justly be regarded as the father of the theory of probability.[1]

SUMMARY OF PASCAL'S MATHEMATICAL WORK

In 1631 Blaise Pascal's father Etienne (himself an able mathematician who gave his name to the '*limaçon* of Pascal') moved his family

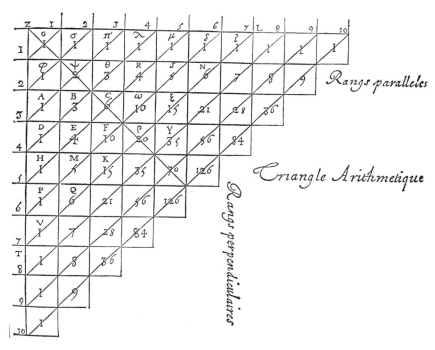

Fig. 1 Pascal's arithmetical triangle from the *Traité*

to Paris in order to secure his son a better education. In 1635 he was one of the founders of Marin Mersenne's 'Academy', the finest exchange of mathematical information in Europe at the time. To this informal academy he introduced his son at the age of 14, and Blaise immediately put his new source of knowledge to good use, producing (at the age of 16) his *Essay pour les coniques*, a single printed sheet enunciating Pascal's Theorem, that the opposite sides of a hexagon inscribed in a conic intersect in three collinear points.

Mersenne's *Harmonicorum libri XII* of 1636, and the two-volume French version *Harmonie universelle* published in 1636 and 1637, contain the first accounts of the mathematical theory of permutations and combinations in recognisably modern form, applied to musical notes. Included is a table of the number of permutations of r things of one kind and s things of another kind for $r = 0$ to 12 and $s = 0$ to 25. This form of 'arithmetical triangle' was used by the younger Pascal in due course, and became known as 'Pascal's arithmetical triangle' (see figures 1 and 2). It is almost certain that Pascal

```
1   1   1   1   1   1   1   .   .   .

1   2   3   4   5   6   .   .   .   .

1   3   6  10  15   .   .   .   .   .

1   4  10  20   .   .   .   .   .   .

1   5  15   .   .   .   .   .   .   .

1   6   .   .   .   .   .   .   .   .

1   .   .   .   .   .   .   .   .   .

.   .   .   .   .   .   .   .   .   .
```

Fig. 2 Pascal's arithmetical triangle

learnt of it and its combinatorial uses from the Mersenne books, for in them the author paid tribute to Etienne Pascal's knowledge of music, having previously dedicated his treatise on the organ to him.

At the age of 18 Pascal turned his attention to constructing a calculating machine to help his father in his calculations, and within a few years he had built and sold fifty of them. Some still exist. (The computer programming language PASCAL is named in honour of this achievement.) In 1646 he started work on hydrostatics, determining the weight of air experimentally and writing on the vacuum (leading ultimately to the choice of 'Pascal' as the name for the SI unit of pressure).

In 1654 Pascal returned to mathematics, extending his early work on conics in a manuscript which does not now exist, though it was seen by Leibniz. In the same year he entered into correspondence with Pierre de Fermat of Toulouse about some problems in calculating the odds in games of chance, and this led him to write the *Traité du triangle arithmétique, avec quelques autres petits traitez sur la mesme matière*, probably in August of that year. Not published until 1665, this work, and the correspondence itself which was published in 1679, is the basis of Pascal's reputation in probability theory as the originator of the concept of expectation and its use recursively to solve the 'Problem of Points', as well as the justification for calling the arithmetical triangle 'Pascal's triangle'. His advances, considered to be the foundation of modern probability theory, are described in detail below.

Later in 1654 Pascal underwent a religious experience as a result of which he almost entirely abandoned his scientific work, although in 1656 he posed Fermat a problem in probability which later became well known as the 'Gambler's Ruin' problem. He devoted his remaining years to writing the *Lettres provinciales* and the *Pensées*. The latter includes his famous 'Wager'. In 1658–9 he briefly returned to mathematics, writing on the curve known as the cycloid, but his final input into the development of probability theory arises through his presumed contribution to *La Logique, ou l'art de penser* by Antoine Arnauld and Pierre Nicole, published in 1662 and often referred to in English as the *Port-Royal Logic* through the association of its authors, and Pascal himself, with Port-Royal Abbey. The Gambler's Ruin, the Wager and the *Port-Royal Logic* are considered below.

CORRESPONDENCE WITH FERMAT, 1654

The centrepiece of Pascal's correspondence with Fermat in the summer of 1654 is a gambling problem known in English as the Problem of Points. Also known simply as the 'division problem' (*Problème des partis*), it involves determining how the total stake should be divided in the event of a game of chance being terminated prematurely.

Suppose two players X and Y stake equal money on being the first to win n points in a game in which the winner of each point is decided by the toss of a fair coin. If such a game is interrupted when X still lacks x points and Y lacks y, how should the total stake be divided between them? In the middle of the sixteenth century Tartaglia famously concluded that 'the resolution of such a question is judicial rather than mathematical, so that in whatever way the division is made there will be cause for litigation'. A century later the correct solution was derived by three different methods during the correspondence between Pascal and Fermat, after the problem had been brought to Pascal's attention by Antoine Gombaud, chevalier de Méré.

The first method involves a straightforward enumeration of the possible ways the game could have been completed. At most $(x + y - 1)$ more tosses would have settled the game, and if this number of tosses is imagined to have been made, the resulting $2^{(x+y-1)}$ possible games, each equally probable, may be classified into those which X wins and those which Y wins, the stakes then being divided in this proportion. Thus the real game, of indeterminate length, is embedded in an imaginary game of fixed length. This method of solution depends upon the peculiar fact that the order of occurrence of the heads and tails is of no significance, only their total numbers, as both Pascal and Fermat had realised. The solution thus involves counting combinations and summing binomial coefficients, which will be explained more fully in the next section. 'But', wrote Pascal, 'because the labour of the combinations is excessive I have found a shortcut or, more exactly, an alternative method which is much quicker and neater' (*OC* 1, 146). This method involves the path-breaking procedure of computing expectations recursively.

Pascal's key advance was to understand that the value of a gamble is equal to its mathematical expectation computed as the average of the values of each of two equally probable outcomes and that this precise definition of value lends itself to recursive computation, because the value of a gamble that one is certain to win is undoubtedly the total stake itself. Thus, if the probabilities of winning a or b units are each one-half, the expectation is $\frac{1}{2}(a + b)$ units, which is then the value of the gamble. In *Ars conjectandi* (1713) James Bernoulli called this 'the fundamental principle of the whole art'. Pascal has invented the concept of 'expected value', that is the probability of a win multiplied by its value, and has understood that it is an exact mathematical concept that can be manipulated.

In his letter to Fermat of 29 July (*OC* 1, 146), Pascal develops the recursive argument applied to expected values in order to find the correct division of the stake money, and thus computes the 'value' of each successive throw. As I shall show, in the *Traité* the same idea is more formally expressed, and in particular Pascal there gives as a principle the value of the expectation when the chances are equal. He remarks at one point that 'the division has to be proportional to the chances' (*OC* 1, 305), but in the solution to the problem when the players have equal chances the question of computing an expectation for unequal chances does not arise; that extension was first formally made by Huygens in his *De ratiociniis in ludo aleae* of 1657. It is known that when Huygens spent July–September 1655 in Paris he had the opportunity to discuss Pascal's work on probability problems with Roberval, and presumably learnt of the concept of mathematical expectation then, though it is often attributed to him.

The easiest way to understand how Pascal used expectation and recursion to solve the problem of points is to visualise the event tree of possible further results. Each bifurcation corresponds to a toss, one branch for X winning it and the other for Y, and successive bifurcations must lead eventually to tips corresponding to the whole game being won by either X or Y. Considering now the expectation of X (say), each tip can be labelled with his expectation, either S (the total stake) or o, as the case may be. Applying now Pascal's expectation rule for equal chances, each bifurcation has an expectation associated with it. Working recursively down the tree from the tips to the root, we arrive at the solution to the problem. If $E(x, y)$ be the expectation of player X when he lacks x points and Y lacks y, then the recursion is

$$E(x, y) = \tfrac{1}{2}E(x - 1, y) + \tfrac{1}{2}E(x, y - 1)$$

By these methods, and his knowledge of the arithmetical triangle, Pascal was able to demonstrate how the stake should be divided between the players according to the partial sums of the binomial coefficients, a result which he had already obtained by enumeration, for both he and Fermat had realised that the actual game of uncertain length could be embedded in a game of fixed length to which the binomial coefficients could then be applied.

Pascal formally proved his solution in the third section of part 2 of his *Treatise on the Arithmetical Triangle*, to which we now turn.

TRAITÉ DU TRIANGLE ARITHMÉTIQUE, 1654

The *Traité du triangle arithmétique* itself is 36 pages long (setting aside *quelques autres petits traitez sur la mesme matière*) and consists of two parts. The first carries the title by which the whole is usually known, in English translation *A Treatise on the Arithmetical Triangle*, and is an account of the arithmetical triangle as a piece of pure mathematics. The second part, *Uses of the Arithmetical Triangle*, consists of four sections:

Use (1)... *in the theory of figurate numbers*
    (2)... *in the theory of combinations*
    (3)... *in dividing the stakes in games of chance*
    (4)... *in finding the powers of binomial expressions*

Pascal opens the first part by defining an unbounded rectangular array like a matrix in which 'The number in each cell is equal to that in the preceding cell in the same column plus that in the preceding cell in the same row' (OC 1, 284), and he considers the special case in which the cells of the first row and column each contain 1 (see figure 2). Symbolically, he has defined $\{f_{i,j}\}$ where

$$f_{i,j} = f_{i-1,j} + f_{i,j-1}, \quad i,j = 2, 3, 4, \ldots,$$
$$f_{i,1} = f_{1,j} = 1, \quad i,j = 1, 2, 3, \ldots,$$

The rest of part 1 is devoted to the demonstration of nineteen corollaries flowing from this definition and concludes with a 'problem'. The corollaries include all the common relations among the *binomial coefficients* (as the entries of the triangle are now universally called), none of which was new. Pascal proves the twelfth corollary

$$(i - 1)f_{i,j} = jf_{i-1,j+1} \text{ in our notation}$$

by explicit use of mathematical induction. The 'problem' is to find $f_{i,j}$ as a function of i and j, which Pascal does by applying the twelfth corollary recursively. Part 1 of the *Treatise* thus amounts to a systematic development of all the main results then known about the properties of the numbers in the arithmetical triangle.

In Part 2 Pascal turns to the applications of these numbers. The numbers thus defined have three different interpretations, each of great antiquity (to which he does not, however, refer). The successive rows of the triangle define the *figurate numbers* that have their roots in Pythagorean arithmetic. Pascal treats these in section 1.

The second interpretation is as *binomial numbers*, the coefficients of a binomial expansion, which are arrayed in the successive diagonals, their identity with the figurate numbers having been recognised in Persia and China in the eleventh century and in Europe in the sixteenth century. The above definition of $f_{i,j}$ is obvious on considering the expansion of both sides of

$$(x + y)^n = (x + y)(x + y)^{n-1}.$$

The fact that the coefficient of $x^r y^{n-r}$ in the expansion of $(x + y)^n$ may be expressed as

$$\frac{n(n - 1)(n - 2) \ldots (n - r + 1)}{1.2.3 \ldots r} = \binom{n}{r}$$

was known to the Arabs in the thirteenth century and to the Renaissance mathematician Cardano in 1570. It provides a closed form for $f_{i,j}$, with $n = i + j - 2$ and $r = i - 1$. Pascal treats the binomial interpretation in section 4.

The third interpretation is as a *combinatorial number*, for the number of combinations of n different things taken r at a time, ^nC_r, is equal to

$$\binom{n}{r}$$

a result known in India in the ninth century, to Hebrew writers in the fourteenth century, and to Cardano in 1550. Pascal deals with this interpretation in section 2, giving a novel demonstration of the combinatorial version of the basic addition relation

$$^{n+1}C_{r+1} = {}^nC_r + {}^nC_{r+1},$$

for, considering any particular one of the $n + 1$ things, ^nC_r gives the number of combinations that include it and $^nC_{r+1}$ the number that exclude it, the two together giving the total.

In section 3 Pascal breaks new ground, and this section, taken together with his correspondence with Fermat, is the basis of his reputation as the father of probability theory. In it he amplifies and formalises the solution of the Problem of Points which he had discussed with Fermat, calling it *La règle des partis*. As I have shown, they both arrived at the combinatorial solution involving the counting of all the ways in which the game could have been completed. Pascal, however, does not refer to this method explicitly in the *Traité*, preferring to prove the same result by mathematical induction based on his method of expectations. I cannot give the mathematical details here, but it is a brilliant display using the results recorded earlier in the *Traité*, and is justly prized as the birth of modern probability theory.

We should, however, record the words in which Pascal formalised the principle involved (*OC* 1, 305):[2]

The first principle leading to a knowledge of the way in which one should make the division is as follows:

If one of the players finds himself in the position that, whatever happens, a certain sum is due to him whether he loses or wins and chance cannot take it from him, he should not divide it but take it all as is his right, because the division has to be proportional to the chances and as there is no risk of losing he should get it all back without division.

The second principle is this: if two players find themselves in the position that if one wins he will get a certain sum and if he loses then the sum will belong to the other; and if the game is one of pure chance with as many chances for the one as for the other and thus no reason for one to win rather than the other, and they want to separate without playing and take what they are legitimately due, the division is that they split the sum at stake into half and each takes his half.

Pascal was justly proud of his solution to the Problem of Points. In his letter of 1654 to the Académie Parisienne, presumably Mersenne's academy, he mentions a little treatise he proposes: La géométrie du hasard (*Aleae geometria*). 'This stunning title' will show how 'proper calculation masters fickle fortune' (*Anceps fortuna aequitate rationis reprimitur*) so that for the Problem of Points 'each player always has assigned to him precisely what justice demands' (*OC* I, 172).

THE GAMBLER'S RUIN, 1656

In 1656 Pascal posed Fermat a problem, eventually to become known as the 'Gambler's Ruin' problem, that played a central role in the development of probability theory through being the first example of a problem about the duration of play. Let two men play with three dice, the first player scoring a point whenever 11 is thrown and the second whenever 14 is thrown. Instead of the points accumulating in the ordinary way, let a point be added to a player's score only if his opponent's score is nil, but otherwise let it be subtracted from his opponent's score. The winner is the first to reach twelve points. What are the relative chances of each player winning?

As the famous Gambler's Ruin problem it has come down to us in the simpler, but equivalent, form, in which each player starts with twelve points and a win transfers a point from the loser to the winner. The overall winner is then he who bankrupts his opponent. The new feature, not present in the Problem of Points, is that the game has no certain end to it, which was perhaps why Pascal tried it on Fermat.

Fermat did in fact obtain the correct answer, but probably not by the method Pascal used. Though this must remain a matter for speculation since no record of it has survived, it seems likely that

Pascal once again used his method of expectations to derive a set of equations, which he then solved by an ingenious method. This not only gave the correct answer, but also incidentally proved that the probability of the game never finishing is zero. In the later history of probability this question of the 'duration of play' led to many further advances. Huygens included the problem in *De ratiociniis in ludo aleae* (1657). It found its way into Montmort's *Essay d'analyse sur les jeux de hazard* (1708), De Moivre's *De mensura sortis* (1712) and James Bernoulli's *Ars conjectandi* (1713), and thence into prominence.

THE WAGER, *CIRCA* 1658

In the *Pensées* Pascal used his concept of expectation to argue that one should bet on the existence of God because, however small the probability of His existence, the value of eternal salvation if He does exist is infinite, so that the expected value of assuming that He does exist far exceeds that of assuming that He does not. Subsequent writers have regarded this, 'Pascal's Wager', as an example of decision theory, though it is doubtful if it had any influence on the origin of the modern theory. In the present *Companion* the Wager is discussed by Jon Elster in chapter 4.

Pascal discusses the implication of what he calls *la règle des partis* in fragment L 577/S 480 of the *Pensées*. Unfortunately the Krailsheimer translation renders this as 'the rule of probability' without connecting it with Pascal's use of the phrase in the *Traité*, and is in other respects misleading as well. It is better to have 'Now when we work for tomorrow and take chances we are behaving rationally for we ought to calculate the chances according to the division rule which has been proved. St Augustine saw that we take chances at sea, in battle, etc. – but he did not see the division rule which shows how one must do it' (L 577/S 480). As I shall show below, these thoughts recur in the *Port-Royal Logic*.

THE *PORT-ROYAL LOGIC*, 1662

Pascal greatly influenced the probability arguments in the *Port-Royal Logic*, in the last chapter of which there is a clear understanding of the importance of judging an action not only by the possible gain or loss, but also by the probability of each of these, as in modern decision theory.

The chapter entitled 'The Judgements we Ought to make Concerning Future Accidents' emphasises the supremacy of expectation as a guide to action. First Pascal (for surely it was he) points out the error in ignoring the probabilities: 'The flaw in this reasoning is that in order to judge how one should act to obtain a benefit or avoid a loss, it is necessary not only to take into account the benefit or loss itself, but also the probability that it will or will not come about, and to consider mathematically the magnitudes when these things are multiplied together' (Arnauld and Nicole 1996, p. 273). This is the first occasion in which the word '*probabilité*' is used in its modern sense. A simple example of a fair gamble follows, with an explanation of how lotteries are unfair because the expectation of each player is less than his wager.

But 'Sometimes the success of something is so unlikely that however advantageous it may be ... it is preferable not to chance it. Thus it would be foolish to play twenty sous against ten million pounds, or against a kingdom, on the condition that one could win only in the event that a child, arranging the letters in a printer's shop at random, immediately composed the first twenty verses of Virgil's *Aeneid*' (Arnauld and Nicole 1996, p. 274). Here the authors are using a version of the 'monkeys and the typewriter' argument; no typewriters then, but the image of a contemporary printer's shop with its trays or 'cases' of lead type with a compartment for each size and style of letter of the alphabet. Capitals lived in the top cases ('upper-case letters') and small letters lower down ('lower-case letters'). The greatest crime in a printer's shop was to drop a case of type on the floor, randomising all the letters in a chaotic heap. It was a powerful metaphor in the seventeenth century, and has endured in one form or another ever since, perhaps made popular by its use here. The authors, who show themselves to be familiar with Cicero's works, will have got it from Cicero's *The Nature of the Gods*, where it appears in the argument for the improbability of the Epicurean hypothesis that the world is a chance conglomeration of particles: 'If anybody thinks that this is possible, I do not see why he should not think that if an infinite number of copies of the twenty-one letters of the alphabet, made of gold or what you will, were shaken together and poured out on the ground it would be possible that they should produce the *Annals* of

Ennius all ready for the reader. In fact I doubt whether chance could possibly succeed in producing even a single verse!' (Cicero 1972, p. 161).

This argument that very small probabilities should be ignored appears to be the reverse of the logic of the Wager, but then 'Only infinite things such as eternity and salvation cannot be equalled by any temporal benefit. Thus we ought never to balance them against anything worldly.' Finally, 'This is enough to make all reasonable people draw this conclusion, with which we will end this *Logic*, that the greatest of all follies is to use one's time and life for something other than which may be useful for acquiring a life that will never end' (Arnauld and Nicole 1996, p. 275).

CONCLUSION

Pascal's work on probability, in its maturest form in the *Traité du triangle arithmétique*, took the subject beyond the medieval enumeration of possibilities and computation of chances into the modern form of a calculus embodying the full rigour of mathematical proof, as in classical geometry. It is no accident that Pascal called his projected work *The Geometry of Chance*, nor that the title of the *Traité* has a geometric allusion. By introducing the concept of mathematical expectation as a product of a probability and an outcome, he was able to apply advanced techniques such as induction and recursion to achieve the solution of problems that had seemed intractable, and in so doing laid the foundations of a true theory of probability.[3]

NOTES

1.   The principal work on Pascal's contributions to probability is *Pascal's Arithmetical Triangle* (Edwards 1987, 2002). This describes and analyses the *Traité* in detail, whilst the Problem of Points and the Gambler's Ruin Problem are covered in two appendices, previously separately published (Edwards 1982, 1983). A parallel account is provided in chapter 5 of *A History of Probability and Statistics and their Applications Before 1750* (Hald 1990). These books supersede the pioneering works of Todhunter (1865) and David (1962); although the latter remains a readable introduction to the subject, it should be noted that the author omitted

to mention the *Traité*. *Classical Probability in the Enlightenment* (Daston 1988) is valuable background reading, although it also neglects the *Traité*. *The Emergence of Probability* (Hacking 1975) is especially valuable for its treatment of the Wager and the *Port-Royal Logic*. *Blaise Pascal 1623–1662* (Loeffel 1987) is a monograph in German which may be consulted about the rest of Pascal's mathematical work; it contains an account of the *Traité* which parallels that in Edwards (1987, 2002). Finally, the pioneering description of 'Pascal and the invention of probability theory' should not be overlooked – Ore 1960.

2. Existing English translations of the writings of Pascal and Fermat touching on probability, and of the related material in the *Port-Royal Logic*, are often unreliable. The translations in the present chapter are the work of the author.

3. Digitised images of a copy of *Traité du triangle arithmétique* have been placed on the web by Cambridge University Library and may be found at http://www.lib.cam.ac.uk/RareBooks/PascalTraite/

4   Pascal and decision theory

Suppose there is a plausible model of the atmosphere in which global warming will lead to the extinction of humankind unless the consumption of fossil fuel is reduced drastically. Even though the probability of this outcome is small or indeterminate, it is in some hard-to-explicate sense a 'real' one. The implications for action seem compelling: even if the use of fossil fuel has many indubitable benefits, it ought to be curtailed drastically. No finite gain can outweigh the 'real' possibility of the extinction of humankind. On reflection, however, this conclusion is too quick. For suppose there is also a plausible socioeconomic model in which reduced use of fossil fuel leads to global economic collapse, which leads to nuclear war and to a nuclear winter that causes the extinction of humankind. Now, what do we do?[1]

Readers of this volume are likely to recognise the structure of Pascal's Wager and of the many-gods objection to Pascal's argument. In this chapter I try to reconstitute some of the context of Pascal's Wager and to assess the validity of the argument. I carefully say 'some' of the context, as the theological debates in which Pascal's argument is embedded are highly complex and well beyond my expertise. Although I have been greatly assisted by Leszek Kolakowski's acute and irreverent *God Owes Us Nothing*, I do not claim that standing on his shoulders enables me to see as far as he did.

I shall proceed somewhat indirectly. In the next section I compare the Jesuit strategies that Pascal denounces in *Les Provinciales* with the persuasive strategies he himself uses in *Les Pensées*, arguing that in a caricatural form the key elements of the Wager were already present in the Jesuit writings. In the section entitled 'Decision theory' I sketch some elements of modern decision theory, partly to point out how Pascal had a richer conception of human behaviour than what can be stated within the framework of that theory and partly to prepare the grounds for the discussion of the Wager, which is the object of the final section.

PASCAL AND THE JESUITS

Kolakowski observes that in a 'fundamental sense [Pascal] was following the same rule as the Jesuits'.[2] The words he put in the mouth of his Jesuit interlocutor, 'Men today are so corrupt that since we cannot make them come to us, we must go to them' (OC 1, 640–1), applies to his own strategy in the Wager. The similarities between the Jesuitical and the Pascalian proceedings are in fact striking and numerous, even though ultimately overshadowed by the differences.

1.   The Jesuits as perceived by Pascal (I do not address the historical issue of the real motivations of the Jesuits) and Pascal himself may have addressed the same audience, the so-called 'libertines' who are concerned with nothing but their own interest and honour. In the *Provinciales* Pascal quotes a number of passages from Jesuit sources, the cumulative effect of which is that there is virtually no vice that cannot be construed as being allowed by Christian doctrine. In these passages the Jesuits are largely, but not exclusively, concerned with elite vices, such as selling salvation or justice, duelling, usury and refusing charitable work. To attract an elite obsessed with money and honour to their fold, they had to lower standards of behaviour to a minimal level (see the next paragraph). It is certainly arguable that the Wager argument was addressed to a similar audience.[3] The fact that it is a form of gambling suggests that the intended reader is a gambler. Elsewhere in the *Pensées*, gambling is singled out as one of the main *divertissements* of those who are not forced by their condition to engage in sustained activity.[4]

2.   In the ninth *Provinciale*, the falsely naïve Pascal and his invented Jesuit interlocutor are discussing the devotions needed to 'open heaven's gates' (OC 1, 672). The requirements of the father turn out to be so minimal and undemanding that it would be irrational to refuse them: 'only an utter wretch would refuse to take up one moment of his whole life to put beads around his arm, or a rosary in his pocket, thus making so certain of salvation that those who have tried have never been disappointed, whatever their way of life'

(OC 1, 673). The Jesuit argument is that a small secular sacrifice will ensure salvation with certainty. The Wager argument is that a large secular sacrifice will ensure salvation with some non-zero probability. Both arguments can be stated in terms of the rationality of making a finite sacrifice for the sake of an infinite expected pay-off.

3. The Wager turns crucially on the *decision to believe*. The Jesuits argue for the importance of the *decision to forget*. In the fourth *Provinciale* the discussion turns to the paradoxical Jesuit doctrine that one cannot sin if one does not know that what one is doing is wrong. Summarising the father's argument, Pascal writes:

What an excellent path to happiness in this world and the next! I had always thought that the less one thought of God the more sinful one was. But, from what I can see, once one has *managed to stop thinking of him altogether* the purity of all one's future conduct becomes assured. Let us have none of these half-sinners, with some love of virtue; they will all be damned. But as for these avowed sinners, hardened sinners, unadulterated, complete and absolute sinners, hell cannot hold them; they have cheated the devil by surrendering to him. (OC 1, 617)

The phrase I have italicised ('quand on a pu gagner une fois sur soi de n'y penser plus du tout') implies a deliberate effort and intention to turn away from God and to stop thinking about Him. Once that aim is achieved, salvation is certain. Now, as the classical moralists knew, the decision to forget is intrinsically paradoxical. Montaigne observed that 'there is nothing which stamps anything so vividly on our memories as the desire not to remember it'.[5] For the seventeenth-century *moraliste* La Bruyère, 'the desire to forget someone is to think about that person' (*Characters* IV.38). At the more mundane level, there is a trick that never fails to charm or frustrate small children: tell them that the rug in their room is a magic carpet that will take them anywhere they want to go, on the condition that they never think about giraffes. Similarly, even if one believed that by forgetting God one could sin without risking damnation, this would not by itself enable one to do so – on the contrary. The state of forgetfulness is essentially a by-product.[6] Pascal does not raise this objection. Had he done so, it might have occurred to him that belief, too, is essentially a by-product. I return to that question below.

4. An important component of the Wager is the idea that many have been saved by behaving 'just *as if* they did believe' (L 418/S 680; italics added). Here, too, the Jesuits anticipated Pascal's reasoning. In the tenth *Provinciale* the issue is whether love of God is necessary for salvation or, as the Jesuits thought, fear of damnation together with the sacrament is sufficient. To set up a proper target for his polemic, Pascal quotes from the Jesuit, Antoine Sirmond:[7]

In bidding us to love him, God is content that we should keep his other commandments. If God had said: I will damn you if you do not also give me your heart, would such a motive, in your view, be consistent with the aim that God could and should have had? It is written therefore that we shall love God by doing his will, *as if* we loved him in our hearts, *as if* the motive of charity led us to do so. If that really happens, so much the better; otherwise we shall strictly obey the commandment to love God by having works, so that (observe God's goodness) we are not so much bidden to love him as not to hate him. (*OC* 1, 694–5; italics added)

The crucial difference is that, for Pascal, the inducement of real belief by going through the motions of acting as if one believed is not merely something that may or may not 'happen', but the very aim of going through the motions. Again, a fuller discussion is provided below.

5. Let me now point to an important difference. The Jesuits, as not inaccurately portrayed by Pascal,[8] recommended a very simple, indeed simplistic decision procedure. Suppose there are two possible, exhaustive and mutually exclusive states of the world, A and B, and two possible actions, x and y (see Fig. 3).

Let us suppose, moreover, that the agent ranks the possible outcomes in the following order: I > IV > II > III. In a typical piece of Jesuit casuistry, A and B could be 'God permits a person deliberately to tire himself in order to be dispensed from the fast' and 'God does not permit a person deliberately to tire himself in order to be dispensed from the fast' (*OC* 1, 630), and x and y would be 'eating' and 'fasting' respectively. The recommended decision procedure is that if state A has some substantial probability, the agent can do x even if state B is the more probable one.[9] Probability (perhaps 'plausibility' would be a better term) is proved by the testimony of one or several doctors of the church holding that opinion; hence both A and B may be probable states of affairs. The procedure could perhaps be justified by an implicit theological premise, to the effect that God would never

States

Fig. 3 Decision procedure.

punish – refuse salvation or condemn to damnation – a person who acted against His will as long as the person acted on a probable opinion. Alternatively, it may simply rest on a conflation between an action being 'supported by good reasons' and its being 'supported by the total of all reasons relevant to it'.[10]

Pascal, by contrast, adopts the modern approach to decision-making.[11] In the Wager, A and B represent 'There is a God' and 'There is no God', and x and y represent 'Wager for God' and 'Wager against God'. To decide what to do, the agent has to assign probabilities to the states of affairs and cardinal utilities to the outcomes, to be able to identify the action with the greatest expected utility. The details of the argument will concern us later. Here I only want to note an abstract conceptual virtue of the casuistic argument. Consider again the issue of global warming. The mere, abstract possibility that continued use of fossil fuel *could* lead to the extinction of humankind does not justify drastic policy measures. Even if we cannot quantify the probability, it must in some sense be a 'real' one. To identify a real possibility in what Quine has called the 'slum of possibles', we might, for instance, require that it be based on an explicit causal model rather than on coincidences or on fancy ideas such as that of the Cartesian demon.[12] The Jesuits, for their part, required that at least one doctor of the church had held the belief in question. Whatever else we might think of their approach, they did at least suggest an explicit criterion for distinguishing what is 'really possible' from

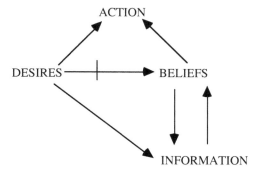

Fig. 4 Rational choice theory.

what is abstractly possible. Pascal, whose argument must presuppose a criterion of this kind, did not propose one.

DECISION THEORY

The modern theory of rational choice is radically subjective. Given the beliefs and preferences with which an agent is endowed, what is the best decision he can make *by his own lights*?[13] Figure 4 shows how the structure of the problem can be set out. There are two – largely equivalent – ways of reading this diagram. First, it may be interpreted as saying that a rational agent chooses the means (the action) that will best realise his end (defined by his desires), given his beliefs.[14] Second, desires may be understood as utilities and beliefs as subjective probabilities. The rational agent chooses the option that maximises the expected utility, that is, the weighted sum of the possible utilities of the possible outcomes associated with each option, the probabilities of these outcomes serving as the weights. In terms of figure 3, the agent has to compare $[p_A \cdot u(I) + (1 - p_A) \cdot u(II)]$ with $[p_A \cdot u(III) + (1 - p_A) \cdot u(IV)]$ and choose x if the former exceeds the latter and (ignoring ties) otherwise choose y.

A rational agent forms his beliefs, which will typically be probabilistic, by considering the evidence at hand, as represented in figure 4 by the arrow from information to beliefs. The evidence is not simply given, however. The agent also has to decide whether and how much to invest in acquiring new evidence. As indicated in figure 4 by the arrows from desires and beliefs to information, the amount of resources he decides to invest depends partly on his prior beliefs about the expected cost and value of new information – beliefs that may be updated in the course of the process of information acquisition itself – and partly on his desires. Although a direct influence of desires on beliefs is unacceptable, as indicated by the blocked arrow from desires to beliefs, an indirect influence that operates through the gathering of information is perfectly acceptable. Other things being equal, the more important the decision the more resources a rational agent would invest gathering information before making up his mind about what to believe and how to act. Since important decisions are often urgent, however, other things may not be equal. In an urgent decision, the opportunity costs of gathering more evidence may count against extensive investment in information.

Pascal is extremely sensitive to the fragility of this model as a representation of how people actually make decisions. In particular, motivated belief formation about our real motives is rampant. Our self-interest leads us into self-deception, as when we believe that we eat for health rather than for pleasure. 'Do we not learn from the saints themselves how many secret snares concupiscence lays for them, and how commonly it happens that, sober as they may be, they yield to pleasure what they think they are only yielding to necessity, as St Augustine says of himself in the *Confessions*?' (*OC* I, 620) For a similar reason, the rich are all too ready to accept the reasons the Jesuits provide them for keeping their money to themselves:

As regards giving alms from what is necessary, which is obligatory in cases of extreme and urgent need, you will see from the conditions that [Vasquez] attaches to this obligation, that the richest people in Paris need never in their lives be bound by it . . . One: 'that it MUST BE CERTAIN that the poor person will receive help from no one else . . . How often will it happen that in Paris, where there are so many charitable people, we can be certain that no one will turn up to help the poor man with whom we are confronted?' (*OC* I, 711–12)

The underlying fallacy here – because I do not know that nobody else will help, I can assume that somebody else will – is not simply a form of moral laxism, although it certainly is that. It is also an instance of a mode of reasoning that Pascal denounces in his polemic with Père Etienne Noël about the existence of a vacuum. Those who deny the existence of a vacuum claim that apparently empty space is filled up with some invisible matter, and 'think they have achieved much when they make it impossible for others to show that it does not exist, by removing from themselves all power to show that it does. But we find that there are better reasons to deny its existence on the grounds that it cannot be proven, than for believing in it merely because one cannot show that it does not exist.'[15] The implications of this burden-of-proof argument for the Wager will concern us later.

For the rational choice model to have normative or explanatory power, desires have to be (i) goal-oriented, (ii) reasonably stable and (iii) causally efficacious. Beliefs, too, have to satisfy the last two conditions. Pascal argues that these requirements are frequently not fulfilled. The *divertissement* argument says that the main force behind much human behaviour is push, not pull. It is motivated by the inability to be alone with oneself in a room; one runs away from that state rather than towards anything in particular. Thus the gambler will not be satisfied with simply getting the money he can win without playing for it, nor with gambling with fictitious money. No one 'imagines that true bliss comes from possessing the money to be had at gaming or the hare that is hunted: no one would take it as a gift' (L 136/S 168). Also, 'Make him play for nothing; his interest will not be fired and he will become bored' (ibid.). We seek the game because of the possibility of *losing*, not of winning.[16]

Pascal argues against the stability of desires and beliefs. For human beings, the grass is always greener on the other side of the fence. 'What causes inconstancy is the realisation that present pleasures are false, together with the failure to realise that absent pleasures are vain' (L 73/S 107). As for beliefs, they are so heavily subject to social influence that one may question whether they have any independent existence at all:

How difficult it is to propose something for someone else to judge without affecting his judgment by the way we do it. If you say: 'I think this is excellent', 'I think it is obscure' or something like that, you either persuade his imagination to agree with you, or you irritate it, in the opposite sense. It is better to say nothing... unless our silence also produces an effect... It is so difficult not to dislodge judgment from its natural basis, or rather this is so seldom firm and stable. (L 529/S 454)[17]

Finally, Pascal argues that some of our desires have no causal efficacy, but are held simply because they make us feel good about

ourselves. 'Pity for the unfortunate does not run counter to concupiscence; on the contrary, we are very glad to show such evidence
of friendship and thus win a reputation for sympathy without actually giving anything' (L 657/S 541).[18] He denounces the feeling of
pseudo-compassion, or sentimental compassion,[19] which is not accompanied by the spontaneous tendency to give or help that is the
mark of genuine compassion.

The need to gather information to improve belief formation is a
central theme in the *Pensées*. Fragments L 427/S 681 and L 428/S 682
in particular expound at length the need to seek illumination about
religion, not simply as a matter of 'duty' but out of our 'interest'.
When the stakes are infinite, any rational being would make 'every
effort to seek [truth] everywhere, even in what the Church offers by
way of instruction' (L 427/S 681).[20] This argument is hardly convincing. For one thing, it begs the question. If Christianity is true, the
stakes are indeed immense, but that fact alone cannot motivate us
to find out whether it is true.

For another thing, Pascal is committed to denying that we can
assess the truth of Christianity in this way. If the existence of God
and the immortality of the soul were empirical hypotheses, they
could not be proven. As Kolakowski emphasises, Pascal had a quasi-
Popperian philosophy of explanation.[21] Writing to Père Etienne Noël,
he affirms that 'to ensure that an hypothesis be evident, it is not
enough that all the observable phenomena can be deduced from it,
while if anything occurs that is contrary to a single phenomenon
it is enough to ensure its falsity'.[22] In a note to this passage, the
Pléiade editor draws a useful contrast to a statement from Descartes'
Principles:

Suppose for example that someone wants to read a letter written in Latin
but encoded so that the letters of the alphabet do not have their proper
value, and he guesses that the letter B should be read whenever A appears,
and C when B appears, i.e. that each letter should be replaced by the one
immediately following it. If, by using this key, he can make up Latin words
from the letters, he will be in no doubt about the true meaning of the letter
contained in these words ... Now if people look at all the many properties
related to magnetism, fire and the fabric of the entire world, which I have
deduced in this book from just a few principles, then, even if they think
that my assumption of these principles was arbitrary and groundless, they
will perhaps still acknowledge that it would hardly have been possible for so

many items to fit into a coherent pattern if the original principles had been false.[23]

Pascal would have to disagree. For any given message there are many codes that could turn it into an intelligible statement.[24] 'Just as one cause can have many different effects, a given effect can be produced by several different causes.'[25] Hence, even if the coincidence between the prophecies in the Bible and what actually transpired at later times can be explained by the truth of Christianity, it might also be open to other explanations. Although many fragments of the *Pensées* claim that miracles and prophecies provide proof of Christianity, others make it clear that these proofs are 'not of such a kind that they can be said to be absolutely convincing' (L 835/S 423). In fact, it would not have been 'right that [God] should appear in a manner manifestly divine and absolutely capable of convincing all men' (L 149/S 182). As I shall show shortly, He only 'convinces' those whom He causes to believe through the grace He confers on them.

In any case, the existence of God and the immortality of the soul are *not* empirical hypotheses. As Kolakowski observes, many of the prophecies have to be understood in a non-literal way to be consistent with later observations. 'Whatever the Scripture says is by definition true, therefore if we find something incredible in them the real meaning must be different from the ostensible one. But then the reader, in order to understand God's word, has to know in advance that this is verily God's word; he has to *"believe in order to understand"*.'[26] The rational procedure would be the other way around: understand (by impartial consideration of the evidence) in order to believe. This is not to say, of course, that beliefs do not enter into the interpretation of the evidence, but in a process of rational belief formation these cannot be the very same beliefs that the evidence is supposed to justify. In modern parlance, the fact that observations are theory-laden does not imply that they are incapable of providing support for theories.

In conclusion, Pascal would probably have said that as a general approach to human behaviour, decision theory is shallow because it ignores the numerous frailties of human nature. Independently of these frailties, he draws on his philosophy of explanation to assert that we cannot *prove* the truth of Christianity by considering evidence from nature (L 463/S 702) or from the Scriptures. In the light of the Wager, it is perhaps surprising that he does not say whether this evidence might nevertheless allow us to assign a non-zero probability to its truth.

THE WAGER

Pascal's argument that it is rational to wager for God is a logico-theological thicket, with important psychological premises as well. The logical aspects are the simplest, which is not to say they are simple. The key passage is the following:

Let us weigh up the gain and the loss involved in calling heads that God exists. [i] Let us assess two cases: if you win, you win everything, if you lose, you lose nothing. Do not hesitate, then; wager that he does exist. [Pascal's interlocutor:] 'That is wonderful. Yes, I must wager, but perhaps I am wagering too much.' Let us see: since there is an equal chance of gain and loss, if you stood to win only two lives you could still wager, but supposing you stood to win three? [ii] Since there is an equal chance of gain and loss, if you stood to win only two lives for one you could still wager, but supposing you stood to win three? [iii] It would be unwise of you ... not to risk your life in order to win three lives at a game in which there is an equal chance of losing and winning. [iv] But there is an eternity of life and happiness. That being so, even though there were an infinite number of chances, of which only one were in your favour, you would still be right to wager one in order to win two; and [v] you would be acting wrongly ... in refusing to stake one life against three in a game, where out of an infinite number of chances there is one in your favour, if there were an infinity of infinitely happy life to be won. But here [vi] there is an infinity of infinitely happy life to be won, one chance of winning against a finite number of losing, and what you are staking is finite. That leaves no choice; [vii] wherever there is infinity, and when there are not infinite chances of losing against that of winning, there is no room for hesitation, you must give everything ... You must be renouncing reason if you hoard your life rather than risk it for an infinite gain, just as likely to occur as a loss amounting to nothing. (L 418/ S 680)

Among the arguments I have numbered i–vii, some are valid; others incomplete; still others invalid or potentially invalid; still others incoherent; and some are essentially indeterminate. The invalid or potentially invalid arguments are flawed because they ignore the agent's attitude to risk as well as his time preferences. The indeterminate arguments are defective because, given the state of seventeenth-century mathematics, Pascal did not have the conceptual resources to spell them out in a convincing manner. The incomplete and incoherent arguments may simply be due to the rapid composition of this fragment.

Argument (i) as it stands is incomplete, as nothing is asserted about the probabilities of the two states of affairs (God's existence or non-existence). Based on the previous exchange, Pascal's interlocutor seems to accept that there is a non-zero probability that God exists, but then questions the premise that there is nothing to lose. If he wagers on God and gives up some of his worldly pleasures, he will have something to lose if God does not exist. Pascal then grants him that he might have something to lose, and goes on to consider various possibilities.

Argument (ii) is valid. If, say, the interlocutor has to stake $100 and has a 50 per cent chance of a gross gain of $200, and therefore a net gain of $100, and a 50 per cent chance of losing his stake, it is not irrational to gamble. A risk-neutral person would be indifferent between gambling and keeping his stakes, and a risk-seeking person would prefer the gamble.

Argument (iii) is invalid. If there is a 50 per cent chance of gaining $300 gross (and $200 net) for a stake of $100 and a 50 per cent chance of losing the stake, a risk-averse agent might rationally keep the $100 and abstain from gambling.

Arguments (iv) and (v) are incoherent.[27] Pascal seems to be saying in (iv) that if you wager on God and he exists you receive twice the stakes *and* an infinite reward, and in (v) that if you wager on God and he exists you receive thrice the stakes *and* an infinite reward. Let us simply ignore the reference to the double and triple gains and focus on the idea, common to (iv) and (v), that it is rational to wager if you will gain an infinite amount if one of an infinite number of possibilities is realised and otherwise lose your stakes. Mathematically, it is not clear what it means that 'out of an infinite number of chances there is one in your favour'. It is possible to assign non-zero probabilities to a countably infinite number of options so that they add up to 1, for example, by assigning the probability $1/2^n$ to the n'th option.[28] In that case, the likelihood of God existing is some definite positive number, which if multiplied by an infinite value will yield an infinite product. Pascal may have had something else mind, however, viz. that the chance of God existing could be infinitesimally small, that is smaller than any positive number but still larger than zero. Although the idea of real infinitesimals was floating around in the seventeenth century, it is not well defined in classical (Cauchy–Weierstrass) mathematics.[29] *A fortiori*, it makes no sense to ask if the product of this infinitesimally small number and the infinitely large value of eternal life is greater than some finite loss.[30]

Perhaps we could use the idea of a lexicographic ordering to make sense of the idea of a number larger than zero but smaller than any positive number you can name. Montaigne writes that

> When one scale in the balance is quite empty I will let the other be swayed by an old woman's dreams: so it seems pardonable if I choose the odd number rather than the even, or Thursday rather than Friday; if I prefer to be twelfth or fourteenth at table rather than thirteenth; if I prefer on my travels to see a hare skirting my path rather than crossing it, and offer my left foot to be booted before the right. All such lunacies (which are believed among us) at least deserve to be heard. For me they only outweigh an empty scale, but outweigh it they do. Similarly the weight of popular and unfounded opinions has a natural existence which is more than nothing.[31]

There are, in other words, two classes of reasons, which are hierarchically or lexicographically ordered. In the first class, there are reasons that are always decisive when they favour one option over another. In the second class, there are reasons so weak that they can never offset reasons in the first class, yet in the absence of the latter (or more generally when the latter are equally balanced for and against a given opinion) they are decisive. Yet supposing our reasons for believing in the existence of God lie in the second class, the question whether their weakness is offset by the infinite value of eternal life remains indeterminate or meaningless.

Arguments (vi) and (vii) may or may not be valid, depending on how we interpret the notion of eternal bliss and on the structure of the time preferences of the agent to whom the argument is addressed. Whereas Pascal discounted rewards by their probability, he ignored the need to discount them also by their degree of temporal proximity or remoteness. Suppose, first, that eternal bliss is understood as involving infinite utility at each moment of time in the future. In that case, the present value of future utility will also be infinite, re-gardless of the nature of time preferences, and Pascal's argument is valid. As it is hard to see how anyone short of God would be capable of experiencing infinite bliss in this sense, this idea may probably be discarded.

Suppose, next, that eternal bliss is understood as a constant fi-nite level of utility over infinite time. If the agent (at the time of choice) values all future times equally, that is, if he does not dis-count future utility to a smaller present value, the value of eternal bliss is indeed infinite.[32] If there is a positive (non-infinitesimal) chance of an infinite gain, the expected gain is also infinite and so will offset any risk of a finite loss. Under these assumptions, (vi) and (vii) are valid. Suppose, however, that the agent discounts future utility to a smaller present value. In that case, the validity of the argument depends on the structure of time-discounting. If the agent discounts the future exponentially, as assumed in most of traditional economic theory, the infinite stream of future utilities will add up to a finite present value and Pascal's argument is invalid.[33] If he dis-counts the future hyperbolically, as assumed in modern behavioural economics the present value will also be infinite and Pascal's argument is valid.[34] To accept the conclusion of the argument, however, we also have to accept the premise of a positive, non-infinitesimal probability of God's existence, a question to which I now turn.

We can quickly eliminate the argument from the principle of in-sufficient reason.[35] It might seem as if Pascal has something like this in mind when he writes that 'Reason cannot decide this question' (L 418/S 680). If there are two possibilities, 'There is a God' and 'There is no God', and we have no positive grounds for assigning proba-bilities to them, why not assume that they are equally likely, each with probability 1/2? But we might also propose a different partition: 'There is a benevolent God'; 'There is a malevolent God'; 'There is no God'. Using the principle of insufficient reason, the probability of there being no God now magically goes down from 1/2 to 1/3. We can also specify the pay-offs such that wagering against there being a God is rational viz. if benevolence and malevolence are defined such that each God will send to hell all and only those who believe in the other.[36]

Moreover, Pascal cannot appeal to a burden-of-proof argument. What he says about invisible matter must also apply to God: 'there are better reasons to deny [His] existence on the grounds that it cannot be proven, than for believing in it merely because one cannot show that it does not exist'. Actually, the burden of proof is on the person who asserts the existence of God. If somebody asserts 'There is a finite sequence of English words such that whoever pronounces it will gain a vast fortune', the natural response is 'Show me!' rather than suspending belief or (a hopeless task) trying to show that there is no such formula. As Michael Scriven writes, 'The proper alternative, when there is no evidence, is not mere suspension of belief: it is disbelief.'[37]

Can the evidence from the Scriptures establish a positive probability for the existence of God? The answer is ambiguous. As mentioned, belief in God precedes the interpretation of the Scriptures that would justify it. Belief in God is a matter of faith rather than of inference:

There is thus evidence and obscurity, to enlighten some and obfuscate others. But the evidence is such as to exceed, or at least equal, the evidence to the contrary, so that it cannot be reason that decides us against following it, and can therefore only be concupiscence and wickedness of heart. Thus there is enough evidence to condemn and not enough to convince, so that it should be apparent that *those who follow it do so by grace and not by reason*, and those who evade it are prompted by concupiscence and not by reason. (L 835/S 423; italics added)

The reasoning in this passage does not line up neatly with the Wager argument. It does not refer to probabilities, nor to the need for considering the possible outcomes before deciding which opinion to 'follow'. What seems clear, however, is that God's grace produces the certainty of His existence, not merely a positive subjective probability. The cognitive state of those whom God refuses grace is more delicate. Are they atheists, agnostics, or 'semi-believers', who attach respectively zero, indeterminate and positive probability to God's existence? If Pascal had the third case in mind, he could have used it to buttress the assumption in (vi) above of 'one chance of winning against a finite number of losing', that is, to provide a criterion for distinguishing 'real possibility' from mere abstract conceivability.

The distinction between these two kinds of possibility is related to the 'many-gods objection' to the Wager.[38] In Diderot's formulation, 'An Imam could reason just as well this way.'[39] Does not the fact that a Pascal of Muslim persuasion could make identically the same argument for wagering on the truth of Islam as the real Pascal offered for wagering on the truth of Christianity refute both conclusions? Pascal may have anticipated something like this objection when he wrote:

It is not by what is obscure in Mahomet, and might be claimed to have a mystical sense, that I want him to be judged, but by what is clear, by his paradise and all the rest. That is what is ridiculous about him, and that is why it is not right to take his obscurities for mysteries, seeing that what is clear in him is ridiculous. It is not the same with Scripture. I admit that there are obscurities as odd of those of Mahomet, but some things are admirably clear, with prophecies manifestly fulfilled. So it is not an even contest. We must not confuse and treat as equal things which are only alike in their obscurities, and not in the clarity which earns respect for the obscurities. (L 218/S 251)

This passage is consistent with the idea that Islam lacks the kind of 'real possibility' that we can impute to Christianity. Yet it is also consistent with the idea that both doctrines lack real possibility. The mere fact that one logically consistent doctrine is more plausible than another does not by itself establish that the former has a positive probability of being true. An explanation that presupposes the violation of one well-established law of nature is more plausible than one that violates two such laws, but that fact does not allow us to conclude that doubts about the first law are in order. If Christianity itself remains merely conceivable, the Wager argument fails. Finally, the passage is also consistent with the idea that the truth of Islam is a real possibility, but less so than the truth of Christianity. In that case, the many-gods objection applies. For the Wager to be persuasive – *neither too weak, nor too strong* – Pascal has to establish that among religions that assign infinitely large rewards to believers, Christianity is the only one to possess real possibility.[40] I think it is fair to say that he did not show this to be the case.

Let me say a few words about the psychological premises of the Wager. Because of the near universally granted impossibility of simply *deciding to believe*,[41] Pascal has to suggest an indirect strategy to his interlocutor:

You want to find faith and you do not know the road. You want to be cured of unbelief and you ask for the remedy: learn from those who were once bound like you and who now wager all they have. They are people who know the road you wish to follow, who have been cured of the affliction of which you want to be cured: follow the way by which they began. They behaved just as if they did believe, taking holy water, having masses said, and so on. That will make you believe quite naturally, and will make you more docile [*vous abêtira*]. (L 418/S 680)

This empirical claim is usually linked to Pascal's Cartesian view that 'we are as much automaton as mind' (L 821/S 661). Yet this fragment goes on to say, somewhat confusingly in light of the Wager, that 'we must . . . make *both* parts of us believe: the mind by reason, which need to be seen only once in a lifetime, and the automaton by habit' (italics added). The idea that habit can *sustain* belief acquired by reason is obviously much weaker than the idea which is needed for the Wager, viz. that habit can *generate* belief without any prior reason to believe. Also, Pascal's argument, to be valid, might seem to require that the process of belief acquisition has a *self-erasing* component. One cannot coherently believe that one believes only because one has gone through the motions of believing. One might conjecture, therefore, that '*vous abêtira*' refers to the capacity of habitual belief to induce forgetfulness about its own origin. In a sense, then, Pascal's programme would include that of the Jesuits that I discussed earlier: deciding to forget, in order to be able to believe.

There is another way of looking at the matter, however. Rather than forgetting the origins of our present belief, we might decide that they are strictly irrelevant. 'True', one might say, 'I did engage in the process of belief acquisition for purely instrumental reasons. I could do so without incoherence because, counting on the fact that people tend to align their beliefs on their actions to avoid cognitive dissonance, I correctly predicted that the process would induce a sincerely held belief. Since I knew that my future reasons for *holding* the belief would be different from those that caused me to *induce* it, I also knew that awareness of the latter would not undermine the former.' I find this argument unpersuasive. Dissonance reduction takes place 'behind the back' of the agent, not in the full glare of self-consciousness. I prefer, therefore, the self-erasing interpretation.

The theological aspects of the Wager are harder to make sense of. Pascal believed in predestination. Why then bother to persuade anyone, when what they do can make no difference to their salvation? More generally, why would a person who believed in predestination bother to do anything for *anyone's* salvation, his own or that of others? If he or the target of his attention is among the elect, there is no need to do anything; if not, nothing he can do will make a difference. Calvin's answer was that those whom God chooses for salvation, he also causes to do good works.[42] Thus, if someone fails to be charitable, he can infer that he has not been chosen. By a well-known form of magical thinking,[43] this belief may indeed induce charitable behaviour, but the rational paradox remains. Although Pascal tried hard to distinguish his views from those of the Calvinists, I agree with Kolakowski that it amounts to a distinction without a difference.[44]

There are two puzzles. Why would Pascal bother to make the argument? And why would his interlocutor bother to take him seriously? Kolakowski argues that Pascal would answer the first question as follows: 'God's way of converting sinners are various, and it is normal, rather than exceptional, that he should employ other people as his tools. I can never be sure that I will be effective working as an instrument, but I must do my duty nevertheless; otherwise why would Jesus have sent his disciples to preach his truth to heathens?'[45] But would the Wager (assuming its mathematical and psychological premises to be true) have any motivating force *for his interlocutor* if Pascal gave this answer? Why couldn't he answer: 'If I am among the elect, God will find some way of converting me. There is no reason for me to do anything.'

The conclusion seems inescapable that the Wager, with the mathematical and psychological features discussed above, would have been much more convincing if offered by a Jesuit.[46] Kolakowski summarises the semi-Pelagian views (which he attributes to the Jesuits) as follows: 'We do need divine grace to do good but "sufficient grace" is given to all, and it needs only our free will to make it efficient. Since this efficient grace is a constant condition of our life, we may say that moral perfection and salvation depend on our effort and will.'[47] If there is a positive probability that we can achieve eternal bliss through our own effort, we obviously ought to make that effort. If our effort makes no difference, why make one? Kolakowski claims that the psychological connection may go in the other direction: 'If there is a technical way to open the door of paradise, it is natural to make it as easy and uncomplicated as possible.'[48] Yet as I demonstrated above, in the section on Pascal and the Jesuits, some effort, however minimal, will still be required. In any case, the Jesuitical doctrine is dissociable from the lax Jesuitical practices. The original Pelagians, who held largely the same doctrine, were rigorous, not laxist.

If this interpretation is correct, it offers an ultimate irony. The culminating argument in Pascal's second major work will work only if we accept the doctrine he spent so much energy demolishing in the first.

NOTES

I am grateful to Alain Boyer, James Franklin, Dagfinn Føllesdal, Isaac Levi and Nick Hammond for comments on an earlier draft of this chapter.

1. Manson 1999.
2. Kolakowski 1995; see also Blanchet 1919.
3. For a summary of the discussion concerning Pascal's interlocutor in the Wager, see Wetsel 1994, pp. 248–75.
4. 'When a soldier complains of his hard life (or a labourer etc.) try giving him nothing to do' (L 415/S 34). For a discussion of Pascal's analysis of the motivation of gamblers, see Elster 1999, pp. 214–16.
5. Montaigne, *The Complete Essays*, trans. M. A. Screech (Harmondsworth: Penguin, 1991), p. 551.
6. For the idea of states that are essentially by-products, see Elster 1982, ch. 2. The Jesuitical idea of 'directing one's intention' to certain aspects of an action so that it will no longer appear as sinful is vulnerable to the same objection.
7. Franklin 2001, p. 251 notes that Sirmond's book *On the Immortality of the Soul* (1637) already had 'the full version of the wager, including explicit discussion of risks and rewards'. The passage quoted in the text is taken from a book published in 1641; according to Franklin it is not known whether Pascal had read the 1637 book.
8. For an historical account, see Franklin 2001, ch. 4.
9. This is referred to as the doctrine of *probabilism* (Franklin 2001 pp. 74 ff.).
10. ibid., p.76. Bartolome de Medina, 'celebrated as the author of probabilism' (p. 74), was certainly guilty of serious conceptual confusion when he wrote that 'It could be argued [that] since the more probable opinion is more in conformity and safer, we are obliged to follow it. Against this is the argument that no one is obliged to do what is better and more perfect: it is more perfect to be a virgin than a wife, to be religious than

to be rich, but no one is obliged to adopt the more perfect of those' (cited ibid., pp. 75–6).

11. Indeed, in the table of contents to Hacking 1975 he calls the Wager 'the first well-understood contribution to decision theory'.

12. An example of a mere abstract possibility of human extinction is the idea that we are all living in a computer simulation that may be shut down at any time, as the result of our actions or by exogenous factors (Bostrom 2001).

13. For a fuller discussion of this subjective conception of *rationality*, and for an analysis of how it differs from ancient and modern conceptions of *reason*, see Elster (forthcoming).

14. The Jesuits added a wrinkle to this general approach by recommending that a rational agent choose the *description* under which he can perform the action without incurring damnation. 'That is how our Fathers have found a way to permit the acts of violence commonly practised in the defense of honour. For it is only a question of deflecting one's intention from the desire for vengeance, which is criminal, and applying it to the desire to defend one's honour, which according to our Fathers is lawful' (*OC* 1, 649). This task of 'deflecting one's intention' is, of course, as self-defeating as the task of never thinking about giraffes. You can fool others in this way, but not God.

15. Letter of 29.10.1647 (*OC* 1, 381). This may be an echo from Montaigne (*Complete Essays*, p. 1165): 'Many of this world's abuses are engendered – or to put it more rashly, all of this world's abuses are engendered – by our being schooled to be afraid to admit our ignorance and because we are required to accept anything which we cannot refute.'

16. The idea that people engage in gambling because it offers the possibility of losing does not imply that they want to lose, as suggested by psycho-analytical theories of gambling, e.g. Bergler 1957.

17. Pascal's *'assiette'*, rendered by Krailsheimer as 'basis', is perhaps better translated as 'equilibrium'. One can imagine three uses of the equilibrium metaphor to describe beliefs. (i) A belief may be in equilibrium like a ball in a closed bowl. Although it can be dislodged by external forces, it will find the equilibrium state when no forces operate on it. (ii) It may be in equilibrium like a ball in an open bowl. If the external forces are sufficiently strong, they may send it over the edge. (iii) It may be in equilibrium like a ball resting on a flat surface. In that case, no particular point is privileged. If we asked 'What does he really believe?', the answer is that *there is no fact of the matter*. This view seems close to Pascal's.

18. Krailsheimer translates 'without giving anything in return'. Pascal's text, 'sans rien donner', does not seem to justify 'in return'. If that is

what he had in mind, he would presumably have written *'rendre'* rather than *'donner'*.

19. In the sense of Tanner 1976–7.
20. The matter is complicated by the fact that the decision is not only important, but urgent, as we may die at any time. When Pascal refers to this aspect of the decision to believe (L 163/S 195), he may (or may not) be suggesting that it justifies believing on insufficient evidence.
21. Kolakowski 1995, p. 151.
22. *OC* I, p. 382.
23. *Principles of Philosophy*, IV. 205, in Descartes, *Philosophical Writings*, I, 290. As Pascal understood well, the Cartesian explanations are largely arbitrary (L 84/S 118).
24. Pascal notes that 'The Old Testament is a cipher' (L 276/S 307) that can be decoded in several ways.
25. *OC* I, 382–3.
26. Kolakowski 1995, p. 143; italics added. For other complications (not mentioned by Pascal) in interpreting prophecies and sorting out the false from the true, see Smith 1986. Many prophets were labelled false merely because their prophecies did not come true.
27. The interpretation proposed by M. le Guern (*OC* II, 1455) is internally coherent, but bears only a tenuous relation to the interpreted text.
28. Aanund Hylland (personal communication).
29. That it is well defined in non-classical mathematics (see, for instance, Robinson 1966) is irrelevant for my purposes. I am asking whether *Pascal* had the conceptual resources to make sense of the idea of real infinitesimals, not whether *we* can make sense of it.
30. Again, this idea was circulating in the seventeenth century; see, for instance, Leibniz, *Mathematische Schriften*, II, 288: 'dx and ddx are magnitudes, since when multiplied by infinite numbers...they yield ordinary numbers'.
31. Montaigne, *Complete Essays*, p. 1046.
32. Even a decreasing utility profile can add up to an infinite sum, provided that it does not decrease too fast. In an early writing, Leibniz ignored this proviso and argued that an infinity of evil however small always offsets the largest temporal gain. Later, he mentions that Torricelli and others 'have found figures of infinite length that are equal to finite spaces' (Elster 1975, pp. 247–8).
33. Assuming discrete time, exponential discounting implies that an amount of utility U t periods into the future has a present value of $U \cdot r^t$, where r is the rate of discounting. The present value of the infinite stream is then equal to the sum $U + U \cdot r + U \cdot r^2 + U \cdot r^3 + \cdots = U(1 - r)$.

34. Strotz 1955–6, Ainslie 1992. With hyperbolic discounting, the present value of utility U t periods into the future is $U/(1 + t)$ (I simplify). The sum $1 + 1/2 + 1/3 + 1/4 +$ does not converge to a finite sum.

35. For criticism of this principle, see notably ch. 4 of Keynes 1921. Ch. 6, on 'The weight of arguments', is also relevant.

36. Martin 1983, p. 60.

37. Scriven 1966, p. 103, cited after Morris 1986, p. 445.

38. For a survey, see Saka 2001.

39. Cited after Hacking 1975, p. 66.

40. The distinctions made in this paragraph can obviously be restated in terms of the lexicographic ordering discussed in the text.

41. See notably Williams 1973.

42. See the texts quoted in Kolakowski 1995, pp. 210–11.

43. Weber 1958, p. 115; Quattrone and Tversky 1986; Elster 1989, pp. 196–200.

44. *OC* 11, 259–60, 308–16; Kolakowski 1995, p. 56.

45. Kolakowski 1995, p. 122.

46. For a forceful argument along these lines, see Blanchet 1919.

47. Kolakowski 1995, p. 13.

48. ibid., p. 65.

5   Pascal's physics

Pascal's contributions to physics might appear limited: his research was confined to the investigation of the vacuum and the statics of fluids, and only a few relatively brief publications resulted. These include the *Expériences nouvelles touchant le vide* (1647), *Récit de la grande expérience de l'équilibre des liqueurs* (1648), and *Traités de l'équilibre des liqueurs et de la pesanteur de la masse de l'air*, which were published posthumously in 1664. However, these works are still admired for their rigour and held up as models of empirical investigation. Pascal's experiments were carefully designed to converge on the causes of phenomena. In his posthumous works especially, equally important to the design of his experiments was the manner in which he presented them to his readers, placing them in an order which, with his accompanying analysis, extended a few simple principles to a wide variety of phenomena and produced an illuminating synthesis of existing knowledge.

BACKGROUND

From the age of 14 Pascal accompanied his father to meetings conducted in the chamber of Marin Mersenne, who was a member of the religious order of Minims. It is well known that Mersenne circulated Descartes' *Meditations on First Philosophy* and collected the objections which were published with that work along with Descartes' responses. However, Mersenne's circle included Gilles Personne de Roberval, Pierre Fermat and Pierre Petit – all friends of Pascal who engaged in heated controversies with Descartes. This group of *savants* regarded Descartes' project of grounding physics in a priori principles and deductive metaphysics as retrograde – of the same stripe as the dogmatic metaphysics of the schools. Mersenne himself was scep-tical of essentialist metaphysical systems, of Descartes' system as much as Aristotle's. He doubted that humans could penetrate beyond sensible appearances to their causes and the inner natures of things and sought to render the phenomena intelligible instead by means of mathematical laws. He was also a great admirer of Descartes' antago-nist, Roberval, and closely associated with him during the 1630s and 1640s. Roberval, a mathematician and physicist, advocated scepti-cism towards physical systems and speculative hypotheses, empha-sising that physics could never advance beyond the application of mathematics to effects whose causes were perpetually hidden. Pascal shared these attitudes. The unconventional education he received from his father, Etienne, did not involve training in metaphysics and produced an 'orientation towards the concrete' (OC 1, 63–7).[1]

THE NEW EXPERIMENTS

The events that led Pascal into the investigation of the vacuum are well documented. In 1644 the Italian physicist and mathematician, Evangelista Torricelli, with the assistance of Michelangelo Ricci, produced an interesting phenomenon by following a suggestion of Galileo. They took a 4-foot long glass tube, sealed at one end, and filled it with mercury. When the tube was inverted with the open end placed in a dish of mercury covered with water, the mercury partially descended, leaving a very small space at the height of the tube. Torricelli suggested that this space was a vacuum. In contrast to previous discussions in which vacua were merely hypothesised to explain such things as the motion of atoms, here was the possi-ble production of a sensible vacuum. Through correspondence with Torricelli, Mersenne learned of this experiment and in December 1644 travelled to Florence, where he assisted Torricelli in repeating the experiment. Upon his return to Paris, Mersenne circulated in-formation about this experiment to some of his friends, including Pierre Chanut, the ambassador to Sweden, who tried with Mersenne to repeat the experiment. But their efforts were unsuccessful because they could not obtain adequate glass tubes.

In 1646 the Pascals were living at Rouen. During the summer they were visited by their friend Pierre Petit. Petit – who had earned Descartes' wrath by circulating objections to his *Dioptrics* – was at that time collaborating with his friend, Pierre Gassendi. On his way to Dieppe where he had some duties to perform as Intendant of Fortifications, Petit brought the news of Torricelli's experiment. He explained that he had tried the experiment himself, with a tube 2 feet in length, but did not have enough mercury to produce a space large enough to deny the hypothesis that it was filled with rarefied air or fine matter. In October, when Petit returned from Dieppe, the three travelled to Rouen, where skilled manufacturers of glass were able to supply them with a tube that was 4 feet in length and they successfully reproduced Torricelli's experiment.

In the winter of 1646/7 Pascal conducted public demonstrations of a number of variations on Torricelli's experiment. In his demonstrations Pascal used not only mercury, but water and wine as well. These fluids, having specific gravities much smaller than mercury, required the manufacture of much longer tubes. Wine was used in order to refute the opinion of those who claimed that the empty space was filled with fine matter. According to this hypothesis, wine, since it is obviously more spirituous, should have produced a larger space in the column than water. These experiments were witnessed by, among others, Florin Périer (Pascal's brother-in-law), Pierre Guiffart, Jacques Pierius, Adrien Auzout and several Jesuits. Pascal's experiments were widely discussed. In October 1646 Pierius published *An detur vacuum natura*, followed on 19 August 1647 by Pierre Guiffart's *Discours du vide, sur les expériences de Monsieur Pascal et le traité de M. Pierius*. Auzout related Pascal's experiments to Gassendi, who was then inspired to write a dissertation, *De nupero experimento circa vacuum*, which used the experiments to support elements of his philosophy. Initially interest was primarily in the space left by the descent of the mercury and whether it was a real vacuum. Only later was curiosity aroused about what caused the mercury to be suspended in the tube, always at the same height.

Pascal moved to Paris in the spring of 1647. On 24 July of that year – while Pascal was working on a treatise to be based on the experiments at Rouen and others he had since made – Mersenne received a letter from Des Noyers, who was stationed at the court in Warsaw. He enclosed a printed account of an experiment performed publicly by the Capucin, Valeriano Magni, which affirmed the existence of a real vacuum in the tube. To protect the priority of his work, in October 1647 Pascal published an 'abstract' of the treatise that he was preparing. This abstract was entitled 'Expériences nouvelles touchant le vide'.

The purpose of the experiments, Pascal would later say, was to disprove the widely held principle that 'nature would suffer its own destruction rather than admit the least empty space'. He claimed that, based on 'observations we make daily of the rarefaction and condensation of air', he had always been of the opinion that 'a vacuum is not a thing impossible in nature and that she does not flee it with as much horror as many imagine'. In addition, it had been proven that air 'can be condensed up to the thousandth part of the place that it seemed formerly to occupy', which could not occur without either vacua between the parts of air or the interpenetration of its parts. His successful replication of Toricelli's experiment only further confirmed his belief. But he discovered that even Toricelli's experiment was insufficient to dispel the prejudice against the possibility of a vacuum, some claiming that the apparently empty space was filled with spirits of mercury, and some that it was filled by a particle of air which had rarefied. Insultingly referring to Descartes' fine matter, Pascal added that there were others who placed in the empty space 'a matter which subsists only in their imagination'. So he resolved to conduct further experiments of such a design that they would be proof 'against all the objections which could be made' against the existence of a vacuum (OC 1, 436–8, 355–7).

The first part of the pamphlet describes the experiments, and then sets out the maxims that could be derived from them. Fanton d'Andon has compared Pascal's experiments and his analysis and presentation of them to that of his contemporaries, with special attention to Roberval, and concluded that Pascal's presentation introduces a 'new philosophy of experience' and a new kind of demonstration.[2] Peter Dear, in contrast, argues that Pascal's experiences are constructed according to the demands of Aristotle and what came to be known as the 'subordinate', 'middle', or 'mixed' sciences which required premises or principles that are conceded by all because they are evident from common experience. On this interpretation, Pascal's 'experiences' are not intended to be singular events produced in the privacy of a laboratory. Rather, Pascal relates them in such a way as to strip them of particularity in order to give them the status of common and unchanging experience that makes evident universal statements about nature.[3] Historians of science have been especially interested in analysing the order in which Pascal's experiments were presented. It has been suggested that they form a rigorous chain in which 'the result of each experiment is suggested or implied by an hypothesis founded on the results of the preceding experiments'.[4] Each experiment is ingeniously illuminated by all the others. One liquid is replaced by another, while the apparatus remains unchanged, or the apparatus is changed, but not the liquid. The effects produced by liquids singly are compared to mixed liquids.

The first two experiments are designed to refute the opinion of those, such as Jacques Pierius in his *An detur vacuum in rerum natura* (1646), who claimed that 'the force which nature uses when it wishes to impede the vacuum is unlimited and infinite'.[5] Pierius had tried to explain the experimental results which he witnessed in Rouen by defending the notion that rarefaction and condensation involve changes in the volumes of bodies without admitting or excluding any corpuscle. At the same time he argued that the humidity of mercury, water and wine – the fluids used by Pascal in the experiments – produced an emission of vapours in the height of the tube. To address this, a glass syringe, with its piston depressed and its mouth blocked by a finger, is placed in a vessel of water. When the piston is retracted, which requires only a moderate force, an apparently empty space appears in the syringe without drawing water from the vessel. The volume of the space can be varied by further retraction of the piston, but an increase in volume produces no noticeable increase in the amount of pull felt by the finger. This first experiment suggests that the creation of a small vacuum requires only a small force. Replacing the syringe with a bellows shows that there is no greater sensible resistance to the formation of a larger vacuum. The third experiment replicates Torricelli's experiment on a grand scale, with a glass tube 46 feet in length and filled with wine which visibly descends to a height of around 32 feet leaving an apparently empty space, approximately 13 feet in length, at the top of the tube. The fourth experiment involves a scalene siphon with one leg 50 feet in length and the other 45 feet in length. The siphon is filled with water and the mouths of both legs are stopped and immersed to a depth of 1 foot in vessels of water which differ by 5 feet in their height above the ground. When the legs are unstopped, the siphon draws no water from one vessel to the other. Instead, the water in each leg descends to a height of 31 feet above the surface of the water in its vessel,

leaving an apparently empty space. When the siphon is inclined to
31 feet it draws water from the higher to the lower vessel, showing
that the siphon's ability to function is related to the height of the water in the tube. In addition, the claim that vapours or spirits occupy
the space at the top of the tube is addressed: wine is granted to be
more spirituous than water, yet water produces a smaller space at the
top of the tube. The fifth and sixth experiments use pistons of cord
and wood to draw mercury and water, singly and in combination,
into vertical glass tubes and glass siphons to ingeniously determine
that the height of a liquid in a tube is proportionate to its weight. The
seventh and eighth experiments extend insights of the first five experiments by systematically varying the liquids used and the length
of the siphon's legs, showing that varying the shape of the tube does
not vary the effect and that the whole spectrum of effects produced
by the experiments are the same if one takes account of the differences between the weights of the liquids. As Guiffart explained in his
Discours du vide, some of the experiments also suggested nature's
limited horror of the vacuum, since the mercury is so heavy that it
did not seem likely to mount in the tube by its own inclination and
must be drawn there by some force.

Pascal concludes this section by stating that the unabridged treatise which he will eventually produce will include other experiments, 'with tubes of all lengths, sizes, and shapes, charged with
different liquids, diversely immersed in different liquids, transported
from one to another, weighed in several ways, and in which are noted
the different attractions felt by the finger which blocks the tubes in
which there is an apparent vacuum.' Pascal does not speculate on the
inner nature of the phenomena he has produced. Instead, the descriptions of the experiments are followed by a set of maxims which convert the observations of specific phenomena into generalised claims.
The maxims are 'deduced' from them in the sense that they are 'a
recapitulation of that which has been seen' (*OC* 1, 362, 357).

These maxims only concern the 'apparent vacuum' and make no
claim about whether the vacuum is real. Nature's abhorrence of a
vacuum is employed as a kind of shorthand for the tendencies of the
fluids made manifest by the experiments. The first two maxims gen-
eralise the experiences produced with the syringe and bellows. All
bodies resist separation, which would produce an apparent vacuum
between them, and this is what it means to say that 'nature abhors

an apparent vacuum'. This 'horror' is no greater towards admitting a large apparent vacuum than a small one. The third maxim sets out the measurement of the force of the horror: it is 'limited, and equal to the force with which water of a certain height, which is around thirty-one feet, tends to flow downwards'. The fourth, fifth and sixth maxims recapitulate the first three, but replace resistance to separation with an inclination of bodies on the boundaries of a vacuum to fill it. This inclination is not greater for filling a large apparent vacuum than a small one. The force of this inclination is limited, and is always equal to that with which water of a certain height, which is around 31 feet, tends to flow downwards. The seventh maxim states that any force greater than this is sufficient to produce an apparent vacuum (OC 1, 362–3).

The maxims about the apparent vacuum are followed by a set of propositions that the longer treatise will establish about the matter which can be said to fill the apparent vacuum: it is not filled with air from outside the tube, with air 'enclosed in the interstices of atoms of corpuscles composing the liquids', or with an imperceptible particle of air left in the tube accidentally and rarefying to fill the empty space. Nor is it filled with a vaporised bit of mercury or water. The empty space is filled with no matter known in nature or perceptible to the senses. In the conclusion Pascal asserts that until he is shown that some substance fills the apparently empty space, he will take the maxims he posed in the first part to be true not only for the vacuum which is apparent, but also for 'the absolute vacuum' (OC 1, 363–5).

The publication of Pascal's *Expériences nouvelles* was followed immediately by a letter from Jesuit father, Etienne Noël, who was rector of the College of Clermont, Paris. Formerly Noël had been rector of La Flèche, where Descartes had been one of his students. Descartes seems to have sent him copies of the *Discours de la méthode* (1637), with its accompanying essays, and the *Principes de la philosophie* (1646). Noël had developed a natural philosophy that combined eclectically principles of Cartesian and Aristotelian physics. This was not the odd combination it might seem, since both denied the existence of a vacuum and constructed essentialist metaphysical systems.

Noël argued that the space produced above the mercury must be a body 'because it has the actions of a body: it transmits light with reflections and refractions and it retards the movement of another body', since it takes time for the mercury to fill the space when the tube is upended. What appears to be an empty space is then really a body. Noël went on to explain the Torricellian phenomena. The natural state of ordinary air, he claimed, is a mixture, which includes fire, water and earth. The light's penetration of the glass tube clearly shows it to possess many fine pores. The weight of mercury introduces violent changes in the air outside it, by pulling the fire, or subtle matter, through the minute pores of the glass, which acts as a filter. The mercury is suspended in the tube because the subtle matter strives to return to its natural state of mixture with the elements trapped outside of the glass, thus counterpoising the downward force of the mercury's weight. Besides this, the term *empty space* is contradictory. The definition of a body is 'a composite of parts outside of parts', of 'such a length, magnitude' and 'figure'. Consequently, 'all space is necessarily a body' (*OC* I, 372–6).

In his response, Pascal quickly shifted the debate on to epistemological grounds by insisting on 'a universal rule which applies to all particular subjects which involve recognition of the truth'. This rule constitutes the 'principal part of the way in which the sciences are treated in the schools'. The rule is to 'never make a decisive judgment affirming or denying a proposition', unless it meets one of two conditions. It must 'appear so clearly and distinctly to the senses or the reason, as it is subject to the one or the other, that its certitude cannot be doubted' – and these are 'what we call principles or axioms', as, for example, 'if equal things are added to equal things, the totals will be equal'. Failing this condition, it must be a necessary consequence of a principle that is known with such certitude. Any proposition which cannot meet these requirements is 'doubtful and uncertain', more to be doubted than affirmed, until convincingly demonstrated (*OC* I, 377–8).

Returning to Noël's claims, Pascal pointed out that rays of light penetrating the tube have no refraction other than what is produced by the glass alone. So if there is a body in the space it does not act sensibly on the rays of light. Besides this, any contradictions involved in the term *empty space* only result from Noël's presupposed definitions of 'empty space, light, and motion', which yield contradictions in claims such as 'Light penetrates an empty space, and it takes time for bodies there to move'. But these definitions are not based on real knowledge of the nature of these things. Likewise, Noël's explanation of the mercury's suspension and of what fills the apparently empty space are merely based on 'ideas', not demonstrations, and 'all things of this kind, whose existence is not manifest to any of the senses, are as difficult to believe as they are easy to invent'. To establish that an hypothesis is true, it is not enough to show that it can be used to explain the phenomena. However, if from an hypothesis only one thing follows which is contrary to the phenomena, then that is enough to demonstrate it as false (*OC* 1, 378–82).

Pascal attempted to clarify the distinction between *body* and an *empty space*. To define body Noël used only relative terms, such as '*top, bottom, right, left*', which actually constitute the definition of space, not body, and 'only apply to a body as it occupies space'. And 'what we call an *empty space* is a space having length, breadth, and depth, immobile and capable of receiving and containing a body of the same size and figure'. This is the same as 'what is called a *solid* in geometry which only considers abstract and immaterial things'. Consequently, the 'essential difference' between empty space and body is that 'the one is immobile and the other mobile, and the one can receive into itself a body which penetrates its dimensions, whereas the other cannot'. An empty space is not a nothing, but 'holds the middle between matter and nothingness'. Noting the similarity between Descartes' notion of subtle matter and the matter that Noël claimed was in the space above the mercury in the tube, Pascal closed with a mocking reference to Descartes: this physicist, one of the most celebrated of the day, fills the whole universe with a kind of matter which is 'imperceptible and unheard of, which is of the same substance as the sky and the elements' (*OC* 1, 384–5).

In his second letter Noël especially criticised the coherence of Pascal's conception of empty space: Pascal had attributed real existence to quantity separated from all its individual conditions by an abstraction of the understanding which could only exist in the mind of a geometer. Pascal commented upon this criticism in a letter to Le Pailleur. After explaining why he broke off correspondence with Noël, Pascal defended his definition of absolute space. It is 'neither mind nor body, but it is space; as time is neither body nor mind; and as time does not cease to be, although it be not either of these things, so space can be, although it be neither body nor mind'. If substance is taken to include only mind and body, then space, like time, is 'neither substance nor accident', for 'in order to be it is not necessary to be either substance or accident' (*OC* 1, 388–9, 396–7, 400–1, 413–25, 1082–3). It has been noted that Pascal's explanation of space, and the analogy between space and time, seem to have been directly influenced by Gassendi, perhaps by reading a manuscript of *Animadversiones*, which would be published in 1649.[6]

THE GREAT EXPERIMENT OF THE EQUILIBRIUM OF FLUIDS

While most of the initial interest in the experiments centred around the possibility of a vacuum, these experiments raised questions about what caused the suspension of the liquids in the tubes. Some time after the spring of 1647, when he moved to Paris, Pascal had become aware of Torricelli's explanation for the mercury's suspension in the tube. In a letter to Ricci, Torricelli had reasoned that 'we live submerged at the base of an ocean of elementary air and we know by indubitable experience that the air has weight', more weight in the lower regions and less on the tops of mountains, where it is thinner. He attributed the cause of the mercury's suspension to the weight of the 'column of air' above the dish into which the tube was inserted. The analogy between air and an ocean would play a central role in Pascal's *Traités de l'équilibre des liqueurs et de la pesanteur de l'air*. In a letter written to Périer on 15 November 1647 Pascal claimed that at the time he published *Expériences nouvelles* he had accepted Torricelli's hypothesis, but lacked convincing proof (*OC* 1, 446–7, 426).

The explanation by the 'column of air' was initially disputed by Roberval, Mersenne and other contemporaries because it was generally believed that the weight of the air was so great that the mercury would not descend in the tube at all if that were the cause of its suspension. However, by September 1647, when he was writing the preface of his *Reflexiones physico mathematicae*, Mersenne adopted this hypothesis and proposed an experiment, perhaps suggested by Descartes, to compare the level of mercury in the tube at the base of a mountain and at the summit. A little later, however, Mersenne dropped this hypothesis and adopted Roberval's theory that an attractive force held the mercury in the tube.

Meanwhile, early in 1648 Roberval was conducting experiments which cast doubt on the reality of a vacuum in the tube. For example, he found that heating the apparently empty space produced a slight descent of the mercury, suggesting that the space contained a rarefied body. He filled the tube partly with water and partly with mercury. When he reversed the tube, the mercury descended to the bottom, with the water above it and an apparently empty space on the top. But he observed innumerable small bubbles descending from the mercury through the water. When he inclined the tube to make the space disappear, the bubbles joined in a small volume, leading him to suspect the presence of air, which dilates, in the tube.

Roberval conducted further experiments which convinced him that air is compressible, expandible and elastic. In one of these a carp's bladder was inflated and found to expand when placed in the space above the mercury. Reflecting on this he abandoned his previous belief that an attractive force held the mercury in the tube and took up the hypothesis that it was caused by the pressure of exterior air, the air in the tube dilating more as the pressure of the exterior air on the mercury in the bowl was less. To test this hypothesis he invented the experiment of the vacuum within the vacuum. According to Auzout, this experiment, in June 1648, convinced the *savants mathématiciens* of Paris that the mercury was suspended by the weight of a column of air. Auzout went on to construct his own variant of this experiment.[7] Earlier Pascal had conducted a similar experiment in the presence of his brother-in-law, Périer, prior to 15 November 1647. This was done by placing one of Torricelli's tubes inside another. Pascal described the results.

You saw that the mercury of the inner tube remained suspended at the height at which it is held in the ordinary experiment, when it was counter-balanced and pressed by the weight of the entire mass of air. You also saw that, to the contrary, the mercury fell entirely, with no height or suspension when, having surrounded it with a vacuum so that it was deprived of air on all sides, it was no longer pressed or counter-balanced by any air. You saw then that this height or suspension of mercury increased or diminished as the pressure of air was augmented or diminished, and that finally all the different heights or suspensions of the mercury were found to be always proportionate to the pressure of the air. (*OC* 1, 428)

It appears that at the time Roberval recorded his own experiment of the vacuum within the vacuum he was unaware of Pascal's earlier experiment. The delicacy of the operations required by his apparatus made it difficult to replicate this experiment, but Pascal later devised an easier version of the experiment which was illustrated in *Traités de l'équilibre des liqueurs et de la pesanteur de la masse de l'air*.

Pascal considered the phenomena produced by these experiments, as well as those in his *Expériences nouvelles*, to be 'only particular cases of a universal proposition on the equilibrium of fluids'. However, even though the effects could be 'explained so naturally by the weight and pressure of air alone', they could 'yet be explained with some probability by the abhorrence of a vacuum', so further proof was required. For that purpose he requested that Périer perform an experiment on the mountain called the puy-de-Dôme near Clermont (*OC* 1, 427–8). The results were described in *Récit de la grande expérience de l'équilibre des liqueurs* (1648).

This experiment has been called one of the 'two most famous event experiments in the seventeenth century' (the second being Newton's experiments with prisms).[8] Pascal claimed priority, but Descartes insisted that he was the true inventor of the experiment and had mentioned the idea to Pascal when visiting him and Roberval on 23 and 24 September 1647 (*OC* 1, 15, 446). Mersenne was actually the first to propose the project in a publication. In fact, the idea of the experiment would have been suggested rather directly by Torricelli's letter to Ricci in which he compared the atmosphere to an ocean, for in that same letter (which Pascal read shortly after arriving in Paris in the spring of 1647) Torricelli suggested that the weight of air caused the mercury's suspension and was greater near the surface of the earth than on the upper reaches of mountains.

Pascal's doubts about nature's horror led him to devise what he called 'the great experiment on the equilibrium of fluids'. Because Clermont in Auvergne was one of the few places in France that was physically suited for the experiment, he asked his brother-in-law, Périer, who lived nearby, to conduct the experiment on his behalf. The letter in which he made this request was included in the *Récit* and is dated 15 November 1647. Pascal directed Périer 'to make the ordinary experiment of the vacuum several times in the same day, in the same tube, with the same mercury, sometimes at the base and sometimes at the summit of a mountain at least five or six hundred fathoms high'. There is certainly more air pressing down at the base of the mountain than at the top, but it cannot be said that nature abhors a vacuum more at the foot of the mountain than at the summit.

Consequently, if the height of the mercury is less at the top of the mountain than at the base, then 'it will follow necessarily that the weight and pressure of the air is the sole cause of this suspension of the mercury, and not horror of the vacuum'. This letter is followed by Périer's response, on 22 September 1648, after he was finally able to conduct the experiment, which he did numerous times with several priests and lay people as witnesses. He left one Torricellian tube at the monastery to be observed frequently by the monks. With the witnesses, he carried the other tube up the puy-de-Dôme, which was about 500 fathoms high. Various heights of mercury were recorded at different places on the mountain. He also repeated the experiment at the foot and the top of the highest tower of Notre-Dame de Clermont and at other altitudes around the city. The results were consistent with Pascal's predictions. Analysing Périer's data, Pascal concluded that a difference in altitude of 6 or 7 fathoms varied the height of the mercury by about $^1/_{24}$ of an inch, which he further confirmed by conducting the experiment on buildings of different heights. Pascal claimed that 'many consequences' could be drawn from the experiments, of which he mentioned three. The experiment showed that the tube of mercury could be used to compare altitudes of distant places. It also revealed the inaccuracy of thermometers, since the height of their fluids could vary according to atmospheric pressure as well as temperature. Finally, the experiment showed the unequal pressure of the air at the same temperature, which is always greatest in the lowest places. Pascal promised to deduce these and other consequences in his longer treatise on the vacuum. In a final address to the reader, Pascal announced that the experiments justified departing from the ancient maxim that nature abhors a vacuum (OC I, 1090, 428–9, 435–7).

In fact, nature's limited horror of a vacuum could explain the phenomena produced in this experiment. Assuming that the parts of air in the upper portions of the atmosphere are farther apart than the parts below, nature would have already expended some of its force in pulling the parts of air together resisting the formation of empty spaces between them. This would leave nature with less force to support the mercury at the top of a mountain. While such explanations remained possible, Mersenne concluded that Pascal's experiment provided 'a clear enough proof' that atmospheric pressure caused the mercury's suspension in the tube.[9]

88   DANIEL C. FOUKE

THE EQUILIBRIUM OF LIQUIDS AND OF
THE MASS OF AIR

The *Traités de l'équilibre des liqueurs et de la pesanteur de la masse de l'air* were composed in 1654 but published in 1663, not long after Pascal's death. The first of these two treatises has been called 'the third of the great founding texts of hydrostatics, after Archimedes' *On Floating Bodies* and books IV and V of the *Statics* written by Simon Stevin (1548–1620) (*OC* 1, 1102). It is interesting to compare the treatises of 1654 with Pascal's projected treatise on the vacuum. This work remains only in fragmentary form. Part of the treatise was to be an historical reconstruction of the experiments he had conducted and reported on in his earlier works. The various experiments were to provide the starting points for the investigation of hypotheses, as in the *Expériences nouvelles*, with more general principles derived gradually from detailed analysis of the experiments. In contrast, the *Traités de l'équilibre des liqueurs et de la pesanteur de la masse de l'air* present the phenomena produced in the experiments as the results of general principles that are first applied to the equilibrium of liquids and which are then extended to the weight and pressure of the atmosphere. The equilibrium between the weight of air and a column of liquid is a result of the general principles governing the equilibrium between two columns of liquid in communicating vessels.

The influences on Pascal's analysis of hydrostatic phenomena are well documented. Mersenne's encyclopedia, *Universae geometriae mixtaeque mathematicae synopsis* (1644), included the propositions from Archimedes' *On Floating Bodies*. In his *Cogitata physicomathematica*, also published in 1644, Mersenne included an account of Galileo's study of hydraulics and reproduced the definitions and theorems used by Simon Stevin in his ground-breaking study of hydraulic phenomena. Mersenne was also in possession of a treatise on statics that Descartes had sent to him on 13 July 1638 and which led to a sustained correspondence. Mersenne published Descartes' foundational axiom in the *Cogitata*. It seems that Mersenne was also familiar with a letter on hydrostatics written by Giovanni-Batista Benedetti and published in 1583. Torricelli's *De motu gravium* was also well known in Mersenne's circle. Mersenne made his own contribution to the analysis of hydraulic phenomena as well. In his

Cogitata physico-mathematica Mersenne began with Stevin's law that the pressure exerted by water on the surface below it will be equal to the weight of the column of water with this surface as base and, for height, the vertical distance rising to the upper surface of the water. From this law he derived the hydrostatic paradox: a single pound of water can exert the same amount of pressure at the base of a vessel which contains it as one thousand pounds of water, 'indeed as much as the whole ocean', exerts on the base of its container. For suppose the ocean and a pound of water are contained in two vessels with bases of equal size. Suppose now that the vessel that contains a pound of water narrows just above the base to become a tube so narrow that the pound of water mounts as high as the ocean. Then the pressure that each exerts at the base of its own vessel will be equal. Mersenne went on to consider the transmission of pressure through fluids by imagining the entire ocean to be entirely enclosed in a vessel with a hole in the cover through which a piston could be inserted. Duhem has pointed out the similarities between these passages and the first three chapters of Pascal's *Traité de l'équilibre des liqueurs*, which develop the principle of the hydraulic press.[10]

The first chapter of *Traité de l'équilibre des liqueurs* announces that fluids (*liqueurs*) weigh, or exert vertical pressure, in proportion to their height independently of their total weight. The principle is illustrated in figures I, II, III and IV (see Fig. 5). If these differently configured vessels are filled to the same height and have plugged openings of the same size in their base, then the downward pressure of water in each will be equal. Figure I shows a straight cylinder. Of the vessels shown in the figures this is the simplest and it gives the measure of the downward pressure of the water in the four other vessels which are represented on the same horizontal line of the plate. Figure II shows the same volume of water, held in a cylinder of the same size as the first, but canted at an angle shortly above its base. Figure III shows a much larger volume of water in a vessel, which swells to a bowl just above the stopper. Figure IV shows a vessel with a smaller volume in a vessel that tapers inward. The same amount of force is required to keep the stoppers from coming out of each vessel, and the measure of this force is determined by the first vessel. The water contained in this vessel, which is a cylinder of the same diameter as the opening at its base, is 100 pounds. Figure V shows the experiment by which 'to prove exactly' this principle. The illustration

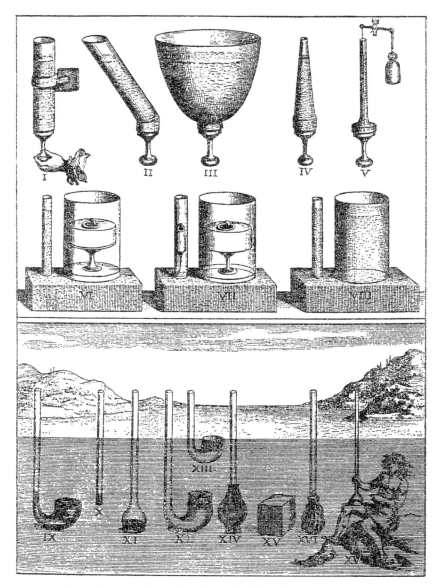

Fig. 5 Plate I of Pascal's *Traité de l'équilibre des liqueurs.*

is of the third experiment described by Stevin in order to demonstrate one of his principles of hydrostatic practice. A tightly fitted
stopper is placed in the aperture at the base of the fifth vessel, which
narrows sharply to a thin tube just above the base. A cord is attached

to the stopper, passed through the vessel and affixed to the arm of a balance. A weight of 100 pounds on the other arm of the balance establishes equilibrium with the water, weighing only 1 ounce, which is in the narrow vessel. Having varied the shapes of each vessel to establish his principle concerning the measure of downward force, he then varies the state of the water. If the water in the vessel in figure V is frozen, its equilibrium with the weight is destroyed. Water frozen in that vessel requires a weight of only 1 ounce to balance it. Melt the ice and again a weight of 100 pounds is required, so that the principle is shown to apply only to fluids (1: 468–71, 1105).

Pascal further generalises the principles established by the experiments in figures I through V by varying the locations of the openings in figure VI, which shows a vessel with two apertures in the top, one of which is one hundred times smaller in diameter than the other. To each aperture a tube is soldered. If the smaller tube is filled with water and a piston is placed in the other, it will be necessary to place a great weight on the piston to keep the water from pushing it up. This is analogous to the measure of downward force by the balance in figure V. The fluidity of the water ensures that, provided the height of water is the same, the vertical pressure will be constant in every direction and on every point of the inner surfaces. If the water is poured to twice the height, then twice as much weight will have to be placed on the piston in order to establish equilibrium – a principle that will not apply to compressible fluids, such as air is shown to be in the second treatise.

The second chapter explains 'why liquids weigh in proportion to their height'. The explanation begins with figure VII, which shows an 'expérience' labelled 'Nouvelle sorte de machine pour multiplier forces'. The physical system represented in the engraving is identical to that in figure VI, except that the water in the narrow cylinder has been replaced by a weight on a piston in equilibrium with the larger weight on the larger piston. The system is in equilibrium when the pistons are at the same height and that is achieved when a weight of 100 pounds is placed on the piston in the large aperture and a weight of 1 pound on the small one. So 'one person pushing the small piston will equal the force of one hundred people pushing the one which is one hundred times larger, and will overmaster ninety-nine', and there will always be equilibrium if the forces applied to the pistons are as the ratios of the openings. If the smaller piston is depressed, the path it travels is in the same ratio to the path of the larger piston as the areas of their apertures, and this is the same ratio as that of the forces exerted on each piston. Here, then, is the hydraulic press by which a person can multiply forces to lift any load. The incompressibility of the water – what Pascal calls its 'continuité' – assures that the pistons are so joined that one cannot move without moving the other and the larger piston must be displaced by a volume of water equal to that displaced by the smaller piston. If the small piston moves one inch, then the water it pushes finds an opening a hundred times greater, so that the larger piston can only be moved a distance which is hundredth of the smaller piston's. The fluidity of the water assures that all its parts are displaced equally so that the same pressure is exerted in every direction and is felt equally on every part of the inner surface of the vessel and pistons. While the larger piston is one hundred times heavier than the smaller, it is also in contact with one hundred times as many parts of the water, each part exerting an equal pressure. The result is that paths of the pistons are to each other as the forces which move them, it being obvious that to move 100 pounds of water 1 inch is the same thing as to move 1 pound of water 100 inches. Pascal links the hydraulic press to the lever, wheel, endless screw and other such machines – the distance (chemin) covered is increased in the same ratio as the force applied (what we would now call work). This mathematical relationship can even be taken 'for the true cause of this effect' (1: 471–5).

Pascal then offers another proof 'which only geometers will be able to follow', that being those, such as Mersenne and his circle, who had read Torricelli's Opera geometrica (1644), which contained De motu gravium. This work began with the theory of the inclined plane and derived from it the principle that when two weights are united together by means of a lever, pulley or any other mechanism, so that the movement of one produces movement in the other, these weights cannot be moved of themselves unless their common centre of gravity descends. Pascal uses this principle to prove that the two pistons represented in figure VII are in equilibrium. He also mentions a 'little treatise on mechanics', which he had written but which is lost to us, in which he proved that the cause of all multiplication of forces by mechanical instruments is that 'the unequal weights which are placed in equilibrium by the machines are so disposed by the construction of the machines that their common centre of gravity could never descend, whatever position they take, so that they must always remain at rest, that is, in equilibrium'.

Liquids weigh according to their heights, and not their expanse, because of a general principle that governs all statics. To show this, Pascal returns to figure VI in which the smaller piston of figure VII is replaced by a column of water of the same weight. Looking at this from the perspective of figure VII, it is clear that equilibrium is established because the water in the tube is equivalent to a piston the weight of which is in the same ratio to the weight on the larger piston as the size of their apertures. The principles of the hydraulic press revealed in figure VII can also be used to analyse figure V. In the lower portion of the vessel a fine tube flares at its base to become the same diameter as the stopper which is tied by a string to the arm of a balance. The flared portion of the tube can be understood as a closed vessel with two openings, like the hydraulic press. As in figure VI, the water in the narrow part of the tube can be understood to be a piston inserted into the smaller of two openings. The weight of this piston exerts a force that is in the same ratio to the weight on the balance (which holds the stopper in the bottom) as the area of the smaller opening is to the larger opening at the bottom of the vessel. Consequently, water in these tubes does the same thing as pistons of equal weight and the multiplication of forces is not caused by the liquidity of the water in these tubes but by the water's extension from one opening of a closed vessel to another.

In his third chapter Pascal uses the principles he has developed to explain further examples of the equilibrium of liquids. Figure VIII shows the same apparatus as figure VII, but with both the pistons re-placed with straight tubes filled with water. They are in equilibrium when the heights of the water are the same. The amount of water is therefore proportional to the area of the openings below each column and, according to what was established in chapter II, the water in the two columns is equivalent to pistons inserted into openings of the closed vessel below which are in equilibrium when their weights are proportional to the openings. And because liquids weigh only accord-ing to their height above a surface and not according to the expanse of the vessel, all these conclusions can be extended to vessels of all kinds. For a vessel of any shape with two openings, O_1 and O_2, the pressure exerted on the base of the vessel by the liquid above each opening will depend only on its height. If two different liquids, such as water and mercury, are placed in each tube, then they will be in equilibrium when their heights are proportional to their weights.

The principle of the equilibrium of fluids has been established: at any given level a fluid exerts a pressure which is determined by the height of the fluid above it and which is constant in every direction. In the remainder of the first treatise Pascal deduces what phenomena would be produced in a set of nine further experiments. Figures IX and X are analysed as variants of figure VIII, in which equilibrium is established between two different liquids, water and quicksilver. Figures XI, XII and XIII are analysed as variants of figure VI, which showed a column of liquid in equilibrium with a piston. In figure XI a glass tube, flared at one end, is immersed in water. A copper cylinder is suspended in the tube by the pressure of water beneath it. Figure XII shows 'this tube we have just described', but curved upward to receive a wooden cylinder which is pressed into the tube by the weight of water above it. In figure XIII the tube is raised until the cylinder is flush with the surface of the water, so that it is held in place by its weight alone. Figures XIV, XVI and XVII show how fluids exert pressure on immersed, compressible bodies. Figure XIV shows a bellows with a tube of 20 feet. The bellows is immersed so that the opening of the tube is above the water. If the holes in the wings are stopped, so that all the pressure of the water is exerted against the outside of the bellows, they will be hard to open. In Figure XVI the same tube is placed in a balloon which is filled with mercury and immersed in water. The pressure of the water makes the mercury in the tube visibly ascend until it reaches a height at which it is in equilibrium with the water pressing the balloon. In figure XVII a man is immersed in water with a tube, 20 feet in length and cupped at the lower end, pressed against his leg. Where the cup meets his leg the flesh will swell, because the pressure of the water is exerted against every other part of his leg except there. Figure XV shows an immersed body and is used in Pascal's discussion of Archimedes' principle. Because a body in water is counterpoised by an equal volume of water, the body is carried in the water 'as if it were in the pan of a balance whose other pan carried a volume of water of equal weight'.

In the second treatise, *Traité de la pesanteur de la masse de l'air*, Pascal establishes an analogy between liquids, and their behaviour as analysed in the first treatise, and air. The link between pneumatics and hydraulics had been suggested by Torricelli's letter to Ricci, which Pascal read shortly after his arrival in Paris and was already suggested in the name he gave to the experiment on the puy-de-Dôme. He called it 'the *great experiment on the equilibrium of fluids*' because it showed 'the equilibrium of air and mercury, which are the lightest and heaviest of all the fluids which are known'. The treatise begins with the assertion, which 'no one denies today', that 'the air is heavy', of which there is ample proof in the fact that a balloon weighs more when inflated than it does when empty. From this simple fact, Pascal draws a series of consequences that creates an analogy between the effects of air and of water: not only each part, but the whole mass of air, has weight and this weight is finite. As the mass of water in the sea presses the earth with its weight, so does the mass of air press every part of the surface of the earth. As the bottom of a bucket is pressed more by water when full than when half-empty, so the tops of mountains are pressed less by air than are the valleys, where the air is deeper. As bodies immersed in water are pressed on all sides, so are bodies immersed in the air. We do not feel this pressure for the same reason that fish do not – because we are pressed equally on all sides. These properties of air establish that it is a fluid governed by the principle discovered in the first treatise: at any given level air exerts a pressure that is determined by the height of the air above it and which is constant in every direction (*OC* 1, 426).

Pascal then introduces an analogy, previously drawn by Descartes and Torricelli, which distinguishes the behaviours of air and water. In contrast to the incompressible fluids discussed in the first treatise, air can be compared to a great heap of wool compressed more at the base than the top. From the fluidity and compressibility of air it follows that 'if we took a balloon only half filled with air' and carried it up a mountain, it would inflate more at the top than it did at the bottom. He then reports that he had actually confirmed this by experiment. As the fluidity and incompressibility of water explained the *expériences* discussed in the first treatise, fluidity and compressibility of air explain the *expériences* that had been attributed to nature's horror of a vacuum. Pascal systematically draws, when relevant, on the hydrostatic laws he had produced in the first treatise. These laws when applied to the mass of air explain why a bellows with a closed aperture is hard to open, why two polished bodies that have been placed together are hard to separate, why a hat on a table is hard to snatch up, why water flows into a syringe placed in water when

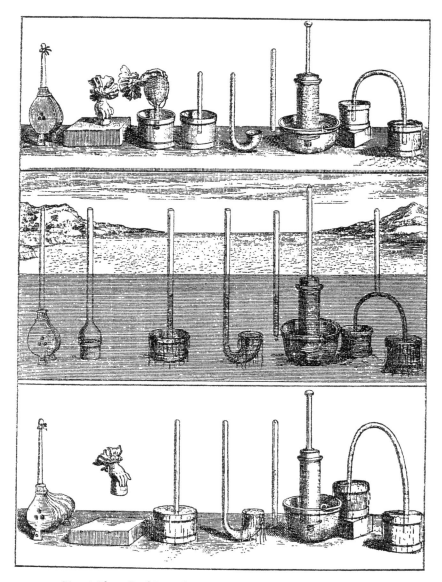

Fig. 6 Plate II of Pascal's *Traité de l'équilibre des liqueurs*.

the piston is withdrawn, why water remains suspended in a bottle which was filled with water and placed with its mouth down in a vessel, and so on. The fourth and fifth chapters examine *expériences* which establish that the effects produced by the weight of air vary according to humidity and height (*OC* 1, 489–93, 1108).

In the sixth chapter Pascal concludes that all the phenomena he has attributed to the weight of the mass of air would cease entirely 'if we were above the air or in a place where there were none'. He reasons that, since a difference in the weight of air at the foot and the top of the mountain caused the mercury in a Torricellian tube to fall, were one able to raise the tube entirely above the height of the atmosphere, the mercury – no longer suspended by the weight of air – would entirely fall from the tube. So would it happen were the experiment conducted in a room from which all air had been removed. In place of these experiments, which were impossible to conduct, Pascal describes a modified version of his earlier experiment of the vacuum within a vacuum. A glass tube is recurved at the bottom, closed at end A, and left open at end B. Another tube is made entirely straight and open at both ends, M and N. End M is inserted and soldered into the recurved end of the other, as shown in figure 7. B is stopped with a finger and the two soldered tubes are filled with mercury and inverted so that N is immersed in a basin of mercury. The mercury flows entirely out of the upper portion of the tube into the basin formed at the recurved end B, while the mercury in MN remains suspended at a height of 26–27 inches. The explanation for this phenomenon is that the air weighs upon the mercury in the basin to establish equilibrium with the mercury in the tube MN, but no air weighs on the mercury of AB, so that the mercury is free to fall. And if one's finger is removed from the opening near B, so that air enters, the mercury at the recurved end will rise to the level at which it is at equilibrium with the air.

Pascal goes on, in his seventh, eighth and ninth chapters, to calculate how far water can rise in pumps at different altitudes, how much each of these altitudes is pressed by the weight of air, and the total weight of the mass of air. In his conclusion he claims to have 'demonstrated' by means of 'arguments and experiments absolutely convincing' that the weight of the mass of air is singly responsible for all the effects that had been attributed to nature's horror of the vacuum, so that it is 'now assured that in the whole of nature there is no effect produced by her in order to avoid a vacuum'. His proof consisted in making nature's horror extraneous. By linking effects produced by water and air and other fluids, and relating these in turn to general principles of statics, every introduction of nature's horror to explain an effect has been made to appear ridiculously *ad hoc*. Pascal makes this point in his conclusion by returning to the bellows

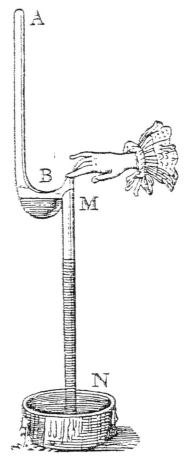

Fig. 7 'The experiment of the vacuum within a vacuum', from
Traité de l'équilibre des liqueurs.

represented in figure XIV of the *Traité de l'équilibre des liqueurs.*
The bellows are immersed with their wings stopped and with a tube
of 20 feet projecting above the water. The wings are difficult to open
because of the pressure of the water, with the difficulty increasing
as the bellows are more deeply submerged and decreasing as it is
brought closer to the surface. The difficulty ceases when the holes in
the bellows are opened so that the water is free to come in. It is possible to explain this effect by horror of air – a horror which ceases once

the wings are opened to allow water to come in, but 'there is no one who would not laugh at such an inference' because another explanation is available – the pressure of the water – and that explanation is obvious (*OC* 1, 526). By connecting diverse phenomena explained by nature's horror to general principles of statics, Pascal has made their cause obvious.

Pascal's character and originality as a physicist are most evident in the only complete treatises that have come down to us – the *Traités de l'équilibre des liqueurs et de la pesanteur de la masse de l'air*. These are remarkable not only for their rigour but also for their penetrating use of the visual imagination to assist in an analysis of relationships – also characteristic of Pascal's work in projective geometry. The fundamental notion of projective geometry is that 'point of view' or perspective can discover unities that do not appear upon first view. Imagining an eye perched at the summit of a cone discloses that points, a straight line, a circle, an ellipse, a parabola (or other metrically distinct figures produced by planes intersecting the cone) are images of one another. Taking a circle as the image that is projected, circumscribing figures around or inscribing figures within the circle and projecting the points from those figures onto the other sections of the cone reveals their common properties. The simplicity and symmetry of the circle makes it easy to grasp its properties, which, when projected on to the other conic sections, enable one to unlock the properties of the cone (*OC* 1, 111–28).[11] Compare this to Pascal's use of the figures of plate I in the first two chapters of the *Traité de l'équilibre des liqueurs*. The text takes the reader back and forth between the engravings. Figure I shows the simplest apparatus. The sequence of figures that follow it systematically vary the shapes of the vessels and the volumes of water while keeping the water's height constant. Figure I becomes the model for understanding the *expériences* which follow, and figure V, the last in the row, quantifies the relationship that has been disclosed. In the next row, figures VI through VIII take the relationship established in figures I through V and show that the pressure exerted by the height of water is exerted not only on the base of the vessel, but also upon all the inner surfaces. An analogy is established between figures V and VI. Figure VI moves the location of the openings from the top and bottom of a vertical tube to the two openings of communicating vessels. Figure VI compares the piston placed in one of the apertures to the weight on the arm of the balance in figure V, and introduces a transition to the hydraulic press represented in figure VII. After the principle of the hydraulic press is analysed, and linked to a general principles of statics, the text then leads the reader, with this principle in mind, back through figures VI and V, using this principle to further clarify these earlier moments in the process leading up to its discovery. As in Pascal's projective geometry, reason aided by the visual imagination leads to the discovery of a few simple relationships that unite complex phenomena.

CONCLUSION

Pascal's debt to others has been well established, as well as the degree to which he shared the presuppositions of a group of philosophers in Mersenne's circle. For example, Shôzô Akagi has shown that Pascal's emphasis on the role of knowledge derived from the senses was posed in nearly the same terms by Roberval, Petite, Auzout and Mersenne.[12] Peter Dear has situated Pascal within an evolving tradition (which can be traced back through the schools to Aristotle) of treating physics as a mixed mathematical science. Pascal did not discover truths that were entirely new, but commandingly synthesised isolated pieces of existing knowledge. As Duhem expressed it, comparing the work on the statics of fluids done by Stevin, Benedetti, Torricelli, Descartes and Galileo with that of Pascal shows that Pascal alone 'constituted a logical and harmonious doctrine from scattered materials'.[13] He organised common experience to make a few principles evident and rigorously linked them to a large number of phenomena, some of which might even seem to be contradictory, as when mercury suspended in the Torricellian tubes seems to contradict the tendency of heavy bodies to fall.

Some have suggested that Pascal did not actually perform a good number of the experiments he described,[14] and that may be the case. But that does not detract from their ingenuity or penetration. Pascal's experiments, whether real or imagined, build one upon another, like chains of reasoning. Relationships are analysed and experience is organised to establish conclusions with great force and clarity. The most powerful examples of this are found in the *Traités de l'équilibre des liqueurs et de la pesanteur de la masse de l'air*. The experiments are represented by engravings that stand somewhere between geometrical abstractions and realistic representations of physical instruments. By leading the reader back and forth between these images, constants are established, analogies developed, models constructed and principles revealed with the force of a demonstration. Pascal not only systematically integrated existing knowledge, but developed a remarkable method of rigorous and illuminating analysis out of a controlled interplay between experience, reason and the visual imagination.

NOTES

1. Le Guern 1971, pp. 89–92.
2. Fanton d'Andon 1978, pp. 22–3, 25, 33.
3. Dear 1995, pp. 39, 42–3, 180–7.
4. Harrington 1982, p. 50.
5. Quoted in Fanton d'Andon 1978, p. 26.
6. Bloch 1971, pp. 196–8.
7. L. Brunschwicg et al. (eds.), Oeuvres complètes (Paris: Hachette, 1904–25), II, 287–90; Akagi 1968, pp. 171–8, Dugas 1958, pp. 229–33.
8. Dear 1991, p. 180.
9. Brunschwicg et al., Oeuvres complètes, II, 306.
10. Duhem 1905, pp. 599–612.
11. Pascal showed that a hexagon inscribed in a circle has three pairs of opposite sides which meet in a straight line, and then established the projectivity of this property, extending the relation to all the other sections of a cone.
12. Akagi 1964, pp. 20–36.
13. Duhem 1905, p. 609.
14. For example, Koyré 1968, pp. 150–6.

6   Pascal's philosophy of science

Pascal's philosophy of science did not result from a detached philosophical reflection on the scientific achievements of others. It was honed, instead, in his intense, personal involvement in the religious and philosophical controversies that convulsed the kingdom of Louis XIV in the middle of the seventeenth century, and in which this notoriously combative defender of Jansenism played a leading role. The scope of Pascal's own scientific work was modest, and was primarily concerned with pneumatics. However, the experimental character of his research was such that it provoked discussion of a number of important issues that were implicit in the new mechanical philosophy, including its relationship to traditional metaphysics. In fact, Pascal's appeal to experimental evidence in support of his scientific theories against critics provided an ideal vantage point from which to address critically the epistemology of science, and to compare the certainty or otherwise of its theoretical claims with dogmatic religious teaching and with the traditional philosophy of the schools. This focus on the relative certainty of competing types of belief – scientific, religious or philosophical – and on alternative strategies for resolving apparent conflicts between them, was not unique in the scientific revolution. Many scientists, from Galileo to Newton, addressed similar questions. In the case of Pascal, however, the intensity of his personal faith and his public commitment to the rigorous piety of Jansenism made it impossible for him not to reflect on the status of scientific results that were confirmed by what appeared to be incontrovertible experimental evidence. It is easy to understand, in retrospect, how the focus of Pascal's philosophy of science was the role of experimental evidence in the confirmation and disconfirmation of scientific theories.

One of the central issues in confirmation theory was the apparent conclusiveness of crucial experiments, such as the 'great experiment'. On 19 September 1648, on the mountain called the puy-de-Dôme near Clermont, Pascal's brother-in-law, Florin Périer, conducted a series of tests using glass barometric tubes that were subsequently recognised as being among the best designed and well-executed experiments of the scientific revolution. Pascal was living in Paris, and he had neither the health nor the appropriate conditions to do the experiment himself. Accordingly, he asked Périer in November 1647 to perform the experiment on his behalf and to report back the results. Professional duties and poor weather conditions delayed the experiment for almost ten months, until the following September. Périer described the experiment as follows.[1] He prepared for the tests by purifying 6 pounds of mercury for three days. He then set out early in the morning, accompanied by five reliable witnesses, to measure the height of mercury in Torricelli tubes at the bottom of the mountain and at various intermediate stages up to the top. He began with two exactly similar glass tubes, filled them with mercury, and then inverted each of them in the usual way in a dish of mercury. Both showed the same height, which was measured and recorded. Périer left one of the tubes in position, and he asked Father Chastin (a member of the Minim friary, where this first measurement was made) to watch it continuously during the day and to record any changes in the height of the mercury. Meanwhile Périer and his witnesses climbed the puy-de-Dôme, carrying the second tube, and measured the height of the column of mercury on the mountaintop.[2] The mercury had dropped 'three inches and one and a half lines'. The observers were so overcome 'with wonder and delight' that they decided to repeat the experiment. They did so five times, in various weather conditions, on the mountaintop and always got the same result. Périer and his witnesses then descended the mountain, taking similar measurements at two intermediate places. They found that the height of mercury in the tube rose in proportion to their descent. Finally, when they rejoined Father Chastin near the bottom of the mountain, they repeated the test once more using the barometer they had carried up the mountain. The mercury column was the same height as that morning, and Father Chastin reported that the mercury in the second tube had remained steady during the whole day 'despite the fact that the weather was very changeable, sometimes calm, sometimes rainy, sometimes very foggy and some-times windy'.[3] The different heights of the mercury column were tabulated with estimates of the height, above sea level, of the various experimental sites, and they revealed a drop in the mercury in propor-tion to its height above sea level. This seemed to show unequivocally that mercury in a Torricelli tube is supported by the weight of the atmospheric air, rather than by nature's fear of a vacuum as proposed by Scholastic philosophers.

Before discussing the implications of this famous experiment and, in particular, the concept of scientific knowledge that Pascal formu-lated when defending his interpretation of its results, it is necessary to outline some of the methodological constraints within which any such defence could be mounted.

DEMONSTRATION AND CERTAINTY

De l'esprit géométrique (1655) represents the nearest approxima-tion, by Pascal, to an explicit theory of knowledge. This essay anal-yses procedures for convincing anyone, either oneself or others, that some belief is true. Pascal uses the metaphor of truths being intro-duced into the soul, to which they have access by only two routes: through the will or the understanding. What Pascal calls 'divine truths' fall exclusively within the scope of the first faculty (although those are not the only truth candidates that enter through the will). All other truths – what he calls 'truths within our reach', includ-ing scientific truths – enter the human mind through the faculty of understanding.[4] Pascal is unusually frank in acknowledging that our success in convincing anyone of some belief depends as much on the state of mind of the potential believer as on the objective evidence that supports the belief itself. For example, one has to identify what someone already believes, and the kinds of belief to which they are receptive. In the case of natural truths, there are two ways into the soul, through the 'mind' or the 'heart', each of which has characteris-tic principles on which it depends.[5] The principles or 'prime movers' of natural truths that successfully enter the mind are 'natural truths, common to everyone, such as: that the whole is greater than its part' (OC 11, 177).[6]

When knowledge of the natural world is involved, therefore, the art of persuasion consists of finding appropriate connections between whatever truth claim is proposed for belief and the principles (already accepted by the new believer) on which they depend. Thus, the likelihood of success, in this enterprise, depends both on the range of principles of which someone is already convinced and the skill of the persuader in finding appropriate links between those principles and the truths proposed for acceptance. Unfortunately, according to Pascal, 'there are few principles of this kind'. Apart from geometry, which concentrates exclusively on very simple shapes, 'there are almost no truths about which we remain always agreed' (OC 11, 174).

This method is evidently a foundationalist one, even if it recognises that the relevant foundations may vary from one person to another and that they may be few in number. Every demonstration depends on first 'identifying the evident principles that it requires. For, if one does not guarantee the foundations, one cannot guarantee the building' (OC 11, 175).[7] Once the foundations are in place, knowledge building may commence. It is not necessary to examine here the three sets of building instructions proposed by this epistemological engineer for constructing our beliefs on reliable foundations. They include providing unambiguous definitions of terms, formulating axioms that are perfectly obvious, and then deducing from them whatever can be shown to follow necessarily.[8] It is clear that these methodological rules are more suitable for traditional geometry than for other disciplines that might benefit from a 'geometrical spirit' in some wider sense of that term.

The proposal that we construct our belief system step by step, on secure foundations, is readily recognisable as a Pascalian version of the theory of *demonstration*. This had been proposed originally by Aristotle and had been refashioned, with indefinitely many variations, by generations of authors who were primarily concerned with the certainty of belief. It is a simplification (although possibly a useful one) of this complex historical development to summarise one of its conclusions as: the scope of human knowledge is inversely proportional to the certainty required of our beliefs. At the limit, if genuine knowledge requires absolute certainty, then we *know* very little. Pascal draws this conclusion in *De l'esprit géométrique*: 'everyone seeks the method for not erring. Logicians claim to guide us to it, but only geometers find it; and apart from their science and whatever imitates it, there are no true demonstrations'

(*OC* II, 180). Our beliefs about the natural world, therefore, cannot become demonstrated knowledge unless they result from a method that imitates geometrical demonstration.[9]

This pessimistic conclusion about the uncertainty of human knowledge reflects Pascal's debt to Montaigne and Charron, and the influence of ancient Greek scepticism on his thought. It also coincides neatly with his complementary conviction about the necessity of faith as a foundation for religious belief, and the relative immunity of such belief to rational critique. This is particularly clear in the *Entretien de Pascal avec M. de Sacy*, according to which a critical evaluation of our natural cognitive powers shows 'the little use that Christians can derive from these philosophical studies' (*OC* II, 95).[10] Even more explicitly he argues that, once we realise how little we know with certainty, we are less likely to question the mysteries of faith by arrogantly using our natural knowledge as a criterion of what is credible in religion.

> Montaigne is incomparable for confounding the pride of those who, lacking faith, pretend to a true justice; for disabusing those who cling to their beliefs and believe they have found unshakeable truths in the sciences; and for convincing reason so effectively of its minimal understanding and of its straying [from the truth] that, when Montaigne's principles are used properly, one is not easily tempted to find anything objectionable in mysteries. (*OC* II, 97)

These reflections on knowledge and belief suggest, in summary, that genuine knowledge must be demonstrated; that sceptical arguments show the extremely limited capacity of human beings to know anything with certainty; and that there is therefore no justification for the pride and arrogance of those who mistakenly apply criteria that are relevant to natural knowledge in the context of religious belief. They also raise serious questions about the epistemological status of scientific knowledge.

THE CONFIRMATION OF SCIENTIFIC THEORY

Pascal accepted, as did most of his contemporaries, that we should distinguish between the mere description of natural phenomena or experimental results and the hypothetical or theoretical causes that we postulate to explain them.[11] In a typical case, we observe some phenomenon, agree about its correct description and then try to imagine some hypothetical cause that could explain it. For example – one discussed by Descartes ten years before the puy-de-Dôme experiment – we see a rainbow (its shape, colours, etc.), we notice that it occurs in a rain shower when the sun is shining, and we construct some hypothetical explanation in terms of the refraction and/or reflection of light in raindrops. This division of labour between describing and explaining raises at least two related issues: one was where to draw the demarcation line between the two phrases. The second challenge was to test the veracity of one's hypothetical explanation, and one of the preferred ways for doing so was to use experiments. Evidently, in disputed cases the two issues overlapped.

The limitations of experimental tests for confirming hypotheses were widely discussed in Pascal's time, both by those who favoured the new experimental philosophy and especially by critics who argued that its role was exaggerated. In particular, it was almost universally recognised that if any hypothesis to be tested, H, implies a particular experimental result, O (in specified conditions), then the fact that O occurs as expected cannot confirm the truth of H. The fallacy of assuming otherwise was so well known, from the time of Aristotle, that it acquired its own proper name.[12] Pascal acknowledges this awkward feature of confirmatory tests on a number of occasions. For example, in the *Entretien avec M. Sacy* he acknowledges that principles 'may well be different and, nevertheless, lead to the same conclusions, for everyone knows that truth is often concluded from falsehood' (*OC* 11, 90).[13] Thus, in the puy-de-Dôme experiment one hypothesis that was being tested was that mercury in a Torricelli tube is supported by the weight of the atmospheric air. This implies (if one makes other assumptions, to which I return below) that the weight of the air should be reduced on top of a high mountain, and that the height of the mercury column should diminish accordingly. While Périer and his witnesses welcomed such a positive result, it could not in principle have confirmed the truth of their hypothesis. They might have been tempted to conclude, therefore, that their hypothesis was at least not disconfirmed, assuming that no drop in the height of the mercury column would have implied a definitive rejection of Pascal's theory. Unfortunately, that would not follow either.

It is now widely recognised that there are no crucial experiments in science, if these are understood as experiments that conclusively disprove hypotheses.[14] This is called the Duhem–Quine thesis today, to acknowledge its independent formulation by Pierre Duhem, based on an extensive study of the history of science, and by W. V. O. Quine, based on an analysis of the logic of scientific argument. An idealised crucial experiment might be imagined to function as follows. Assume some hypothesis to be tested, H, and assume that if H were true then experimental result O would occur in specified conditions. The experiment is done and O is false; hence, since H implies O and O is false, H must also be false. In contrast with the argument for confirmation mentioned above, this is logically valid. However, it is impossible to separate any single hypothesis from other assumptions or hypotheses in which it is normally embedded in order to test it experimentally in isolation, as envisaged in the argument just mentioned. In Quine's words, 'our statements about the external world face the tribunal of experience not individually but only as a corporate body'.[15] Every real experiment presupposes many supplementary and often unstated hypotheses – minimally, about the good working order of one's experimental equipment – so that failure to obtain the expected result can be attributed to the falsehood of at least one of those supplementary hypotheses rather than to the falsehood of the principal hypothesis, H, that was the intended subject of the test.

This feature of the logic of disconfirming arguments, although now named after two twentieth-century authors, was also recognised in the seventeenth century. As one might expect, those who were skilled in performing experiments were among the first to notice some of the reasons why experiments may fail to deliver expected results. For example, in *Two Essays, Concerning the Unsuccessfulness of Experiments* (1661) Robert Boyle outlined a number of factors that can go wrong in an experiment because of failures in equipment, etc.[16] Once he understood the implications of poorly performed experiments for apparently disconfirming results, Boyle was emboldened not to reject his most cherished hypotheses even in the face of recalcitrant experimental tests. He was more likely to blame his equipment, or his assistants, than to suspect the fundamental hypothesis about 'the spring of the air, which most of my Explications suppose'.[17]

Thus, proponents of the new experimental philosophy in Pascal's time had to accept that hypotheses could be neither confirmed nor definitively disconfirmed by experiments, no matter how accurately or frequently they were performed. When disputes arose, therefore, about which theory best accounts for a set of experimental results, each side could exploit these complementary limitations of the logic of confirmation and disconfirmation. If Pascal thought that his 'great experiment' confirmed his theory, critics reminded him that the same results could be explained by an alternative hypothesis. If he cast doubt on others' theories because they failed to match experimental results, they reminded him of the familiar reasons why a negative experimental result need not imply that the hypothesis being tested is false.

The discussions that followed Pascal's 1647–8 experiments were informed by an awareness of these unavoidable limits to the logic of confirmation. Consequently, in assessing the certainty or otherwise of hypotheses, Pascal had three options. One was to withdraw from all speculation about causes or explanations, and merely to record correlations between phenomena. The opposite strategy was to adopt the suggestions of *De l'esprit géométrique* and to confront critics by presenting scientific theories as mathematical demonstrations. The third option – one that might seem in retrospect to have been most attractive for someone who contributed significantly to the theory of probability[18] – was to accept the conclusion to which many of his contemporaries were reluctantly forced, viz. that no scientific theory can ever be absolutely certain. The most one can hope for is more or less probability.

Pascal seems to have been incapable of accepting this third option, even if he were persuaded by the logic of confirmation. That left him with the two other possibilities mentioned above: (i) some form of empiricism, or (ii) a reconstruction of physics in the guise of mathematics. His exploitation of both options emerged during the debates about the vacuum in the late 1640s.

NEW EXPERIMENTS AND THEIR INTERPRETATION

Pascal had published a short pamphlet entitled *New Experiments Concerning the Vacuum* in 1647, at the age of 26, and an even shorter pamphlet describing the puy-de-Dôme experiment the following year.[19] He seems to have assumed that these experiments were so clear and uncontestable that they would confirm definitively his explanations of the relevant phenomena. What happened, however, was very much the opposite. Rather than resolve the disagreements, these pamphlets and their subsequent discussions revealed the extent to which Pascal was either confused or disingenuous about the philosophical challenges he faced.

In a twin strategy that is repeated so frequently in scientific disputes, Pascal's critics raised objections both to his reported results and to the theory proposed to explain them. The descriptions of experiments provided in *New Experiments* were too brief to enable readers to repeat them and check their results. Thus, beginning in the seventeenth century, even sympathetic readers expressed doubts about whether the experiments were actually performed at all.[20] Boyle was among the first to express this doubt publicly, in his *Hydrostatical Paradoxes* (1666), where he pointedly mentioned that 'I remember not that he [Pascal] expressly says that he actually try'd them'.[21] He went on to suggest that one of the experiments was almost impossible, for it required a man to sit 15 or 20 feet under water, with the end of a tube in contact with his thigh. Boyle also raised questions about the availability of glass tubes of sufficient strength, and brass plugs that were sufficiently uniform and smoothly finished, to carry out the experiments as described.[22] Koyré revived these queries in 1956. He argued that scientists in Paris had failed to replicate Torricelli's experiment when Mersenne first reported its result in 1644, because the local glass-makers could not provide glass tubes with sufficiently strong walls to support a 3-foot column of mercury.[23] While the glass-makers at Rouen were presumably more successful with a 3-foot tube in 1646/7, it was unlikely that they could have produced a glass tube of 30 or 40 feet (which was required for one of Pascal's experiments using water or wine). Even if they had done so, it seems impossible for Pascal to have tilted such a lengthy tube without breaking it, as he claims in one of his experiments to illustrate variations in the length of the empty space at the top of the tube. Even the puy-de-Dôme experiment has not escaped the suspicion that the results reported by Périer may have been adjusted to preclude questions about their validity.[24] Of course, many natural philosophers in the seventeenth century invoked thought experiments to support their theories; Pascal was not unique. However, even if the experiments had all been done as reported rather than imagined, there was a more intractable problem about drawing theoretical conclusions from their results.

When in 1660 Boyle published his experiments on the 'spring of
the air', in *New Experiments Physico-Mechanicall, Touching the
Spring of the Air, and its Effects (Made for the most part, in a
New Pneumatical Engine)*, he provoked a lengthy controversy that
included, among his critics, Hobbes, More and the little-known
Jesuit, Father Linus.[25] This dispute focused on how to describe the
apparently empty space at the top of an inverted Torricelli tube,
either as a vacuum or as some kind of subtle matter. When Pascal
published his results, thirteen years earlier, he attracted criticism
from another Jesuit, Etienne Noël, who had previously taught at the
college at La Flèche. Noël's correspondence and Pascal's replies were
written in the autumn of 1647, immediately after publication of the
New Experiments but before the puy-de-Dôme experiment. Noël
accepted Pascal's experimental results, and Pascal, Noël and
Descartes all agreed that mercury in the tube was supported by the
weight of the air rather than by nature's 'fear of a vacuum'. But Noël
and Descartes resisted the conclusion proposed by Pascal, that the
apparently empty space at the top of an inverted Torricelli tube was
completely empty of all matter. Thus the focus of the Pascal–Noël
controversy was essentially the same as that between Boyle and
Hobbes. They accepted the experimental results, but they disagreed
about their interpretation with respect to the apparent vacuum at
the top of the Torricelli tube.

   Noël summarises his position elegantly in the first sentence of
his initial letter. 'I read your experiments about the vacuum, which
I find very good and ingenious but I do not understand this apparent
vacuum which appears in the tube . . . I say that it is a body, because it
acts like a body, in that it transmits light with refractions and reflections, it retards the movement of another body' (*OC* 1, 373). Noël
argued that every space is a body and, in a subsequent letter, that
Pascal's vacuum was a very odd reality that was neither a substance
nor an accident, nor anything else that we can describe using traditional categories. In fact, according to Pascal's criterion of accepting
only what is observable, the vacuum should be rejected because it
was invisible, inaudible, etc.[26] Despite these objections Noël confirms, at the conclusion of his second letter, that he accepts Pascal's
experimental results, that he has learned much from them, and had
even adjusted his own scholastic views accordingly. But he could not
accept the reality of a vacuum.[27]

It would be easy, in retrospect, to characterise Noël as an unre-
formed Aristotelian who was more tolerant of suspiciously metaphysical entities, such as subtle matter, than the robustly realistic
and innovative experimentalist, Pascal. However, Noël was not the
only one to support that side of the debate. Descartes argued likewise. Whilst he agreed with Pascal and Noël that it is the weight of
air, rather than fear of a vacuum, that supports the column of mercury in a Torricelli tube, he still wished to claim that the apparently
empty space at the top of the tube was filled with subtle matter.[28]

The historical context of the Pascal–Noël debate is also important for understanding the philosophy of science adopted by the various contributors. Pascal had published results for experiments that
may not have been performed as described and, even in the case of
those that were performed, he may not have got the unequivocal
results that he reported. He also published them at a time when
Torricelli had already made public the results of his experiment,
and when others, such as the relatively obscure Capuchin friar,
Valeriano Magno, had reported similar results in Warsaw.[29] In subsequent correspondence, both Pascal and his father appear very defensive about suggestions that some of the results were mere thought
experiments.[30] In this highly charged atmosphere, which included
priority disputes and questions about the trustworthiness of the experimenter, Pascal focused his arguments, not on the plausibility or
otherwise of two alternative explanations of the Torricelli results –
viz. the weight of the air or fear of a vacuum (about which all his critics agreed) – but on a different question entirely, namely, whether the
apparent vacuum in a Torricelli tube is a real vacuum or whether it
contains some kind of subtle matter. When challenged about this,
Pascal seemed initially to retreat into empiricism and to limit his
claims to reports of experimental results. But he also tried to re-
structure the presentation of his results – in the essays promised in
1647 but published only posthumously – to conform to the logical
structure of a demonstration.

PASCAL POSITIVIST?

Pascal is often presented as an empiricist or a positivist. For example,
Dugas, in his history of mechanics in the seventeenth century, refers
to 'Pascal's organizing and executive positivism',[31] and Jean Laporte

endorses his description as a 'Christian positivist'.[32] Evidently, these characterisations result from suggestive cues in the Pascalian corpus. For, on numerous occasions the young, confident experimenter attempted to define his approach to the natural world in contrast to scholastic philosophers and those whom he classified as their modern followers. In doing so, he emphasised the extent to which he wished to avoid metaphysical disputes about interpreting experiments and to focus exclusively on the phenomena. Since some of the most telling declarations of empiricism occur in the context of disputes with critics, one might interpret them as a rhetorical retreat into a minimalist interpretation of experiments to increase the certainty that he can justifiably claim for his own views.

Thus, in his first reply to Noël, in 1647, Pascal writes about the liberty assumed by his correspondent in assuming both the existence and the properties of an invisible matter at the top of the Torricelli tube. If that were allowed, he argues, one could easily explain anything one wishes, including such baffling natural phenomena as the tides or magnetic attraction. Pascal rejects what he classifies as dubious theoretical entities that seem to have been invented in an *ad hoc* manner in order to explain specific natural phenomena: 'all things of that nature, the existence of which is not manifested to any of our senses, are as difficult to believe as they are easy to invent' (*OC* I, 380). He associates Noël's subtle matter with the metaphysical prodigality of other theorists, to whom in general he addresses the following challenge:

If one asks them, or you, to make us see this matter, they reply that it is not visible. If one asks that it make some sound, they say that it cannot be heard, and likewise for all the other senses. Thus they think that they have achieved much by making others incapable of showing that subtle matter does not exist, thereby depriving themselves of any chance of showing that it does exist. But we find more reason to deny its existence because it cannot be proved, than to believe in it for the sole reason that one cannot prove that it does not exist. (*OC* I, 381)

These remarks imply that one should not accept any theoretical entity in science unless it can be seen, heard or otherwise made sensible. This argument anticipates the criterion proposed by George Berkeley, almost seven decades later, when he argued that there is no reason to believe in the existence of a material substance. Berkeley argued, in the *Three Dialogues Between Hylas and Philonous*: 'It is to me a sufficient reason not to believe the existence of any thing, if I see no reason for believing it.'[33] As in the quotation above from Pascal, Berkeley's criterion was underpinned by a strongly empiricist criterion of what could provide a 'reason for believing it', which he expressed as follows: 'I am of a vulgar cast, simple enough to believe my senses, and leave things as I find them. To be plain, it is my opinion, that the real things are those very things I see and feel, and perceive by my senses.'[34]

During these same controversies, Pascal also drafted a preface for the longer work on the vacuum that he promised and for which the 1647/8 pamphlets were an interim report of results. In this *Préface sur le Traité du vide* (1651) he wrote:

The secrets of nature are hidden. Although nature is always active, its effects are not always noticed. Time reveals them from one era to another, and although nature is always equal in itself, it is not always known equally. The experiments that provide us with an understanding of nature constantly proliferate; and, since they are the only principles of physics, their consequences proliferate accordingly. (*OC* I, 455)

The phrase that catches one's eye here is that experiments are 'the only principles of physics'. This prompted Brunschvicg and his fellow editors, when working on their edition of Pascal's works, to comment that 'the whole of physics, for Pascal, is a science of fact. This understanding is the opposite of the Cartesian school, for which experiment could be only an auxiliary and provisional stage that is guaranteed by mathematical deduction, which alone would be constitutive of science.'[35]

As a final example of Pascal's apparent empiricism, one might consult the conclusions drawn from the two posthumously published treatises, the *Treatises on the Equilibrium of Liquids and of the Weight of the Mass of the Air*. The final paragraph of this work challenges the followers of Aristotle to assemble the strongest possible arguments from his writings to explain, if they can, how all the phenomena discussed could be explained by nature's abhorrence of a vacuum. 'Otherwise, let them recognize that experiments are the real masters that one should follow in physics; that the experiment done in the mountains has overturned the universal belief that nature abhors a vacuum' (*OC* I, 531).

It cannot have escaped Pascal's notice that his disagreement with the critics was not about experimental results, but about the plausibility of hypotheses that were invented to explain them. As already indicated, his most able critics were not defending nature's fear of a vacuum, but rather were disputing the status of the apparent vacuum at the top of inverted Torricelli tubes. Pascal could have appeased those critics by acknowledging the theoretical status of his own (plausible) account. Instead, he fudged the distinction between observation and theory to his own advantage, and borrowed on the alleged certainty of the former to protect his scientific theories from criticism. While appearing to retreat into a minimalist empiricism, Pascal was simultaneously defending the possibility of science as demonstration.

SCIENCE AS DEMONSTRATION

The third alternative available to Pascal, in addition to empiricism or the apparently unacceptable option that scientific theories are merely probable, was to reconstruct scientific knowledge in the form of a demonstration and thereby to avail of the possibility, canvassed in *De l'esprit géométrique*, that physical theory could 'imitate' the demonstrative certainty of geometry. This is Pascal's predominant approach in disputes about the vacuum.

The foundationalism of *De l'esprit géométrique* appears at the very beginning of the first reply to Noël. Pascal argues that no proposition is certain unless (a) it is so clear and distinct either to sense or reason, as appropriate, that it is indubitable (these are called axioms or principles), or (b) 'it is deducible by infallible and necessary logical steps from such axioms or principles, on the certitude of which depends all the certitude of the consequences that are properly deduced from them' (*OC* I, 378). Pascal realises that both Noël and himself are constructing hypotheses to explain experimental results, and his objective is to highlight how *ad hoc* are those of his Jesuit critic. He appeals to this criterion of certainty to distinguish between (his own) plausible hypotheses and (Noël's) *ad hoc* speculation, and he argues as follows. There are three kinds of hypotheses. Some are such that their negation implies an absurd conclusion, and these must be true. In other cases, the affirmation of hypotheses implies something absurd and those must be false. Finally, if we fail to draw any absurd conclusion from either affirming or denying an hypothesis, it remains doubtful until further examination. Pascal then relies, mistakenly, on the alleged asymmetry between the logic of confirmation and of disconfirmation. He concedes that the mere fact that some hypothesis implies all the known experimental results does not confirm it. But, he claims, 'if something incompatible with even one of the phenomena is implied by an hypothesis, that alone is enough to confirm its falsehood' (*OC* I, 382). Unfortunately, the fact that one's hypothesis implies the negation of a given experimental result does not disconfirm it. Pascal's critics took refuge in this familiar feature of the logic of confirmation, and so did Pascal himself (as indicated below).

There are also signs of Pascal's attempting to reconstruct physical theories as putative demonstrations in the *Traité de la pesanteur de la masse de l'air*. At the beginning of this treatise he borrows the language of principles (from *De l'esprit géométrique*) and proposes, as something that is already generally accepted, that 'air has weight' (*OC* I, 489). The next step is almost predictable: 'Having set down this principle, I will do nothing more than draw certain consequences from it' (*OC* I, 489). Pascal deduces seven numbered conclusions from the principle that air has weight, leaving the reader perplexed about whether the principle confirms the consequences or, on the contrary, whether the experimentally established truth of the consequences confirms the (hypothetical) principle. For example, he argues in the first chapter that, if we had a very high stack of wool, the wool at the top would compress the wool towards the bottom. If one were to take out part of that compressed wool and move it elsewhere, it should expand to its original size. Air acts in the same way. The very high mass of air above us compresses those parts of the air that are nearer the earth. Therefore if someone were to move a fixed volume of such compressed air – for example, the air in a balloon – from its position near the earth to the top of a mountain, it would certainly expand. Pascal provides the following philosophical commentary on what he had just claimed:

There is such a necessary connection between these consequences and their principle that the principle cannot be true without the consequences being true also. And since it is guaranteed that the air that stretches from the earth to the height of its sphere has weight, everything that we have deduced from it is equally true. (*OC* 1, 491)

This sounds as if the 'principle' provides evidence for believing that the consequences are true. However, Pascal adds immediately that, despite the certainty of the conclusion, there is no one who would not wish to see it 'confirmed by experience'. If we found that a balloon (such as he had described) expanded when transported to the top of a mountain, then the various hypotheses about the weight of the air would be confirmed because 'there is nothing else that could cause it to inflate' (*OC* 1, 491). Pascal's analysis of the structure of this argument shows a clear understanding of the logic of confirmation and an ability to exploit it to his own advantage. He claims that, if the experiment works (i.e., if a balloon filled with air inflates as it is moved up a mountain), that confirms his theory. But if it fails to inflate, that must be due to some defect in the experiment!

That [the inflation of a balloon] would *prove absolutely* that the air has weight ... that it presses by its weight on all the bodies that it encloses; that it presses more on lower places than on higher places; that it compresses itself by its weight; that the air is more compressed at low altitudes than at high altitudes. And since in physics experiments have much more power to convince than reasoning, I have no doubt that people would wish to see the latter confirmed by the former. But ... if there were no expansion in the balloon on top of the highest mountains, that would not destroy what I have deduced, for I could say that the mountains were not high enough to cause a perceptible difference. Whereas if a very considerable difference occurred ... certainly that would be *completely convincing* for me and there could be no more doubt about the truth of everything that I showed. (*OC* 1, 492; italics added)

If the balloon experiment were to succeed, he claims, that would provide an absolute proof of the truth of his hypothesis – which is false.[36] But if the experiment failed to produce the expected results, he could appeal to what is now called the Duhem–Quine thesis to explain how such negative results do not disconfirm his hypothesis – which is true.

The text, then, informs the reader that the balloon experiment had in fact been done and that the balloon inflated as expected.

Pascal's conclusion underlines the confusion into which he had led his readers: 'this experiment proves, with completely convincing force, everything that I have said about the mass of the air. And it was also necessary to establish it well, because it is the foundation of this whole discourse' (OC 1, 492). Having established this principle as a 'foundation', Pascal was then free to build a new theoretical explanation of phenomena that had previously been explained by nature's alleged fear of a vacuum. All these phenomena could now be explained by the weight of air, and each is introduced with the same formula: 'To explain how the weight of the air can cause...' (OC 1, 497, 498, 500, 501, 503, 506). The explanations are all deduced from a single principle, and physics thereby assumes or, at least, imitates the demonstrative character of geometry.

It is difficult to escape the conclusion that, in the philosophy of science, Pascal's quest for certainty enticed him, against the acknowledged implications of his own insights, to reconstruct scientific theory in the form of geometrical demonstrations. The same motivation explains why he adopted the rhetoric of positivism; that would also protect his physics from criticism, but only at the expense of reducing significantly its explanatory scope. Inspired by Montaigne's scepticism, and mindful of the need to insulate religious faith against criticism, Pascal emphasised the limited scientific results that could be expected from a mere 'thinking reed'. However, his explicit reflections on scientific theory, the conviction displayed in his polemical debate about the nature of the apparent vacuum in barometric tubes, and the final presentation of his scientific results in the two *Traités* of 1663, all suggest that physics could emulate the demonstrative rigour of geometry. Pascal was by no means unique, in the seventeenth century, in considering that view. Descartes was also attracted to this position, but argued that it was an unrealisable ideal: 'to require me to provide geometrical demonstrations about a question that depends on physics is to ask me to do the impossible'.[37] Instead, he accepted, rather reluctantly, that physical theories could never be more than probable. Pascal rejected this option. By doing so he was left to choose between an unrealisable ideal of demonstrated knowledge and a form of empiricism that is usually associated with Berkeley.[38] The subsequent history of the underlying issue – about the confirmation of scientific theory by experimental evidence – shows that it remained a central problem in philosophy of science for at least two more centuries. While Pascal did not resolve this problem, he brought it sharply into focus on the puy-de-Dôme, an experiment of such originality and elegance that one could easily excuse its inventor of the associated conflation of experimental results and their theoretical interpretation.

NOTES

1. I have simplified the description to some extent, by omitting some instances where Périer claims to have repeated a given reading, and I have also omitted similar tests in various towers by Pascal himself.
2. The top of the mountain was estimated at 500 fathoms (or about 5,000 feet) higher than the site of the first measurement near its base.
3. *OC* 1, 433.
4. cf. the *Preface to the Treatise on the Vacuum*, where Pascal distinguishes between the role of authority in religious belief and its complete lack of relevance in scientific work. In the case of scientific claims, 'authority is useless; reason alone is relevant to knowing them' (*OC* 1, 453).
5. The similarity between Pascal's 'heart' and Descartes' 'intuition' is examined by many authors, e.g., Laporte 1950, pp. 80–5.
6. This is axiom 9 of Euclid's *Elements of Geometry* (part I).
7. The idea that human knowledge is like a building and that its reliability depends completely on the foundations that support it was developed by Descartes among others. See his *Discourse on Method* (part II), and the *Meditations on First Philosophy* (*Oeuvres*, VI, 13–14 and VII, 18). In the latter he writes: 'Once the foundations of a building are undermined, anything built on them collapses of its own accord.'
8. For a detailed discussion of this tripartite method, see Descotes (1993).
9. The same conclusion is drawn by John Locke in the *Essay*. He argues in IV, iv, 6 that 'the knowledge we may have of mathematical truths, is not only certain, but real knowledge' and (in IV, iv, 7) 'that moral knowledge is as capable of real certainty as mathematics'. In contrast, it is 'vain... to expect demonstration and certainty in things not capable of it', such as scientific knowledge of the natural world (IV, xi, 10).
10. cf. *Pensées* L 84/S 118: 'we do not think that the whole of philosophy is worth one hour's effort'.
11. This is reflected in Pascal's phrase, the '*raison des effets*'. Cf. Carraud 1992, pp. 255 ff. for a discussion of this concept.
12. The fallacy of affirming the consequent.
13. cf. *Pensées* L 109/ S 141: 'one often derives the same consequences from different suppositions'. In the conclusion of the two *Traités* published in 1663, Pascal notes, in rejecting criticism, 'there is no one who does

not laugh at this conclusion, because it can happen that there is another cause' of the same phenomenon (*OC* 1, 526).

14. cf. Shapin and Schaffer, 1985, pp. 186–7.
15. Quine 1953, p. 41.
16. R. Boyle, *The Works of Robert Boyle* (London: Pickering and Chatto, 1999), 1, 35 ff.
17. 'Defence against Linus', ibid., III, 9.
18. See Hacking (1975).
19. *Récit de la grande expérience de l'équilibre des liqueurs* (1648) in *OC* 1, 426 ff. The original pamphlets were 31 and 20 pages respectively in length.
20. The issue was not whether Pascal personally (rather than, for example, his assistants) carried out the experiments. The question was whether anyone performed the experiments *as they were described*.
21. *Works of Boyle*, v, 206.
22. Boyle also gives an example of an experiment that did not work as Pascal had reported, and concludes: 'It tempts me much to suspect, that *Monsieur Paschall* never actually made the Experiment, at least with a Tube as big as his Scheam would make one guess, but yet thought he might safely set it down, it being very consequent to those Principles, of whose Truth he was fully perswaded... But Experiments that are but speculatively true, should be propos'd as such, and may oftentimes fail in practise.' *Works of Boyle*, v, 224.
23. Koyré 1956, pp. 270–1.
24. Conant 1957, 8–9: 'One cannot help, however, but be somewhat skeptical of the high degree of accuracy reported by Périer. To be able to repeat the Torricellian experiment so that there was less than a twelfth of an inch (one "line") difference in successive readings, as Périer claimed, is remarkable... it may be that Périer... succumbed to the temptation of making his argument appear convincing by recording exact reproducibility of his results on repeated trials.'
25. The significance of this debate is admirably explained in Shapin and Schaffer (1985).
26. *OC* 1, 394–5, 387.
27. *OC* 1, 396.
28. Descartes to Mersenne, 13.12.1647 (*Oeuvres*, v, 99) in which Descartes claims to have suggested the puy-de-Dôme experiment and asks Mersenne whether Pascal had yet performed it (he hadn't). See also Descartes to Carcavi, 11.6.1649 (*Oeuvres*, v, 349).
29. Magno's *Demonstratio ocularis* appeared in Warsaw in July 1647, and a copy was sent to Roberval, a close friend and supporter of Pascal, in July

1647. See Desnoyers to Mersenne, in M. Mersenne, *Correspondance du P. Marin Mersenne* (Paris: CNRS, 1969–88) xv, 311–14.

30. This is particularly evident in his letter to M. de Ribeyre (12.7.1651), in which he complains about another Jesuit, Jean-Paul Médaille, who has raised doubts about the originality of Pascal's experiments and thereby implied plagiarism. Among other replies, Pascal claims that the puy-de-Dôme experiment 'is my invention' and that 'the new knowledge that it has revealed to us comes entirely from me' (*OC* i, 446).

31. Dugas 1958, p. 229.

32. Laporte 1950, p. 27. Guenancia 1976, p. 29 describes scientific knowledge as 'relative, limited to the world of phenomena that are observable and on which we can experiment'. He contrasts 'empirical science, reduced to the sole and strict observation of phenomena' espoused by Pascal, with the a priori method of Descartes (p. 102). O'Connell 1997, p. 111 refers to Pascal's scientific method as 'inductive, direct, individual, experimental'. Harrington 1982, pp. 78–9 rejects the positivist interpretation.

33. *The Works of George Berkeley, Bishop of Cloyne* (Edinburgh and London: Nelson, 1949), ii, 218.

34. ibid. ii, 229.

35. L. Brunschvicg *et al.* (eds.), *Oeuvres complètes* (Paris: Hachette, 1904–25), ii, 136.

36. The resonances of absolute certainty recur a number of times. For example, in part ii of the *Treatise on the Weight of the Mass of the Air*, Pascal claims that 'it is absolutely certain' that an experimental result is explained 'solely by the weight of the air' (*OC* i, 498).

37. Descartes, *Oeuvres*, ii, 142.

38. cf. Baird (1979) for a critical analysis of Pascal's scientific method.

7   Pascal's theory of knowledge

In a letter of 1660 to Pierre Fermat, Pascal describes geometry in the following terms:

> For to speak frankly to you of geometry, I find it to be the highest exercise of the mind; but at the same time I know it to be so useless, that I make little difference between a man who is only a geometer and an able craftsman. Therefore I call it the finest occupation [*métier*] in the world; but after all, it is only an occupation; and I have often said that it is good for the trial but not for the employment of our strength, so that I would not walk two steps for geometry, and I am persuaded that you are strongly of my opinion.[1]

This paradoxical praise of geometry addressed to a man he considered a great mathematician is one of many texts where Pascal expresses doubts regarding human knowledge. The criticism of reverence towards the ancients in the preface to his *Treatise on the Vacuum* is well known:

> Those whom we call 'the ancients' were in fact young in all things, and it was they who properly speaking constituted the 'infancy' of mankind. To their knowledge we have added the experience of the intervening centuries, and so it is in ourselves that we ought to find the maturity that we so much revere in those others.[2]

The examples mentioned afterwards are significant: the ancients had no telescopes and, therefore, unable to see the multitude of stars that composed the Milky Way, mistook it for a solid region of the heavens. They thought that celestial bodies and their movements were eternal and that corruptible life was limited to the sublunar sphere because they had no means to observe cases of generation

or corruption beyond that sphere. As regards the earth, they did
not believe in the existence of the vacuum because they had had
no opportunity to produce and therefore to observe it. Thus, physical science has to be experimental, which means that it is based
not on observation but rather on the construction of conditions
for meaningful observations: 'experiments are the true masters that
we must follow in physics' (*OC* 1, 531). Indeed, as well as being a
gifted mathematician,[3] Pascal was one of the great experimental-
ists of the time. To *measure* the intellectual excitement that surrounded his enterprises, one needs to read the *Récit*[4] of the *grande
expérience*, for which he imagined conducting experiments at the
same instant at several heights of the puy-de-Dôme, over several
days, using long glass pipes filled with quicksilver and plunged in vessels of water. Florin Périer, who conducted them, writes that, when
seeing what could only be a vacuum, all those present at the summit
were 'ravished with admiration and astonishment, and surprised in
such a manner that for our own satisfaction we decided to repeat
the experiment'. The consequences Pascal derives are both theoretical (atmospheric pressure explains away the 'abhorrence of vacuum',
which nature was supposed to suffer) and practical: he invented the
barometer, the altimeter and related inaccuracies in thermometric
measurements to variations in atmospheric pressure.[5]

The admiration contemporaries also had for Pascal's practical
genius is reflected in a passage of Fontaine's *Mémoires*, which refers
to his invention of the calculator:

It was common knowledge that he seemed able to animate copper, and to
give to brass the power of thought. Little unthinking wheels, each rimmed
with the ten digits, were so arranged by him that they could give accounts
[*rendre raison*] even to the most reasonable persons, and he could in a sense
make dumb machines speak . . .[6]

In his study of Pascal's invention of the first urban public transport system, Eric Lundwall has shown to what extent even his
entrepreneurial thought is experimental.[7] The first commercial enterprise, the Machine Arithmétique, which was a technological
wonder but a commercial failure, was succeeded by a management
system that was based on risk distribution and which we would
consider very 'modern'. Pascal saw in it an instrument for the
redistribution of wealth.

PASCAL AND DESCARTES

But however involved he may be in the new sciences and technology, Pascal does not spare them his criticisms. Here is, for instance, his opinion of Cartesian mechanics, and, by extension, physics:

> *Descartes.* In general terms one must say: 'That is the result of figure and motion', because it is true, but to name them and *assemble the machine* is quite ridiculous. It is pointless, uncertain and arduous. Even if it were true we do not think that the whole of philosophy would be worth an hour's effort. (L 84/S 118)

When one looks beyond the enthusiasm found in the scientific works, or the mordant irony used against his opponents,[8] Pascal's theory of knowledge is, in fact, a 'negative epistemology': it constantly tells us what knowledge cannot be, and in particular stresses the vanity of efforts towards a *comprehensive* knowledge of nature.

Descartes is a crucial target. Pascal repeats this criticism: 'Descartes, inutile et incertain' (L 887/S 445) – a violent attack when aimed at a philosopher who set out 'to acquire a clear and certain knowledge of all that is useful in life'.[9] *Le Monde* describes the universe (as well as the human body, in the appended treatise *L'Homme*) as a mechanism, a composition of figure and motion. Pascal wrote to Mersenne that in this work, 'instead of explaining only one phenomenon, [he has] resolved to explain all the phenomena of nature, i.e. all of physics' (November 1629).[10] This treatise was not published (news had arrived of Galileo's trial), and instead Descartes published the *Discours de la méthode* (1637), where the emphasis moves from object to subject and where he presents his scientific results as mere applications of a new universal method of reasoning. But when one looks at these essays it is clear that in spite of their apparent diversity and the reversal of the order of enquiry, proceeding now from effects to principles, they form a system: light is reduced to pure geometrical calculation (*Dioptrique*); following a discussion of telescopes, the same reduction is operated concerning celestial bodies, their movements and the effects of light in nature (*Météores*); and geometry itself is reduced to algebra, or the operations of a pure mind (*Géométrie*). The movement is the same, a detachment from vision towards pure concept, the construction of a *Mathesis universalis*, that is, equally, a universal knowledge and a mathematical system of the universe: 'Those long chains composed of very simple and easy reasonings, which geometers customarily use to arrive at their most difficult demonstrations, had given me occasion to suppose that all the things which can fall under human knowledge are interconnected in the same way.'[11]

Now, according to a contemporary, 'M. Pascal appelait la philosophie cartésienne le roman de la nature, semblable à peu près à l'histoire de Don Quichotte' (OC II, 1087). It is not simply that a novel is a fiction – Descartes himself presented his *Discours de la méthode* as a 'fable', and his *Traité du monde* as the description of a fictional world (out of caution, but also because knowledge implies the construction of rational models). A novel is also the pursuit of noble dreams or chimeras, born from the pride of a solitary, adventurous and now archaic *ego*, hence the comparison with Don Quichotte. More importantly, it is the meaningful (but secular) unification of a multiplicity of events, characters and places, a way of '*composer* la machine'.[12]

By contrast, Pascal's scientific essays are astonishingly diverse.[13] He keeps on designing and tackling new problems as if to generate new areas of research within established ones, or inventing new perspectives upon the same objects (as in projective geometry). And when he links different regions within nature, the link is often strategic rather than scientific. Thus, the *Treatise on the Vacuum* links hydrostatics to atmospheric pressure: quicksilver fills the tube plunged in water because its weight is balanced by the pressure of the atmosphere on the water in the vessel, at least until we reach an altitude where the air is too rarefied. In a sense, we have not gained much knowledge, but we have dispelled a myth born from the application of the psychological notions of 'tendency' or 'repulsion' to nature and, by extension, all teleological or tautological explanations (Father Noël's *horror vacui*, or his definition of light as 'a luminary movement of rays composed of lucid, that is to say luminous, bodies'; OC I, 385). Seen in this light, the *Treatise* can be read in parallel with all the passages in the *Pensées* that question the very idea of personhood or of the substantial unity of the subject. In order to analyse *divertissement* and our consciousness of time or notions such as merit or love, and all the qualities and feelings which apply to persons, Pascal constructs experiments (a king left alone in a room; a man at his window; smallpox, which kills beauty but not the person, etc.). Again, what is unveiled is a real void, previously masked by the illusion of intentionality.[14]

This also explains why, when he deals with astronomy, Pascal pays little attention to the new, heliocentric model (speaking of the sun, he mentions 'the vast arc this star describes'; L 199/S 230). It is clear that for him, the interest of the new sciences is not in replacing one system with another, but in decentring all human points of view, so much so that the visible universe ends up being pictured as '*un petit cachot*': 'let us, from within this little prison cell [*cachot*] where we find ourselves, by which I mean the universe, learn to put a correct value on the earth, its kingdoms, its cities and ourselves' (L 199/S 230).

Again, this is a reversal of perspective: it is the consciousness of the infinite *outside* that constitutes the prison. The true question in astronomy is not whether the centre is the earth or the sun, but whether the notion of centre still makes sense. The images of *recoin* and *cachot* have replaced it: humanity 'without light' (that is, the light of religion) is now 'abandoned to itself, lost in this nook [*recoin*] of the universe'.[15] Hence the dismissal of Copernicus:

> Beginning. Prison cell. I think it is a good thing that Copernicus' opinion is not explored further. But this:
> It affects our whole life to know whether the soul is mortal or immortal. (L 218/S 196)

If there is no centre to the universe and nature can no longer be comprehended as a totality, then the question of the regional centre is secondary. By contrast, the question of the immortality of the soul truly determines each instant and thus the totality of human life. Our position on this question and our correlative awareness or obliteration of death continuously structure(s) our relationship to the present, if only to divert our minds towards a past or a future (in both cases, towards void rather than being). Deciding consciously and constantly on this question can make existence something other than a simple role or *métier*.

Immortality is the central question, and this chiasmus between the necessity of the point of view of the whole in human matters and its impossibility in natural science will inform the *Apology*:

> For it is beyond doubt that this life's duration is but an instant, that the state of death is eternal, whatever its nature may be, and that therefore all

our actions must follow such different paths according to the state of that eternity, that it would be impossible to take a sensible, well thought out step without measuring it against the aim of the point which must be our final objective. (S 682)

It is easy to see that like empirical beliefs, which are grounded on habit, faith produced by human means is first of all a function of time, of the disciplining of passions (*la machine*) advocated at the end of the 'wager' argument. This explains why, when dealing with fundamental questions, Pascal does not use the geometrical method (by demonstrating the existence of God and the immortality of the soul). When aiming at transforming life, we need a teleological approach.[16] It is probability theory, based on projections of the outcome of the totality of the game, which will determine the choice of existence.

Nevertheless, it is true that when scientific knowledge is authentic, it can unify by finding a *'raison des effets'* – that is, by linking, under a common point of view, facts previously perceived as unrelated or even contradictory. The work on the vacuum made sense of apparently unrelated hydrostatic phenomena by linking them to the idea of atmospheric pressure.[17] The *Essay on the Generation of Conical Sections* shows that apparently unrelated geometrical curves can be generated in a regular succession when they are conceived as projections of a circle on a plane intersecting a visual cone. In his works on the cycloid, Pascal stresses how his method for calculating the area of this curve can be used to determine 'toutes sortes de grandeurs', lines, surfaces and solids. And in the proportions between numbers distributed according to the necessary disposition of the *Triangle arithmétique*, he finds a method for distributing gains in a game of chance.

But all these methods for finding a reason behind the effects only unify regions within being according to local points of view. While *horror vacui* seemed a universal and unifying principle (and could be linked to a metaphysics of being[18]), the fact that the vacuum had not so far been observed simply derives from conditions of observation specific to this corner of the universe (the earth has an atmosphere). If local experimentation is necessary to produce truth, it is because truth is never given directly, neither to reason, nor to the senses, and in revealing what could not be observed, experiments produce new perspectives and remove men further away from their spontaneous belonging to the world. But the multiplication of the relative does not produce the absolute. Men simply lose their *milieu*, there is no longer any sympathy between them and the world, upon which they can no longer project their own nature.

> Almost all philosophers confuse the ideas of things, and speak spiritually of corporeal things and corporeally of spiritual ones. They boldly say that bodies are pulled downwards, that they tend towards their centre, that they flee their destruction, that they fear emptiness. They say bodies have inclinations, sympathies and antipathies, things which belong only to spiritual beings. And when speaking of minds, they consider them as if they were in a particular place, and attribute to them the powers of movement from one place to another, a function purely of bodies.
>
> Instead of accepting the idea of these things in their pure state, we tint them with our qualities and imprint our composite nature onto all the simple things we see. (L 199/S 230)

Thus for projective geometry, it is important to note that the differing features of curves are explained as variations of a singular point of view, not as the inner properties of ideal forms.[19]

And with probability, it is the calculation of likelihood or uncertainty when experience cannot decide, as when a game of chance is interrupted and gains have to be distributed in exact proportion to the likelihood of winning, calculated on the number of rounds to come on each side. Such a calculation presupposes that the odds are considered equal by hypothesis: 'Indeed, the ambiguous results of fate are justly attributed to fortuitous contingency rather than to natural necessity.'[20]

Everywhere we find the same separation, the impossibility of an absolute knowledge: the strategies of knowledge Pascal invents keep on revealing the infinity of the unknown.

One now starts to understand why, for Pascal, the true utility of science lies in exercising our minds ('faire l'essai de notre force'), that is, providing us with tools for thinking the really important questions, such as a method for finding the right point of view or the *raison* (Pascal rarely speaks of cause) *des effets* in human matters. This is the problem of the *Pensées*: find a particular point of view from which all the effects (*divertissement*, irrationality of political and ethical systems, survival of the Jewish people, power of imagination and custom over reason, etc.) will make sense, and demonstrate its superiority over all other possible ones. Such a point of view will soon appear to be beyond the plane of immanence of our world, devoid of absolute points of reference in man as well as in nature. But how can we determine it from within this world? This will require ingenious indirect modes of thinking and Pascal's answer will be to insist on the radical nature of contradictions within nature and man, far from masking them, and to propose among all the solutions that fight for pre-eminence in the world the only one that inscribes contradiction at its heart, the Christian one.[21]

Many had disagreed with the Cartesian aim of a *Mathesis universalis* conceived as a complete mechanical system of the universe. Fermat, for instance, objected to the reduction of optical laws to purely mechanical ones, and thought that physical explanations required additional principles (such as principles of economy). But Pascal was the first scientist to ground this criticism in a theory of knowledge and certainty, and thus to drive it at the heart of Descartes' philosophical enterprise. If the new sciences show that knowledge is structurally limited and divided, it will be pointless to look to them for a universal method for finding what is truly important for man.

PASCAL AND SCEPTICISM

Still, if Pascal attacks the ideas of a universal method and of a coincidence of mind and nature, he is far from being a sceptic. Whenever he insists that no proof is ever certain, he invariably adds that scepticism is untenable because we have reasons to believe which are more robust than any rational proof. Scepticism presupposes a rationalist conception of truth which he precisely questions:

Instinct, reason
We have an incapacity for proving anything which no amount of dogmatism can overcome.
We have an idea of truth which no amount of scepticism can overcome.
(L 406/S 25)

Now this contradiction itself, or 'constant swing from pro to con'[22] within the theory of knowledge, is perhaps more essential to the apologetic project than the humbling of man's attempts at absolute knowledge. It reveals man's dual nature or 'monstrosity', which is an essential point, since the aim is to show the superiority of a religion different from all others precisely in this assertion of the essential corruption of nature, physical as well as human.

Hence: 'Instinct and reason, signs of *two natures*' (L 112/S 144).

The 'and', instead of a simple comma, as in (L 406/S 25), is important: those two natures limit each other and in their contradictory coexistence, which Pascal calls *contrariété*, in the same hypothetical '*sujet*', '*substance*' or '*suppôt*', they constitute man as a monster.[23] So here, in the context of thoughts on the 'Grandeur' of man, that is, largely, thoughts against pyrrhonism, reason is not to be dismissed:

> If he exalts himself, I humble him.
> If he humbles himself, I exalt him.
> And I go on contradicting him
> Until he understands
> That he is a monster that passes all understanding.
> (L 130/S 163)

Or

Let us then conceive that man's condition is dual. Let us conceive that man infinitely transcends man, and that without the aid of faith he would remain inconceivable to himself, for who cannot see that unless we realise the duality of human nature we remain invincibly ignorant of the truth about ourselves?

It is, however, an astounding thing that the mystery furthest from our ken, that of the transmission of sin, should be something without which we can have no knowledge of ourselves. (L 131/S 164)

The collapse of cosmological thought, the revelation of a divided world devoid of God and the definitive split between science and philosophy, all this is essential in the demonstration of the superiority of Christianity as such. Descartes thought that his method would allow us to reach an absolute certainty concerning three objects, the world, man and God. For Pascal, structural limits within the knowledge of the world reveal contradictions within man (and the impossibility of grounding ethics and politics on rational principles).[24] Knowledge of God would be the only way to make sense of man, but it clearly must be of a different kind than the sort of finite knowledge of the world which is within our reach. Totality will be regained but within time, not space, through a hermeneutics based on signs, prophecies and figures in history, a knowledge necessarily based on a religious tradition.

But before considering this shift in method, what is it, precisely, that makes totality in nature inaccessible? In an essential text, *De l'esprit géométrique*, Pascal presents his own discourse on the method. The argument can be summarised thus.

1. We have the idea of an ideal method in science, which would consist in clearly *defining* the meaning of all the terms we use, and *demonstrating* all propositions by means of truths already known.

2. This method is impossible because we have to stop at some point in the *regressus* of definition and demonstration. We therefore have to settle for geometry, where definitions are *nominal*, simple abbreviations *within* discourse, for the sake of economy and clarity, abbreviations which indicate what we are referring to without telling us what it is. Such definitions, which do not give us the essence of things, are thus conventional or arbitrary ('*très libres*').[25]

3. Now, in the course of abbreviating our descriptions we will necessarily end up with some primitive words, which cannot be defined further without obscuring what we are referring to, and we simply have to accept the fact of these limits within knowledge. This is not a problem with geometry, which does not have to assume that the entities it works with have any existence beyond the mind or discourse.[26] But it is a fundamental limit for physics, which deals with nature and still is entirely based on terms of which we do not know the meaning, such as 'light', 'time', 'movement', etc.

4. How, then, do we know what we are really referring to if primitive terms cannot be defined? Through a natural, instinctive and thus irrational knowledge of what we are referring to and which we do not understand:

From what has been said, it is sufficiently clear that some words are not susceptible to definition; and if nature had not supplied the deficiency by providing a parallel idea which she has made known to all men, all our expressions of that notion would be nothing but confusion; whereas we all of us do in fact use words with assurance and certitude, as though all our interpretations were perfectly free from equivocation; for nature has herself given us without any use of words, an understanding of the meaning of them, more precise than anything our human arts have acquired for us, with all our explanations.

...I do not say that the nature of these things is known to everybody; only that there is a certain appropriate relation of the name and the thing; so that when we hear the expression 'time', we all turn our thoughts to the same thing. This is enough, and it disposes of the need to find a definition for this word, although afterwards, when we want to investigate the nature of time, once we begin to think about it, differences of opinion will arise; for a definition is only constructed to designate the thing named, and not to explain its nature.[27]

That there should be many things of which we know the existence but of which we cannot understand the nature is important for Pascal's project:

> *Infinity-nothing.* Our soul is cast into the body where it finds number, time, dimensions; it reasons about these things and calls them natural, or necessary, and can believe nothing else... We know that the infinite exists without knowing its nature, just as we know that it is untrue that numbers are finite. Thus it is true that there is an infinite number, but we do not know what it is. It is untrue that it is even, untrue that it is odd, for by adding a unit it does not change its nature. Yet it is a number, and every number is even or odd. (It is true that this applies to every finite number.)
>
> Therefore we may well know that God exists without knowing what he is.
>
> Is there no substantial truth, seeing that there are so many true things which are not truth itself? (L 418/S 680)[28]

The usefulness of geometry lies, therefore, not so much in the truths it finds (and which are not important), as in its revealing simultaneously in our nature the aspiration to a fixed point, substance or principle, and our inability to reach it. From the apologetical point of view, this epistemological paradox is analogous to the historical paradox of the survival of a people through endless and unimaginable persecutions during the millennia, which Pascal takes as proof of the importance of the book they preserve and serve, and of their inability to understand its meaning.

5.   What was said of definitions can also be said of fundamental propositions: when justifying first principles, there is a point where demonstration has to stop and propositions too obvious to be demonstrated further have to be accepted as axioms.

> These three things [movement, number and space] comprise the whole of the universe, in accordance with these words: *Deus fecit omnia in pondere, in numero, et mensura;* and they have a reciprocal and necessary relation. For we cannot imagine movement without something that moves; and this thing being one, this unit is the origin of all numbers; and since movement cannot take place without space, we see that these three things are included

in the first. Time itself is also comprised in it, for movement and time are relative to one another: speed and slowness describe different modes of movement, and they each have a necessary relation to time.

Thus there are certain properties common to all things, and the knowledge of these opens the mind to the greatest marvels in nature. The chief of these is a twofold infinity, comprising those two infinities which are found in all things: the infinitely great, and the infinitely small.

... This means, in one word, that however swift the movement, however great the conceivable number, space or interval of time, there is always another that is yet greater and one still smaller, and all are sustained in the intermediate between the void and the infinite, and are at all times infinitely distant from both extremes.[29]

The universality of this principle of division has two anti-Cartesian consequences: human knowledge cannot have a firm foundation, and it should be subjected to the same analysis as any other natural phenomenon.

The first principles of things are neither *distinct*, since there is a permanent circulation between the first notions, nor *clear*, since they display contradictory properties that are indubitable and still incomprehensible. Instead of finding rest, at the centre or in the foundation of knowledge, as the geometrical method seemed to imply, we only find movement (*liaison réciproque et nécessaire*) within discourse. Hence the famous conclusion: 'men are by nature eternally powerless to deal with any science in an absolutely accomplished order'.[30]

Most philosophers accept that there will always be an unknown beyond the limits of current science, but Pascal adds that there is also, necessarily, a void within it, at its foundation, which is precisely what Descartes had set out to remedy in the *Metaphysical Meditations* and the *Principles of Philosophy*, a text Pascal explicitly attacks:

Of these two scientific infinities we are much more aware of that of size, and that is why few people have claimed to know everything. 'I am going to speak about everything', Democritus would say.

But the infinitely tiny is much less visible. The philosophers have been ready to claim to have achieved it, and that is where they have all stumbled. This has given rise to all the familiar titles: *Of the principles of things*, *Of the principles of philosophy*, and other similar ones, as ostentatious in purpose, though seemingly less so, than that other blindingly obvious one, *De omni scibili* ... yet it does not require less capacity to penetrate into nothingness than it does into the whole. (L 199/S 230)

If we can still have some knowledge, it is because knowledge involves two faculties, *discourse* and *instinct* (sometimes called 'heart'), a duality which limits the sovereignty of reason:

> But it does not follow from this that all order must be abandoned. For there is one such order, which is less esteemed, not because it is less certain but because it is less convincing. This is the method of geometry. It neither defines nor proves everything, and for this reason it fails to convince, and yields pride of place; but it assumes nothing but what is clear and constant and according to the light of nature, and for this reason it is perfectly reliable, *la nature le soutenant au défaut du discours*.[31]

If, for Descartes, discourse, or language used appropriately, is a sign that human beings are endowed with a thinking soul, science must be grounded on an evidence beyond the limits of discourse. In the *Meditations*, the first certainty, the knowledge of my existence, is based neither on physical evidence (the whole physical world is still hypothetical) nor on reasoning, as it still was in the *Discourse on Method* ('cette vérité: *je pense donc je suis*'). Rather than the content of a thought, it is a mental experience, actively repeated whenever (*quoties*) I mentally utter or conceive this utterance (*hoc pronunciatum*): *Ego sum, ego existo*. This *performative* function of the *Cogito* explains Descartes' reluctance to present his philosophy in the axiomatic form of a geometrical treatise: it must remain an experience, even if metaphysical. By contrast, keeping the first elements of knowledge within the sphere and limitations of language, Pascal refuses all external or metaphysical anchorage points: discourse is simply one among many human activities.[32] If the ultimate definitions are nominal, knowledge can only deal with effects and aspects, and the idea that it would unveil the essence of things is an illusion – *human, too human*, would have said Nietzsche, who admired Pascal.

As for 'instinct', 'nature' or 'heart', for Descartes a number of truths are *innate*, that is, known by the very *nature* of the mind, namely, 'figures, numbers and other things belonging to arithmetics and geometry'. This is the third step and the pivotal point in the argument of the *Metaphysical Meditations*, following the *Cogito* (*Meditation* 2), which grounds knowledge beyond language, and the demonstration of the existence of a God who created human nature and is benevolent and truthful (*Meditation* 3 and *Meditation* 4). Thus, whenever I know something through my own nature, and neither through the free exercise of judgment nor through experience, I can be certain of its truth. When it is impossible *not* to believe a particular proposition (e.g. that the sum of the angles of a triangle equals two right angles), then I know that this proposition is true. The same can be said of whatever proposition I can derive from it, provided each step of the demonstration is equally evident.

But for Pascal there is no such divine guarantee of the truthfulness of my nature. On the contrary, what we consider natural is simply customary: 'Our soul is thrust into the body, where it finds number, time, dimension. It ponders them and calls them nature, necessity, and can believe nothing else' (L 418/S 680). And thus, the support given by nature to knowledge, '*au défaut du discours*', will become, in the projected apology, a sign of weakness:

> The knowledge of first principles such as space, time, movement, numbers is as certain as any that our reasoning can give us, and it is on this knowledge by means of the heart and instinct that reason has to rely, and must base all its argument. The heart feels that there are three dimensions in space and that there is an infinite series of numbers, and then reason goes on to prove that there are no two square numbers of which one is double the other. The principles are felt, and the propositions are proved, both conclusively, although by different ways, and it is as useless and stupid for reason to demand of the heart proofs of its first principles as it is for the heart to demand of reason a feeling of all the propositions it proves, before accepting them.
>
> So this powerlessness ought to be used only to humble reason, which would like to be the judge of everything, and not attack our certainty. (L 110/S 142)

Knowledge has lost its rational or divine centre and exhibits the same fundamental duality (or corruption) as its objects: the double infinity. It must, therefore, be treated like any other object within the world.

In projective geometry, as in physics, the point of view of the observer was within the domain of explanation, but it could be precisely determined in relationship to the nature of the curves or to atmospheric pressure. At the end of *De l'esprit géométrique*, Pascal announces, in the revelation of the marvels of the two infinites, 'meditations worth more than the entire system of geometry'.[33] Not the majesty of the universe, but rather the difficulty of determining precisely our *site*, or the right point of view in truly important matters, a point the *Pensées* constantly underline:

> If we look at our work immediately after completing it, we are still too much involved in it; too long afterwards and we cannot pick it up again.
>
> Similarly with pictures seen from too far off, or from too close up. And there is only one indivisible point which is the right position. The others are too close, too distant, too high, or too low. Perspective determines it in the art of painting. But in truth and morality who will determine it? (L 21/S 55)

Descartes' method and his metaphysics aimed at going beyond appearances to reach things themselves. For that he invented machines: world-machine, man-machine and animal-machines, models which were not simple representations, since the laws of geometry and mechanics, space and movement *were* the laws of nature. The world could be said to *be* a machine, knowledge went beyond *mimesis* and the representation *was* the thing. Conversely, for him, the world of the senses, which seemed to give us direct access to reality, was a purely conventional world, a sort of language, or, he says, a world of institution (but a divine institution, and useful to our survival). Sense data are signifiers or signals of a reality, and, like linguistic signifiers, they never, in themselves, convey immediately or naturally the knowledge of what they signify. Rationalism thus aims to go beyond the conventionality of all language, towards an absolute reality.

What Pascal shows in his reflections on geometry is that Descartes' project of a direct access to the rationality of the world is meaningless because the foundations of rational thought itself are as contingent as those of the senses. Even geometry shows that we are *embarqués*: this 'nature' in us, on which discourse is grounded, is not divine: 'I am very much afraid that nature itself is only a first habit, just as habit is a second nature' (L 126/S 159).

THE SELF

The knowing subject has thus lost its eminence; it has to be *honnête*, that is, to understand that the only possible distance from the contingence of human roles is in the knowledge of one's own limits.

Geometry is only a *métier*; its limits are just facts, like the reasons which determine the choice one makes of an occupation or an identity.[34] Before, man knew nature through man (*horror vacui*). Now, man knows man through nature (double infinity). And as thought cannot understand itself, how could it understand its union with the body? In other words, the knowledge of man is impossible. While Descartes set out to show that the soul is easier to know than the body, because it is a thinking substance and because knowledge of the physical world presupposes a knowledge of its existence and nature, Pascal reverses the points of view: like the famous piece of wax in Descartes' second *Meditation*, the self is not a substance but, simply, the intersection of contingent qualities.

What is the self?
   ...Where is the self, then, if it is neither in the body nor in the soul? And how can you love the body or the soul except for its qualities, which do not make up the self, since they are perishable? For would we love the substance of a person's soul in the abstract, whatever qualities it contained? That is impossible, and would be unjust. Therefore we never love a person, only qualities.
   So let us stop mocking people who are honoured for their appointments and offices. For we love no one except for his borrowed qualities. (L 688/S 567)

Nevertheless, we can form an indirect knowledge of man. It centres on the notion of *ennui*, or the inability to face one's own emptiness, demonstrated by the analysis of *divertissement* and of the consciousness of time. A good example is the recurring image of the prison cell or *cachot* (L 163/S 195): compared to eternity, the difference between life's duration and an hour is negligible. It would be unnatural to spend an hour playing games if we were locked up in a cell having been told that we only have that hour to find out whether our whole life can be saved. And still this is what we do.
   Thus, the analysis of the self is based on thought experiments. An hour in a room, a cell or a dungeon: the *cachot* could figure among the various experiments invented by Pascal, always attentive to degrees, to measuring the consciousness of spatial-temporal location, or 'existence', on the scales of infinity and eternity, using the experience of duration as evidence. This experience is itself measured as a degree of restlessness on a scale going from the agitation of adolescents

facing *ennui*, to the intellectual competitions of mathematicians, via hunting, games, etc. The *cachot* thus measures the sense of site men have, retain or gain. We end up with an alternating scale, a familiar model in Pascal, going from *'le peuple'* to *'les chrétiens parfaits'* (*peuple/demi-habiles/habiles/dévôts/chrétiens parfaits*).[35] At the centre of the scale stands the projected reader of the apology. He cannot inhabit the totality of this universe he knows to be infinite, and paradoxically feels a prisoner in this *recoin* of the universe:

> I look in every direction and everywhere I see only darkness. Nature offers me nothing that is not a source of doubt and anxiety. If I saw nothing there which indicated a divinity, I would settle on a negative answer; if I saw the signs of a creator everywhere, I would rest peacefully in faith. (L 429/S 682)

Now knowledge is freed from all metaphysics, not only a metaphysics of nature, but also a metaphysics of the self. In other words, all our objects of thought, including thought itself, are naturalised. The image of the cell could thus have been the foundation of an ontology of the self considered not as the substance supporting transient qualities, but as a bundle of sequences of events. It will take a philosopher, Leibniz, to turn the *cachot* inside out and invent the monad, which is 'without door or window', but which expresses, in its very existence, the totality of the universe, with a degree of clarity relative to its position in the scale of all the creatures which concur in forming this world.[36] But Pascal's thought is fundamentally determined by the doctrine of original sin and by the sense of the loss of substantiality.[37] The project of the apology is thus based on the necessity of looking for a point of reference elsewhere than in nature or man, above contingency and confusion, a point we can only infer from the analysis of the diversity and contradictions within what there is here, and not a point of which we would demonstrate directly the necessity, as philosophers try to do in their proofs of God.

If the preface to the *Traité du vide* refused the argument of authority in physics, it announced that in truly important matters, truth is historical. The infinite is everywhere, in the biggest but also in the smallest object of knowledge, in the universe as well as in our thought. But where is God in all this? Nowhere: he hides (*Deus absconditus*), but he has left in the history of humanity many *signs*, which we can decrypt. This is why the bulk of the *Pensées* deal with hermeneutics: messianism, prophecies, figures, miracles, the paradoxical survival of a people created by a book,[38] which makes the whole book a proof of what it says, etc. In the end, 'The history of the church must properly speaking be called the history of truth' (S 641/L 776).

CONCLUSION

For Pascal, the disenchantment of the world is a Christian statement. The science of his time has simply confirmed it and this is what makes this century a moment in the 'history of truth'. The danger is that this new consciousness revives the stoic delusion of a subject free and sovereign within its own sphere. So Pascal endeavours to show that belief in science undermines belief in the self since far from revealing the freedom of man, the nature of science reveals his 'emptiness'. Here, the mathematician turns into his opposite, the apologist, and, renouncing demonstration in favour of hermeneutics, endeavours to show that the limits of mathematics only make sense in relationship to the history of a fall and the perspective of a redemption. Instead of saving God with mathematics, Pascal saves mathematics with God. This is why the project of the apology itself is not futile. Of course, its first aim is to convert to the practice of a religion, even if such conversion can only transform the converted and not cause grace. But its very writing saves the existence of the mathematician from contingency and turns what was only a *métier* into preparation for a possible salvation.[39]

NOTES

1. *OC* II, 43 (trans. Carol O'Sullivan); italics mine.
2. *OC* I, 456.
3. Furthering Arguesian projective geometry and laying the first principles of calculus and of statistics.
4. *OC* I, 428/429.
5. *OC* I, 435.
6. *OC* II, 85. His sister wrote of Pascal's calculator: 'This work has been considered to be a new thing of nature, for having reduced into a machine a science which resides entirely in the mind, and having found the means of making it perform all its operations with complete certainty, without having need for reasoning.' *OC* I, 67. That a machine can think is important from the point of view of the *Pensées*. It is not

L

by pure thought that man is above matter, but by the consciousness of the whole (even when experienced as that of a loss).

7. Eric Lundwall, *Les Carrosses à cinq sols* (Paris: Science Infuse, 2000).

8. See Pascal's correspondence with Father Noël on the vacuum, and the concept of *'matière subtile'* (*OC* 1, 408) or the *Suite de l'histoire de la Roulette*.

9. AT VI 5.

10. Fontaine writes that in Port-Royal, M. de Sacy considered Descartes dangerous because he destroyed the two reasons why God had made the world, 'one, to give a great idea of Himself, and the other, *to use visible things to paint invisible ones'*. *OC* 11, 84.

11. AT VI 19.

12. In S 783 Pascal writes: 'I find nothing so easy than to treat all this like a novel. But I find nothing more difficult than to reply to it.' According to Jean Mesnard, this *pensée* expresses the frustration of those who consider historical proofs of religion to be a fiction, but who cannot refute them. Again, what is at stake here is the unification of a totality. But in this *pensée* the reality involved is of a radically different order, since we are now dealing not with space, as in geometry and physics, but with time, and not fictional time, as in novels ('Homère fait un roman', L 628/S 688), but real human history. The point of view must then change and we shall see that in this order of reality the teleological explanation is the legitimate one for Pascal.

13. In his address 'A la très illustre Académie Parisienne de Mathématiques' (*OC* 1, 169) Pascal draws a list of his scientific works, insisting on the singularity of the problems and properties he has discovered. For instance, probability: 'extreme novelty, the study of a totally unexplored subject', an art 'which justly assumes this stupefying title: *Geometry of chance (Géométrie du hazard)'*. And he goes on: 'I am not talking about gnomics, nor the innumerable, varied subjects that I have quite in hand; in truth, they are neither finished nor worthy of being finished.' We are a long way from the attitude of Descartes deploring the fact that in his youth mathematics was not put to a better use than *'inventions très subtiles'* or mechanical applications.

14. Pascal is not Spinoza. Mathematical thought has not come to save men from anthropocentrism, but rather to diagnose their disease and to humiliate them.

15. For an analysis of the notion of centre in Pascal's scientific and apologetical thought, see Michel Serres, *Le Système de Leibniz* (Paris: Presses Universitaires de France, 1968), 11, 653–4.

16. See S 160/127: 'Man's nature can be considered in two ways: either according to his end, and then he is great beyond compare, or according to the masses ... and then man is abject and vile.'

17. The *Treatise on the Vacuum* (1663) contains '*the explanation of the causes of the diverse effects of nature that have not been well known until now and particularly those that we have attributed to the horror of vacuum*'. One of these *effects* is breast-feeding, explained as a combination of atmospheric pressure on the breast and the vacuum within the baby *OC* I, 507.

18. Though not in the Scriptures, which never infer God from *horror vacui* (L 463/S 702).

19. *Traité des coniques* (1640–54.) Pascal advertises this essay as 'comprehending the conics of Apollonius and innumerable other results, through a single proposition or almost a single proposition'. The theory of perspective in painting falls under this mode of representing curves: 'It evidently follows that, if the eye is at the tip of the cone, and the object is the circumference of the circle which is the base of the cone, and if the painting is the plane meeting, on each side, the conical surface, then the conic, which will be produced by this plane on the conical surface, whether it is a point, a straight line, an angle, an antobola, a parabola, or a hyperbola, will be the image of the circumference of the circle.' (*OC* I, 21.)

20. *OC* I, 172 (trans. Carol O'Sullivan).

21. Two contradictory reasons. We must begin with that: without it we understand nothing, and everything is heretical. And even at the end of each truth, we must add that we are remembering the opposite truth. (L 576/S 479). See also S 614/L 733 and L 449/S 690.

22. *Renversement continuel du pour au contre* (L 93/S 127.) See also L 90/S 124, L 130/163 and L 131/S 164.

23. 'What sort of freak then is man! How novel, how monstrous, how chaotic, how paradoxical [*quel sujet de contradiction*], how prodigious!' (L 131/S 164).

24. See L 60/S 94.

25. Pascal's favourite example is the definition of 'even'. This term does not reveal an inner property that a specific entity or group of entities would possess, but, rather, it abbreviates the description of a procedure: 'divisible in two equally'. The term thus simply *names* a group of numbers we can isolate. Exporting this method from a domain where objects ultimately result from rules instituted within speech (which does not mean that, once the object is named, its properties do not follow with absolute necessity) to domains where reality pre-exists speech, is bound to failure, unless one manages to reduce truth to a divine institution, which is what Descartes attempted.

26. One of the reasons for Pascal's distrust of rational proofs of the existence of God is his scepticism towards mathematical realism: 'Even if someone were convinced that the proportions between numbers are

immaterial, eternal truths, depending on a first truth in which they sub-
sist, called God, I should not consider that he had made much progress
towards his salvation' (L 449/S 690).

27. *OC* II, 159.

28. Knowledge can thus only be indirect: 'It is a disorder natural to man,
     that he should believe himself capable of the direct apprehension of
     the truth; whence it arises that he always tends to deny anything that
     he himself finds incomprehensible; whereas the fact is, that all his
     direct apprehensions are falsifications, and he ought only to accept as
     true those things of which the contraries are evidently false' (*OC* II,
     164).

29. *OC* II, 162.

30. *OC* II, 157.

31. ibid.

32. The role of context in the constitution of meaning confirms this point: 'I
     would like to ask reasonable people if this principle... *I think therefore
     I am*, [is] in fact the same thing in Descartes' mind and in St Augustine's,
     who said the same thing twelve hundred years earlier. Actually I am very
     far from saying that Descartes was not the true author, even though he
     would only have discovered it by reading that great saint. For I know
     how much difference there is between writing something by chance
     without reflecting longer and more deeply about it, and appreciating
     in this statement a valuable sequence of consequences which proves
     the distinction between material and spiritual natures, and making it
     the firm and continuous principle of an entire physics, as Descartes
     tried to do. For, without examining whether he effectively succeeded
     in his attempt, I am supposing that he did, and it is in this supposition
     that I say that this maxim is as different in his writings from the same
     maxim in other people's who put it in as an aside, as is a dead man from
     a fully alive and vigorous one' (*OC* II, 179; trans. Honor Levi). In the
     Entretien avec M. de Sacy, Pascal applied to the projected *Apologie* this
     idea that a statement takes its meaning from the strategy that organises
     its context. This is a defect for the authors of the *Second Objections*
     to the *Meditations* and for Spinoza, who criticises Descartes' 'analytic'
     rather than 'synthetic' order, which starts with the *Cogito* instead of
     deriving the necessity of nature from its main principle, God. But this,
     for Pascal, would have been mere presumption.

33. *OC* II, 170.

34. All the *pensées* about *métiers* occur in the context of a reflection about
     chance and custom. For instance: the most important thing in our life is
     the choice of a career: chance decides it (L 634/S 527). (See also L 129/S
     162; L 35/S 69; L 542/4 59.)

35. These scales operate in synchrony. It is striking that Pascal, a reader of Montaigne, would not apply them to diachrony and develop an historical anthropology of the consciousness of time. This is not his purpose here: the *Apologie* is aimed at a group that has already lost a sense of the cosmos.

36. Leibniz turned Pascal's work on the cycloid, which he published, into the mathematical mastery of the infinitely small. He would then reconcile the two modes of thinking, mathematics as an exercise of the mind and mathematics as knowledge of a true reality, in a philosophy which would show that a number of 'architectonic' principles (beyond the purely mechanical and local laws of Descartes) in fact reflect God's calculation in the creation of the best possible world. His work could be read as an answer to Pascal's challenge to produce a projective geometry of ethics. The result is a *Theodicy*, a justification of God, rather than the *Apology* of a religion.

37. 'Shall the only being who knows nature know it only in order to be wretched? . . . He must not see nothing at all, nor must he see enough to think that he possesses God, but he must see enough to know that he has lost him' (L 449/S 690).

38. See L 481/S 716; L 482/S 717.

39. I would like to thank Bobby Nayyar for his bibliographical help and for his translations.

8   Grace and religious belief in Pascal

Pascal states that faith is a gift of God, not the result of a process of reasoning (*Pensées*, L 7, 588/S 41, 487). In which case, we might ask, what is the point of an apology for the Christian religion? Suppose I am persuaded to adopt Christianity by arguments for the existence of God, and then for the unique status of Christianity as a divine revelation: in that case, my belief will be based on the human faculty of reasoning, and faith is not necessarily a gift of God. Or if faith is a gift of God, why should I trouble to study the proofs of Christianity? If God intends me to have faith, He will give it; if I do not have it, is that my fault? God could have given it to me, and has not. In either case, where is the place for argument?

Another problem. Pascal elsewhere says that the would-be but not-yet believer should fulfil the external rituals of religion: taking holy water and so forth. That will bring about belief: 'Cela vous fera croire' (L 418/S 680). In other words, the way to belief is through forsaking one's human faculty of reasoning (refraining from asking what possible good holy water can do me) and adopting a purely mechanical mode of behaviour that puts one on a level with the animals ('cela vous *abêtira*').[1] In this case also, where is the gift of God?

Analogous difficulties arise with the concept of grace. The so-called Jansenists, with whom Pascal was associated (they called themselves 'disciples of St Augustine'), held that God's distribution of grace must be understood in terms of a rigorous doctrine of predestination. This might be perceived as making moral effort futile.

If these objections were valid, then for Pascal to write an apology, and for his fellow 'disciples of Augustine' to preach moral effort,

would appear futile. So it seems important to discuss how he anticipates them.

In L 703/S 581 Pascal quotes Romans 3.27: there is no room for boast-
ing, since we are justified by faith, not by works (fulfilling the Law).
Fulfilling the Law is within our power, he comments, but if there
is nothing to boast of in faith, it cannot be in our power: it must be
given us in some other way. And the title of the fragment, 'Grâce',
suggests that the gift of faith is modelled on, or is indeed a form of,
the gift of grace. Indeed, St Paul himself says this: 'It is by grace that
you have been saved, through faith' (Ephesians 2.8–9) – a text commented on by St Augustine to prove that faith is not in our control,
and cited also by St Thomas Aquinas to prove that faith is from God,
moving man inwardly by grace; it does not begin in an act of free
will.[2] In the *Ecrits sur la grâce* Pascal notes that Augustine and his
follower, Fulgentius, teach that faith is a gift of grace.[3] So the problem of grace is the proper starting point for a consideration of the
problem of faith.

But no issue was more vehemently debated among early modern
theologians.[4] The basic lines of the orthodox doctrine had been laid
down by St Augustine, especially in his writings against Pelagius and
his followers: because human nature had been radically corrupted by
the Fall, we could not obey the commandments, let alone persevere
in doing so, without grace, an inner influence from God that mod-
ifies the human will, but since it is we, thus affected, who carry
out both acts of will and the acts that result from them, we are still
making some contribution to our own salvation. In the final analysis grace is granted only to those predestined to salvation by God's
mercy. St Thomas Aquinas had reformulated this doctrine for the
medievals while preserving its general outlines. But the Reformers
sought to minimise the contribution of human effort to salvation,
and Calvin, in particular, stressed the absoluteness of the decree by
which God, from all eternity, predestined some to salvation and the
rest to damnation. Certain Roman Catholic theologians reacted by
insisting that our salvation depends, to some extent, on our free
choice; that God distributes to all a 'sufficient grace' that enables
them to fulfil his commandments, but that we choose whether to

avail ourselves of this help or not. Predestination becomes, as it were, retrospective (though there is no past or future in God): he knew from all eternity that Peter would choose to take advantage of grace and that Judas would not, and in this sense Peter's fidelity and Judas' betrayal were fore-ordained by him. This general approach, pioneered by Luis de Molina (1535–1600), won considerable support in the Society of Jesus. It could be synthesised in various ways with the Augustinian-Thomist legacy. But for Pascal, and his fellow 'disciples of Saint Augustine', it was radically vitiated in two ways. It devalued God's grace by making it dependent on human choice, and it flew in the face of the reality of human nature. It assumed that if human beings were merely *enabled* to do right, then there was no reason why they, or some of them, could not do so. But this overlooked the colossal impact on human nature of original sin.

THE *ECRITS SUR LA GRÂCE*

The commitment to Augustinianism was not unproblematic, for one of the most powerful attempts to restate Augustine's doctrine, Cornelius Jansenius' *Augustinus*, published posthumously in 1640, had been the object of bitter controversy. Five propositions, allegedly derived from it (though Jansenius' followers denied that they represented his views), had been condemned by Pope Innocent X in 1653 in the bull *Cum occasione*, and these were mostly connected with the issue of grace. Pascal's friend Antoine Arnauld (1612–94) had committed himself in print to the defence of Jansenius. But in his main writings on the subject, the *Ecrits sur la grâce*, Pascal seems to make very little direct use of Jansenius, no doubt, as Mesnard suggests, in order to avoid being ensnared in the particular controversy over the *Augustinus*.[5] The date of the *Ecrits* is uncertain: Mesnard ascribes them to 1655–6, Le Guern to late 1656 or early 1657. On either view they are close in time to the *Provinciales* (1656–7). The early *Provinciales* have indeed been accused of misrepresenting the theological issues, whether or not intentionally, for the sake of polemical impact.[6] But the *Ecrits* show Pascal to possess a formidable grasp of the issues. They do not, indeed, advance an original doctrine: on the contrary, their purpose is simply to expound Augustine's teaching. But they stand out by the clarity with which they exhibit the underlying logic of the different theological positions and by the rigour with which they analyse the problems and criticise faulty solutions.

The eleventh *Ecrit* (*OC* 11, 287–93) is doubtless the best place to begin, for it contains an exceptionally lucid account (Augustine himself was never more lucid) of the Augustinian doctrine of the two states of human nature, and of God's plan for the salvation of humankind.[7]

God's initial plan was that all humankind should be saved, provided that they obeyed His commandments. And He did not leave them simply with their natural attributes of reason and free will.[8] They were given sufficient grace to fulfil the commandments, which they could choose, or not, to make operative. If they persevered in their obedience, which was entirely up to them, they would have been rewarded with eternal confirmation in grace, beyond any further risk of sin. But Adam's sin did more than cut humankind off from these benefits, present and in prospect. It changed human nature for the worse. The first human beings were created with a will that was particularly attracted neither to good nor to evil (it was 'flexible', as Pascal says). They could act in whatever way they thought most conducive to their happiness. Having sinned, however, their minds were clouded, so that they no longer had a clear perception of good. Moreover, they were infected with 'concupiscence', an ineradicable attraction to created things for their own sake. Since these are now desired irrespective of any relationship to God as the supreme good, the desire for them has become an attraction towards evil. The will has therefore lost its flexibility: evil is now, so to speak, the default (*EG* x1, 287–9). But this degeneration of our relationship to created goods is analogous to, and intertwined with, a reorientation of our relationship with ourselves. For Pascal also sees the Fall as substituting for a healthy love of self, subordinated to the love of God, a boundless love of oneself for one's own sake.[9]

Adam's descendants as a whole have inherited this guilt and this proclivity to sin. They form a corrupt mass, whom God's justice could quite rightly doom to eternal damnation. But He chose, as an act of pure mercy, and for reasons quite unknown to anyone but Himself, to pick out a number of individuals of both sexes, of every age group, rank, temperament and epoch – a minority, though, of the whole human race. These are the elect and their membership of this category does not depend on their own qualities or efforts. They are saved by the grace made available by Christ's sacrifice, under the influence of which they obey the commandments and thus contribute in some sense to their own salvation (*EG* xi, 289–90).

This conception of the Fall as the great dividing line in the history of our species enables Pascal to steer between the Scylla and Charybdis of Calvinism and Molinism. For the Calvinists, the Fall was not a turning-point, but simply a necessary ingredient in God's eternal plan that some should be saved and others damned. Pascal calls this an abominable doctrine. But the Molinists also fail to see the Fall's significance, for they believe that even now God wills all human beings to be saved, and gives them the grace that is the indispensable means of being so, leaving them to decide whether or not to make use of it (*EG* vii, 260–1; xi, 290–3).

The Molinist conception of grace is not intrinsically false, argues Pascal, for the grace granted to Adam was exactly of this type. But such a grace would be useless to us in our corrupt state. We need a positive attraction towards God that will outweigh the attraction of evil. Such a grace is called 'efficacious' in that its effect does not depend on whether we choose to respond to it. It actually brings about the effect for which it was given.[10] This is because it takes the form of a delight in the law of God that outweighs the attraction of evil, so that we infallibly and spontaneously choose to obey the commandments (*EG* xi, 289–90). This theory, derived from St Augustine's late writings, is known as the 'double delectation': the delectation of grace overcomes the delectation of concupiscence.[11] But it is important to note that there is a cognitive element bound up with this affective experience of delight. We feel a greater satisfaction in obedience: not just a greater pleasure, but a sense that obedience is where our happiness and fulfilment truly lie ('le libre arbitre choisit infailliblement la Loi de Dieu par cette seule raison qu'il y trouve plus de satisfaction et qu'il y sent sa béatitude et sa félicité'; *EG* xi, 290).[12]

This conception of grace might be seen as dangerously complicit with Lutheranism and Calvinism, which tended to minimise human freedom.[13] But Pascal denies the imputation. Those who are under the influence of grace are led, of their own free will, to prefer God to created things; those without it are still ensnared by concupiscence, so that they find their satisfaction in sinning rather than in abstaining from sin (*EG* x1, 290). But both parties are doing what they want. The point is made particularly eloquently in the eighteenth *Provinciale*, and here, too, the cognitive and affective dimensions of grace are intertwined:

Dieu change le coeur de l'homme par une douceur céleste qu'il y répand, qui surmontant la délectation de la chair, fait que l'homme sentant d'un côté sa mortalité et son néant, et découvrant de l'autre la grandeur et l'éternité de Dieu, conçoit du dégoût pour les délices du péché qui le séparent du bien incorruptible, et trouvant sa plus grande joie dans le Dieu qui le charme, il s'y porte infailliblement de lui-même, par un mouvement tout libre, tout volontaire, tout amoureux. (*OC* I, 800–1)

God changes the heart of man by a celestial sweetness He infuses within it, which overcomes the delectation of the flesh, and brings it about that man, feeling on the one hand his mortality and nothingness and on the other discovering the greatness and eternity of God, comes to feel disgust at the sinful delights that separate him from the incorruptible good, and hence, finding his greatest joy in the God that so delights him, moves towards him without fail of his own accord, by an impulse that is wholly free, wholly voluntary, wholly born of love.

So the person touched by grace could turn away from God if they wished – grace is not irresistible – but they would never wish to:

Comment le voudrait-il, puisque la volonté ne se porte jamais qu'à ce qui lui plaît le plus, et que rien ne lui plaît tant alors que ce bien unique, qui comprend en soi tous les autres biens? *Quod enim amplius nos delectat, secundum id operemur necesse est*, comme dit saint Augustin. (p. 801)[14]

How could he wish to, since the will only embraces what pleases it most and nothing in this state pleases it so much as this single good that encompasses all other goods within itself? 'For', as St Augustine says, 'we cannot act but in keeping with what delights us more.'

In other words, under the influence of efficacious grace we act by an infallible necessity, and yet our freedom is not destroyed, since we could always act differently *if we wanted to*. We are free, therefore, insofar as and in the sense that we are doing what we want. This theory has the theological advantage of allowing full power to grace, but also leaving room for merit, in keeping with a key Catholic doctrine: because, under the influence of grace, *we* are nonetheless doing *what we want*, we have merits that are genuinely our own, and are making some active contribution to the process of salvation (p. 801).

It follows, though, from this conception that if a hitherto righteous person were to be deprived of grace, he or she would be unable to fulfil the commandments. And Pascal does not shrink from this conclusion. True, the Council of Trent had formally condemned the view that the commandments are impossible to the righteous.[15] Pascal, however, argues that the Council's target is the Lutheran view that they are *always* impossible, whereas the view he upholds is that they are sometimes so.[16]

But there is a refinement here. Pascal accepts that, in a sense, we always have the *possibility* of observing the commandments, since if we wanted to fulfil them, we could do so. What we do not have is an effective *power*, since we cannot want to fulfil them without grace (*EG* v, 247–8; x11, 295–6). But what of the predicament so memorably deplored by St Paul: 'The good thing I want to do, I never do; the evil thing which I do not want – that is what I do' (Romans 7.19)? From Pascal's analysis it would follow that what we call weakness of will (*acrasia*) is in fact an underlying contrary will: I cannot abandon sin, because deep down I do not really want to.

A righteous person may fall temporarily into sin when deprived of grace (such as St Peter, when he betrayed Christ), and then, when grace is restored, recover. But some hitherto righteous people fall into sin and never recover. In theological parlance, they have failed to persevere. Here, Pascal would say, the deprivation of grace is permanent. Abandoned by God, they fall back into the *massa damnata*. Faithful to the rigours of Augustine's last works, Pascal insists that this lapsing is not all their own fault.[17] If they have abandoned God, there is a terrible sense in which He abandons them first. True, Christ said: 'Ask, and it will be given to you; search, and you will find; knock, and the door will be opened to you' (Matthew 7.7). So those who pray for grace will never be denied. But prayer itself requires a gift of grace: it is not altogether within our power. And God sometimes withholds the grace of prayer from individuals hitherto in a state of grace and obedience to His will. Unable to pray, they will inevitably turn away from God. But it was God's denial of grace that caused their abandonment of Him. Why they are cast away, we cannot know, but it cannot be as a result of some action on their part, for if a person in a state of grace could choose, of his or her own initiative, to abandon

God, then the efficacy of grace would depend on the human will, and we would be back in semi-Pelagianism.

Such are the outlines of Pascal's theory of grace, or rather his formulation of contemporary neo-Augustinian theory. For him, this doctrine was anything but purely theoretical: it perhaps reflected, and certainly nourished, his religious sensibility. Thus, he confides to Mlle de Roannez his anguish at the thought that some of those whose piety seems to mark them as of the elect may, in fact, fall away.[18] But some points call for more detailed theoretical comment. Firstly, the conception of freedom. The will is only ever moved towards what pleases it the more, or the most (*EG* VIII, 272–3). The sense of 'pleases' here is ambiguous (in English and in French). If it involves an experience of pleasure, then the notion seems to be false. We often do what pleases less: we reluctantly opt to carry out some tedious administrative task instead of the part of the work we delight in. For the conception to hold, we must, it seems, invoke some notion of unconscious or only partly conscious motivation (you are, in fact, afraid of the hard intellectual work, and are secretly glad to fall back on the mundanities of e-mail exchange) or else take 'pleases' in a weaker sense, so that 'the will inclines only towards what pleases it the most' means no more than 'we always opt for what we most want to do', which is a truism.[19] Most probably, Pascal would take the former view. In any case, it is not difficult to see in this conception of freedom an aspect of what has been well labelled as 'Augustinian naturalism': a tendency to represent human beings as driven by non-rational forces rather than as capable of regulating emotion by reason – a vision that must not be confused with, but that arguably helped to nourish, later non-Christian forms of naturalism.[20] But it is important to note that Pascal is not a straightforward hedonist. Delectation, as presented above, involves a cognitive element, as well as a sensation of pleasure. Indeed, Pascal's theory of choice can by no means be reduced to the rather mechanical model of an individual pulled between two delights: such models, he himself points out, distort since they always imply that the attraction is somehow external to the will, whereas it actually transforms the will (*EG* VIII, 274).

Nonetheless, the view of freedom set out above runs counter to that of many Roman Catholic theologians of the Counter-Reformation period. Molina had argued that a free action requires a prior judgment of the reason: this might seem to be in major contrast to Pascal, but it should not be overrated, for, as I have shown, his theory of delectation involves a cognitive element. More important, Molina, or Suárez, his fellow Jesuit, insisted that human freedom requires 'indifference', the effective power to choose between alternatives. Pascal, indeed, accepts that when we perform an action, we could always have refrained, *if we had wanted*, but Suárez, in particular, holds that both possibilities must be available while we are acting. Above all, in his and Molina's conception, the will does not merely react to the different pulls or pressures on it: it is an active self-determining force, capable of acting or suspending its action. When all the psychological forces – delight, aversion, and so forth – are in play on both sides, the will does not simply follow the force that prevails: it remains capable of moving – moving itself – in either direction.[21] And this is what Pascal denies. The conception of the will as indifferent belies our basic attraction towards evil. If grace merely balanced that attraction, we would remain, like Buridan's ass, in static equilibrium. If it overmasters that pressure, then we must inevitably be led by it and there is an end of indifference (*EG* viii, 272–4).

But the difference in these conceptions of freedom reflects an equally profound difference between the conceptions of grace involved. This becomes clearer if we bring in the temporal dimension.

Pascal insists that grace is not a capacity or power, which once imparted can be subsequently put into action.[22] Its influence must be simultaneous with the action it prompts. Nor does the reception of grace at one moment imply its continuance in the next: 'The continuation of the righteousness of the faithful is nothing other than the continued infusion of grace: it is not a single grace that remains in being.'[23] He offers several converging arguments in favour of this point. Firstly, the Council of Trent has anathematised the view that all the righteous have the power to persevere in righteousness without special help. But this is tantamount to saying that they do not have the power at a given moment in time to observe the commandments in the next moment.[24] Secondly, God never denies grace to those who ask for it, but that does not mean that it is enough to *have asked* for it. It is not enough to ask today, even with a pure heart, for the gift of continence tomorrow. We must go on asking if we are to go on receiving (*EG* vi, 255): we cannot project our moral and spiritual state into the future. But this capacity to ask does not depend on us, for not only major acts of virtue but also prayer and faith, the bases of the religious life, are gifts of God, as is taught by Augustine and his followers. Now if you say that the righteous have a proximate power to pray, then you must admit that this power is intrinsically capable of being actualised by them in their present condition.[25] In that case, prayer would not depend on an efficacious grace but rather on the prior state of the one who prays. But that is contrary to Augustine's teaching (*EG* VIII, 266–7). Again, if there is a proximate power to pray, one could never speak of a righteous person being abandoned in the first instance by God, since they would always have been able to pray for help, and thus by not choosing to pray they fell away of their own accord (*EG* VIII, 269; IX, 280–1). In short, we must say that those who do not have the *act* of prayer, do not have the power to pray (*EG* VIII, 268). The notion of a proximate power to obey the commandments, or to pray for the grace to do so, is contrary both to common sense and to the doctrine of St Augustine (*EG* IX, 275): a formulation that throws light on Pascal's theological method, of using reason to exhibit the implications of authoritative theological pronouncements, whether by the organs of ecclesiastical authority, such as councils of the church, or by a theologian, Augustine, whose teaching has been endorsed by such authorities.[26]

But for all Pascal's fidelity to tradition, there is something in his view of time that is distinctly modern or early modern. In his refusal to think of grace as conferring a power, something akin to the kind of habit or disposition that enables an agent (a teacher, an athlete, a lawyer) to meet the requirements of performance, he exhibits a sense of existence as radically contingent: one moment gives no certainty, or even probability, of the nature of the next. The analogy with Descartes' view of existence as dependent from instant to instant on God's creative force has been aptly drawn.[27] Time as the Augustinian Christian lives it has nothing in common with the rhythms of ordinary human life, based on expectations of gradual and predictable development. And this indeed connects with another feature of the *Ecrits sur la grâce*: what may fairly be called their anti-humanism. Throughout, Pascal is concerned to preserve the primacy of God in the process of salvation: a human contribution there undoubtedly is, but it is God that necessarily supports and mobilises it; His is the dominant will (*EG* VII, 257–9). Pascal sees that the appeal of

Molinism (over and above its strictly theological arguments) lies in
its appeal to our own sense of autonomy: it flatters us by making
us masters of our own salvation or damnation (*EG* VII, 260). In that
sense, it is a humanist doctrine, and for that reason he will have
none of it. Theological reason ought to enforce the lesson that humanity's fate is governed by a logic it can glimpse but never perfectly
understand. God is not to be measured by our standards of justice.

THE *PENSÉES*

The above has obvious implications for Pascal's apologetic project,
and this is where his conception of grace intersects with his conception of faith. The great bulk of humanity will never receive the double
grace that would enable, indeed induce them, to obey the commandments and to persevere in righteousness. However, we cannot know
that any individual, however wicked, is doomed. For that reason,
we must do whatever we can that may contribute to their salvation
(*EG* VII, 262). This might include writing a work of apologetics.

On the other hand, Pascal does not give the impression that he
thinks that any and every human being might respond to his apologetic arguments. His whole understanding of God's plan for the redemption of our fallen race involves the principle that God intended
to enlighten some, but also to blind others (*Pensées*, L 232/S 264).
David Wetsel has drawn on such passages to argue that Pascal did not
aim his apology primarily at hardened unbelievers. They are, rather,
a terrible example to his true target audience of dubious or tentative
unbelievers.[28] For the hardened unbeliever's very lack of interest in
the possibility that there is an afterlife in which he or she will be
held responsible for his or her actions in this life is so irrational that
it cannot be explained in purely natural terms: there is something
supernatural about it – it reflects, Pascal would say, our condition
as a fallen race (L 163, 623, 427/S 195, 516, 681). Wetsel, however,
points out that Pascal does not abandon all hope for such people:
they might possibly be shocked into giving some serious consideration to his arguments; and it is, precisely, a duty to try to arouse
their interest in Christianity, since we cannot know that they are
not, after all, predestined to receive grace.[29] But the argument comes
back: if they are to receive grace anyway, what difference does your
apologetics make?

Pascal's answer to this is that God does not only act directly
on human beings: He acts through other human beings. He quotes
St Thomas Aquinas to the effect that God has established prayer
in order to communicate to His creatures the dignity of causality
(L 930/S 757).[30] St Thomas specifically notes that prayers are among
the means by which the predestination of an individual may be realised. And by analogy the same would apply to argument. Indeed,
the point is clearly made by Pascal in L 7/S 41:

La foi est différente de la preuve. L'une est humaine, l'autre est un don de
Dieu... C'est cette foi que Dieu lui-même met dans le cœur dont la preuve
est souvent l'instrument... Mais cette foi est dans le cœur et fait dire non
Scio mais *Credo*.

Faith is different from proof. One is human, the other a gift of God... Faith
is put into the heart by God himself, but proof is often instrumental in this
process... But this faith is in the heart, and makes us say not *Scio* [I know]
but *Credo* [I believe].

In other words, the rational proofs offered by Pascal cannot of
themselves bring the state of conviction (not knowledge) that is imparted by God. But they can overcome intellectual obstacles to belief and prepare us to listen to the Christian message. Firstly, the
proofs of the first part of the apology, based on the facts of experience, can persuade the honest seeker after truth that Christianity's explanation of the human predicament is the only one that fits
those facts. Natural reason itself shows that nature is corrupted, as
Christianity claims (L 6/S 40). This does not prove it true, for there
might be no explanation – the world might be the result of blind
chance. But it does prepare the seeker to examine intellectually the
second kind of proof, the record of Scripture, which exhibits an intelligible sequence of facts: the promise to the Jews that a deliverer
would come, the prophecies that mark Jesus Christ out as that deliverer, the miracles that attest his divinity. But intellectual conviction is not enough. Our strongest 'proofs' come from custom. It
is custom that determines people's basic religious allegiances and
the values to which they fundamentally adhere, in such matters as
the choice of an occupation. But even such primordial and universal
notions as the regularity of nature or the mortality of humankind
are based on custom: we infer the future from repeated past experience. Custom inclines the body (the 'machine') and carries the mind

unreflectingly along with it. This is no doubt disastrous when the beliefs it supports are irrational. But custom also supports true beliefs (human beings *are* mortal), which is why Pascal suggests that our intellectual convictions need the reinforcement it provides. If we have once seen the truth (in this case, of Christianity), we must try to stabilise our conviction, for left to itself belief ebbs and flows. We cannot always be going over old ground, reviewing the intellectual proofs. We must resort to habit, ritual, repetition, to immerse ourselves wholly in belief, to colour our whole being with it. In that case, belief will have the immediacy and authority of 'sentiment' (L 821/S 661).[31]

This kind of self-conditioning, of course, involves effort. But somewhere along the line, Pascal implies, our efforts have been accompanied by, and indeed absorbed into, the direct influence of God on our hearts, which is called grace. In fact, when we look back on the process, we realise that God was drawing us, unbeknownst to ourselves, all along ('Tu ne me chercherais pas si tu ne m'avais trouvé [You would not be seeking me if you had not already found me]'; L 919/S 751). And the result of this grace is a supernatural state of conviction in the reality of God and in the truth of Christ's message.[32]

That state of conviction needs to be analysed. Faith, it is true, is not knowledge but belief (not *scio*, but *credo*). But it would be *irrational* to proclaim 'I will accept nothing but what I know, that is, what I can prove, to be true.' For knowledge itself, demonstrable rational knowledge, is founded on a set of beliefs that cannot be proved: beliefs in the reality of space, time, movement, and in a common stock of human perceptual experience (we cannot *prove* that if two people both say 'There is a horse running over there' then there is a shared experience underlying the identity of the verbal statement) (L 110, 109/S 142, 141). These unchallengeable but indemonstrable beliefs are classed by Pascal as 'sentiments'. He sometimes associates 'sentiment' with 'instinct' (L 110/S 142); but, since he casts doubt on the antithesis between nature and custom (L 125–6/S 158–9), he can also suggest that such beliefs (in categories such as number, space and movement) are the result of custom (L 418/S 680). But I have already shown that religious belief, even when attained by the intellect, can be transformed by custom into 'sentiment' (L 821/S 661). And the parallel between religious belief and our basic cognitive framework goes further, for the seat of both is the heart (*cœur*) (L 7, 110/S 41, 142). 'This is what faith is. God perceptible to the heart, not the reason' (L 418/S 680). If we take the parallel seriously, as we must, then, if you have this supernatural state of belief, God is as real to you as the physical world, and a doctrine like original sin, however incomprehensible in itself, carries as much conviction as the reality of number, in which we believe even though we cannot grasp the relationship between finite and infinite number (see L 418/S 680).[33] It may, indeed, seem puzzling to locate conviction in the heart, tra- ditionally identified with the seat of emotion. The point is that both conviction and emotion have an immediate self-certifying quality, quite remote from the experience of rational knowledge, in which my perception that proposition p is true depends entirely on the clarity with which I see that it follows from proposition q. Consid- ering it in itself, I may have no idea whether it is true or false. On the other hand, I am as aware of my own joy in the presence of some- one I love as I am of their presence itself. And, if I have faith, my sense of Christ as present in the Eucharist (for example) is as direct as that.

The complex relationship between reason, custom and (divine) inspiration is set forth in L 808/S 655. Christianity has reason on its side, but one whose belief is purely rational is no Christian. One must open one's mind to the proofs and confirm oneself in belief by custom (i.e., self-conditioning), but also lay oneself open to in- spirations. Strikingly, Pascal associates inspiration here with the ex- perience of humiliation: when our individual will is thwarted, our self-love wounded, and our ordinary complacent relationship with ourselves shattered, we are most open to the irruption of God's otherness – that is, to grace.[34]

CONCLUSION

It should be clear by now that reasoning (as in the Apology) can contribute, though a natural process, to the supernatural gift of faith, just as moral effort, though vain without God's grace, is essential for those who receive it. But Pascal's vision of faith throws further light on his conception of grace: for it shows, again, that he goes beyond a narrow hedonistic conception of grace as delectation. This is made admirably clear in the short piece *Sur la conversion du pécheur* (On the conversion of the sinner), which dates from some time in the mid- to late 1650s, and was doubtless nourished by Pascal's own experience:[35]

> The first thing God inspires in the soul that He deigns truly to touch is a quite unaccustomed knowledge and insight whereby the soul considers things and itself in a completely new fashion.
> This new enlightenment is a source of fear, and produces an unsettled feeling that disturbs its untroubled relationship with the objects of its former delight.
> It can no longer enjoy in peace of mind the things that used to bewitch it. A continual anxiety struggles against its enjoyment of them, and this inner insight prevents it from experiencing the accustomed sweetness of the things to which it used to let its heart go out without reservation... The solidity of invisible things affects it more than the futility of those that are visible. (OC II, 99–100)

Although the word *grace* does not appear here, the action of grace is what Pascal is describing. Its effect is not simply to reorder our affections, displacing the urge towards created things as potential objects of satisfaction by a greater urge towards God, as the true source of happiness, and imparting to us a delight in obedience to His law that outweighs that of self-gratification. It presents us with a wholly different picture of reality and of our relationship to it. In this sense, we can see how his theological reflections on the problem of grace have been nourished by and helped in their turn to nourish his epistemological theories on the heart as the source of knowledge, as well as affect. But this remarkable capacity to integrate the most apparently diverse intellectual fields and preoccupations is indeed one of Pascal's strongest characteristics.

NOTES

1. My italics. Pascal shares the Cartesian conception of animals, and of the human body, as machines: see *Pensées*, L 105, 107, 736, 821/S 137, 139, 617, 661. All translations are mine, except that of biblical quotations, for which the Jerusalem Bible is used.
2. St Augustine, *De praedestinatione sanctorum*, VII.12 (*Patrologia Latina* 44, 969–70); St Thomas Aquinas, *Summa theologiae*, II–II, q. 6, a. 1.
3. *Ecrits sur la grâce* (hereafter *EG*), VIII (*OC* II, 266–7).

4. There is a good historical introduction to the problem of grace in Miel 1969, pp. 1–63.

5. See Jean Mesnard's indispensable introduction to the *Ecrits sur la grâce* in his edition of Pascal's *Oeuvres complètes*, III, 487–641 (at p. 558). There is also much valuable material in Le Guern's edition (*OC*, II, 1210–53), and there are very good analyses of the *Ecrits* in Miel 1969, pp. 64–107; Sellier 1970, pp. 229–348; Pasqua 2000.

6. See Duchêne 1985.

7. There is a similar treatment, although the order of exposition is different, in the seventh *Ecrit* (*OC* II, 261–4). References to the *Ecrits* will henceforth be given by the number and page of the text in the Pléiade edition.

8. Augustine thinks that, even in the state of innocence, our free will would not suffice to keep us doing good without God's help. See *De correptione et gratia*, XI.29–32 (*PL* 44, 933–6). This may be because man was destined for a supernatural good (union with God) and so required supernatural assistance (Miel 1969, p. 69). Perhaps also Augustine felt that to conceive of man's normal state as involving merely natural gifts, without any dependence on God's help, smacked too much of Pelagianism.

9. Letter to Florin and Gilberte Périer, 17.10.1651, *OC* II, 20.

10. Alongside 'efficacious grace', there are also weaker forms of grace that prompt us to do good but whose influence is insufficient actually to bring about the action to which they prompt us (*XVIIIe Provinciale*, *OC* I, 800).

11. On the 'double delectation', see Augustine, *De spiritu et littera*, XXIX.51 (*PL* 44, 233).

12. There is a fine analysis of Pascal's concept of grace as delectation in Gouhier 1986, pp. 71–81. See especially p. 72, where he stresses that grace is a 'sentiment' involving a judgment of value.

13. See M. Luther, *De servo arbitrio*, in *Luthers Werke in Auswahl* (Berlin: De Gruyter, 1966–7), III, 94–293 (p. 125) and J. Calvin, *Institution de la religion chrétienne* (Paris: Vrin, 1957–63), II, 30.

14. The source of the quotation from Augustine is his commentary on Galatians, § 49: it is made much of by Jansenius (*Augustinus*, III, iv, 6 (1643, p. 175)).

15. Council of Trent, session 6, canon 18, in Denzinger-Schönmetzer 1973, no. 1568/828. I use 'righteous' here and throughout this chapter to translate the Latin '*justus*' and the French '*juste*', since it seems best to translate a single term with a single equivalent, and 'just' is misleading. A more exact theological term would be 'justified': in Roman Catholic theological parlance, justification involves the forgiveness of sin and an

inner moral renewal in which God's righteousness is communicated to man (not simply 'imputed', as the Reformers held, to a human being who remains basically sinful).

16. On the possibility of the commandments, see *EG* i–v, 211–50; x, 283–7: on the Council of Trent in particular see especially *EG* i, 211–17 and iv, 235–40. But Pascal's solution was a controversial one. The view that the righteous, for all their efforts, can sometimes be deprived of grace, and are then unable to fulfil the commandments is condemned in the bull against Jansenius (see Denzinger-Schönmetzer 1973, 2001/1092). Antoine Arnauld was to be censured by the Sorbonne in January 1656 for arguing that St Peter, when he betrayed Christ, had been deprived of grace (*Seconde lettre à un duc et pair* (1655) in Arnauld, *Oeuvres* (42 vols., Paris: Sigismond d'Arnay, 1775–81), xix, 528–9).

17. It is, though, in a sense their own fault, because if they had wanted to persevere, they would have been able to do so (*EG* vii, 262), even if in the last analysis it was God that wanted them not to want to persevere. On this 'double abandonment' (by God of man, and man by God) see *EG* vi, 251–6; vii, 262; viii, 264–71; ix, 278–83; xii, 296–8.

18. Letter VI to Mlle de Roannez, 5.11.1656 (*OC* ii, 33).

19. For a rebuttal of the notion that Pascal's conception is merely tautologous, see Miel 1969, pp. 102–3.

20. The term *'naturalisme augustinien'* can be found in Lafond 1977, pp. 159–60.

21. L. de Molina, *Liberi arbitrii concordia cum gratiae donis, divina praescientia, providentia, praedestinatione et reprobatione* (Antwerp: J. Trognaesius, 1609), p. 8; cf. F. Suárez, *Disputationes metaphysicae* (1585), in *Disputaciones metafísicas* (Madrid: Gredos, 1960), iii, 362 (xix, iv, 8).

22. Mesnard's commentary is especially illuminating on this point (*Oeuvres complètes*, iii, 600–5).

23. Letter from Blaise and Jacqueline Pascal to their sister Gilberte, 5.11.1648 (*OC* ii, 12).

24. *EG* i, 215–16; cf. pp. 211, 213; *EG* x, 285–6.

25. Pascal is using 'proximate power' (*pouvoir prochain*) here in the sense given it by the followers of Le Moyne: an agent has the proximate power to carry out an action who has all that is necessary to accomplish it: I have the proximate power to call someone if I have a charged-up mobile phone and know their number, and if the signal is adequate. In the neo-Thomist sense, I would have a proximate power even if I were in a railway tunnel and so receiving no signal, since I could make the call if I had the signal. In theological terms, they would say that the righteous always have the proximate power to pray, but cannot pray

in fact without the further help of an efficacious grace. See the first
Provinciale, OC I, 594–5.

26. On the authority of St Augustine in theological matters, see Neveu
1994, pp. 473–90. On Pascal's application of analytical reason to authoritative theological pronouncements, see Mesnard, *Oeuvres complètes*,
III, 612–37. See also Miel 1969, pp. 78–80, 82–3, 94–7.

27. Mesnard, *Oeuvres complètes*, III, 609 n. 1. But the link has also been
made with the view of time held by the spiritual founder of the so-
called Jansenist movement, Saint-Cyran, as studied by Georges Poulet
(1950–68, IV, 33–54): see Mesnard, *Oeuvres complètes*, III, 609 n.1 and
Miel 1969, p. 74 n. 37.

28. See Wetsel 1994, especially pp. 366–86.

29. See L 427/S 681 *in fine*; Wetsel 1994, pp. 321–2.

30. St Thomas Aquinas, *Summa theologiae*, Part I, q. 23, a. 8.

31. 'Sentiment' is difficult to render into English. 'Feeling' suggests a predominantly affective reaction, whereas 'sentiment' in Pascal normally
has a cognitive dimension: it is a direct perception not based on discursive reasoning. See the careful analysis in Norman 1988, pp. 3–17.

32. On this see Wetsel 1994, pp. 351–61.

33. Though most exegetes do attempt to synthesise in some way the different functions of *le coeur* (affective and cognitive, geared to both natural
principles of knowledge and supernatural faith), Gouhier, however, cau-
tions against the assimilation (1986, pp. 60–70).

34. Although Pascal speaks in this fragment of offering oneself to inspira-
tions, it is important to recognise that he would never have allowed that
by preparing oneself for grace, one can cause it to come. The preparation
for grace, the very desire for grace, is already an effect of grace (see *EG*
VIII, 267).

35. The importance of *Sur la conversion du pécheur* and of the letters to
Mlle de Roannez for Pascal's conception of grace is well brought out in
Gouhier 1986, pp. 71–6.

9   Pascal and holy writ

In some real sense, the Bible we read today is not at all the same Bible that Blaise Pascal used to document his apology. The mental universe of the cultivated French person between 1650 and 1700, Philippe Sellier reminds us, is replete with what for us are amazing lacunae. The reader must play ethnologist in order to engage in dialogue with writers or thinkers who date the creation from the year 4004 BC or think they know the exact date of the Flood. Indeed, it is truly impossible to understand fully a Pascal or a Bossuet without knowing their vision of the world and history, a vision in which the Bible not only stands at the centre, but also limits the scope of the inquiry.[1]

Sellier estimates that of the approximately 800 fragments we read as the *Pensées*, about 80 per cent belong to Pascal's unfinished notes for his *Apology for the Christian Religion*.[2] Of those fragments, at least 200 relate directly or indirectly to Pascal's project of scriptural exegesis. Why, then, has this considerable body of material suffered such neglect at the hands of readers and scholars alike?

Such neglect is, in part, owing to the fact that the dossiers in which these fragments figure rarely transcend the stage of documentation. More than any other single part of the apologetic project, these dossiers represent an apology interrupted in the course of its organisation. At the same time, the traditional division of the *Pensées* into philosophical and religious themes has engendered neglect of those fragments deemed to be of merely 'theological' interest. Moreover, Pascal's adumbration of a classical system of scriptural interpretation largely discredited by nineteenth- and twentieth-century biblical science has served to marginalise these fragments further. They presuppose a system of biblical science that has left few traces in the modern imagination, and are founded upon a view of history that is now espoused only by the most fundamentalist of Christians.

Nonetheless, the dossiers of 1658, our chief guide to the shape and direction of the apology, make it acutely clear that Pascal intended to rest his entire case in favour of the historical credibility of Christianity upon a proof constructed from this very body of fragments. 'Excellence' rules out metaphysical proofs of Christian truth in favour of those 'solid and palpable proofs' (L 189/S 221) constituted by the Old Testament prophecies fulfilled in the New Testament. 'Soumission' rejects an apologetic scheme based upon miracles to make way for the notion of the accomplished prophecies as an 'abiding miracle' (L 180/S 211). 'Falseness of Other Religions' advances the theory that the prophecies and their accomplishment set Christianity totally apart from any other religion that the world has ever known.

In order to establish the historical credibility of the Old and New Testaments, Pascal opens the dossiers 'Proofs of Moses' and 'Proofs of Jesus Christ'. Laying the groundwork for proving the truth of the prophecies and their accomplishment will require an accurate system of interpretation. 'In order to understand the prophecies, one must examine them' (L 274/S 305). Dossier xix/xx, 'Figurative Law', seeks to prove the existence of a figurative level of meaning in the Old Testament. Indeed, if the Old Testament prophecies can be shown to have but a single, literal level of meaning, 'it is certain that the Messiah will not have come' (L 274/S 305). 'Foundations' (xviii/xix), in turn, forges a theological rationale, completely Augustinian in inspiration, to explain why the Old Testament contains a hidden level of meaning. The hypothesis of the 'Hidden God' then sets in motion a chain of investigations that lead Pascal's seeker to contemplate the origins of Christian sacred history and in particular the witness of the Jewish people.

DEUS ABSCONDITUS: THE HIDDEN CHARACTER OF REVELATION

In fragment L 223/S 256 Pascal makes a note to himself. 'In the chapter "Foundations" must be put what is in the chapter "Figurations" about the reason for figures...Why Jesus Christ prophesied in an unclear way.' In what might be viewed as the preface[3] to the entire

apology (L 427/S 681), Pascal's seeker protested that he could find
no evidence of God's presence in the world. As the apology moves
onward, Pascal moves him toward the conclusion that if God exists,
He must have hidden himself from human knowledge. In 'Foundations' Pascal insists that the true teachings of Christianity square
precisely with this conclusion. Far from teaching that God's presence is manifest in the world, the Christian religion as affirmed by
St Augustine concludes that God is knowable only through revelation. 'We only know God through Christ Jesus. All contact with God
is severed without this Mediator' (L 189/S 221). Any religion that did
not proclaim God's hidden presence would contradict the whole of
practical human experience:

That God wanted to hide Himself.
If there were only one religion, God would be clearly manifest...

God thus being hidden, any religion that does not say that God is hidden is
not worthy of veneration. And any religion that does not give us the reason
why is not enlightening. Ours does all this. VERE TU ES DEUS ASCONDI-
TUS (L 242/S 275)

Even in revelation, God remains a 'truly hidden God'. Christ Jesus,
in whom was revealed all that can ever be known about God, was far
from 'evidently God' in the incarnation (L 228/S 260). 'Just as Jesus
remained unrecognised by his fellow men, so his truth remained
hidden among ordinary thinking, with no outward difference. Just
like the Eucharist and ordinary bread' (L 225/S 258).
    God's hidden nature extends to that historical evidence appended
to revelation. Although the prophecies said that Christ would be
born in Bethlehem, Jesus did not deny that he was from Nazareth.
And although the prophets foretold that he would be born of a virgin,
Christ never made a point of denying that he was the 'son of Joseph'
(L 233/S 265). Nor do the genealogies of Jesus recorded in the Gospels
make it perfectly clear that he is a linear descendent of David. Indeed,
the prophets themselves had not predicted that the Messiah would
manifestly be the Son of God:

What do the prophets say of Christ Jesus? That he will be obviously God?
No. Rather that he is a *truly hidden God*, that he will be unrecognised, that
no one will think he is who he is, that he will be a stumbling block for many
to fall over, etc.

We should not be accused of a lack of clarity any longer, therefore, since that is what we profess. 'But', people say, 'there are such obscure things without which we would not have stumbled against [believing in] Jesus Christ.' And this [stumbling] is one of the formal intentions of the prophets. (L 228/S 260)

The figurative and obscure nature of the prophecies is a clear function of the fact that God 'wished to hide Himself' (L 228/S 260). Pascal's explanation of why God has hidden Himself in Scripture and the prophecies is founded directly upon St Augustine's doctrine of predestination and election. If God had permitted but a single religion in the world, that religion 'would have been all too recognisable as true' (L 236/S 268). Even the unjust, even those predestined to damnation, would have been able to see its truth. 'If Jesus Christ had come only to sanctify, the whole of Scripture and everything else would tend that way, and it would be quite easy to convince the unbelievers. If Jesus Christ had come only to blind, all his demeanour would have been unclear and we should have no means of converting the unbelievers' (L 237/S 269). God's plan, however, was not to save all humanity. Christ came not only 'in sanctificationem' but also 'in scandalum' (L 237/S 269).

'We understand nothing of the works of God', Pascal writes in fragment L 232/S 264, 'unless we accept the principle that He wished to blind some and enlighten others.' Blinding those not predestined to recognise Christ as God is 'one of the formal intentions of the prophets' (L 228/S 260). Christ came not only to redeem those he was meant to save but to condemn those doomed since the beginning of time: 'Jesus came to blind those who have clear sight and to give sight to the blind; to heal the sick and let the healthy die; to call sinners to repentance and justify them, and to leave the righteous to their sins; to fill the hungry with good things and leave the rich empty' (L 235/S 267).

Echoing the *Magnificat*, Pascal's use of the word *laisser* (leave) to describe the fate of the damned recalls the central principle of Augustine's teaching on predestination. In condemning some and saving others, God does not act arbitrarily or contrary to mercy and justice. By right, all human beings, who fell in Adam, justly merit eternal damnation. God simply *leaves*, abandons, the unjust to a fate that all humanity has always deserved. His mercy in saving

the elect infinitely transcends any pitiful human standard of justice. God has effectively hidden Himself in revelation, and particularly in the prophecies, to separate the elect from the damned:
'There is enough light to enlighten the elect and enough obscurity
to humble them. There is enough darkness to blind the damned and
enough light to condemn them and to render their excuses naught'
(L 236/S 268).

Just as all humanity is by right condemned in the Fall, so, too, has
God been rendered inaccessible to fallen human reason. Yet, just as
God transcends any human standard of justice in saving the elect, so
too, He transcends His own hidden nature in the incarnation. God
has so 'tempered knowledge of Himself' (L 149/S 274), modified His
unknowable and hidden presence, in order to save those who seek
Him. In a passage whose ending has been transposed from the chapter 'A. P. R.' (xi/xii), Pascal envisages the prophecies as a kind of extraordinary dispensation of grace given to those 'who seek Him with
all their heart'. The following key passage is found in L 149/S 182.
According to the Second Copy followed by Sellier's edition, Pascal
transposes the end of the discourse (in italics) to S 274 in the chapter
'Fondements', seemingly indicating that the entire passage would
have been placed there. One needs to read the entire passage in order
to get the full sense of Pascal's argument:

God's will has been to redeem men and open the way to salvation to those
who seek it, but men have shown themselves so unworthy that it is right for
God to refuse to some, for their hardness of heart, what He grants to others
by a mercy they have not earned.

If He had wished to overcome the obstinacy of the most hardened, He
could have done so by revealing Himself so plainly that they could not doubt
the truth of His essence, as He will appear on the last day with such thunder
and lightning and such convulsions of nature that the dead will rise up and
the blindest will see Him.

This is not the way He wished to appear when He came in mildness...It
was therefore not right that He should appear in a manner manifestly divine
and absolutely capable of convincing all men, but neither was it right that
His coming should be so hidden that He could not be recognised by those who
sincerely sought Him. He wished to make Himself perfectly recognisable to
them.

Wishing to appear openly to those who seek Him with all their heart, and
to remain hidden from those who shun Him with all their heart, God *has
moderated the way He might be known by giving signs, which can be seen*

*by those who seek Him and not by those who do not. There is enough light
for those whose only desire is to see, and enough darkness for those of a
contrary disposition.* (L 149/S 274; italics mine)

The prophecies are 'visible signs' only for those whose hearts,
fixed on things heavenly, are oriented towards a figurative understanding of them. On the other hand, those who aspire to things
temporal will have their hearts blinded by the veiled nature of figures. In Pascal's scheme of things, God's grace must have somehow
already touched those searching for Him with all their heart. Otherwise they would not be searching. 'You would not be seeking me',
says Christ in a fragment destined for the *Mystery of Jesus*, 'if you
did not possess me' (L 929/S 756).

THE DUAL MEANINGS OF SCRIPTURE

When taken literally, the Old Testament prophecies do not, in fact,
square with the historical Jesus of the Gospels. On the surface, they
predict the coming of 'a great temporal ruler' (L 287/S 319). 'Thus
the whole question is to know whether they have two meanings'
(L 274/S 305). Pascal envisages a fivefold proof that the Old Testament as a whole contains a figurative level of meaning. Four of
these proofs, which would have been drawn from the Talmud and
the Kabala in an attempt to show that the Jewish tradition had always attributed a figurative level of meaning to the Scriptures, are
hardly developed (L 274/S 305). Their only trace resides in the chapter
entitled 'Rabbinism'.

Pascal's documentation regarding the exegetical tradition of the
rabbis is taken from the *Pugio fidei adversus Mauros et Judaeos*, a
thirteenth-century polemic against the Muslims and the Jews written by the Spanish Dominican, Raymond Martini. Unpublished until
the seventeenth century, this work attempts to prove to the other
great monotheistic religions that Jesus Christ was none other than
the Messiah predicted by the Old Testament prophecies. In 1651 the
Hebraic scholar, Joseph Voisin, a friend of Port-Royal, brought out
the first edition of the *Pugio fidei*, to which he added a commentary
on the history and principles of the rabbinical tradition.

Fragment L 278/S 309 in the chapter 'Rabbinism' seeks to document an 'ample tradition of original sin according to the Jews'. By

showing that the rabbis, departing from the literal account of Adam's fall in Genesis, went on to deduce a theory of universal human corruption, Pascal seeks to prove that the Talmudic tradition has always assumed the existence of a dual level of meaning in the Hebrew Scriptures. Indeed, his notes seem to anticipate arguing that the Christian doctrine of original sin is already implicit in the Jewish exegetical tradition:

Ample tradition of original sin according to the Jews. On the word of Genesis VIII, *the imagination of man's heart is evil from his youth*. R. Moses Hadarshan: This evil leaven is put into man from the hour in which he is formed. *Massechet Succa*: this evil leaven has seven names; in the Scriptures it is called evil, foreskin, unclean, enemy, scandal, heart of stone, icy blast, which all represent the wickedness hidden and imprinted in the heart of man. *Midrash Tillim* says the same thing, and also that God will deliver man's good nature from his bad. (L 278/S 309)

The 'Rabbinism' dossier however, never spells out this argument, but instead remains a file of transcribed notes. As set forth in the chapter entitled 'Figurative Law', Pascal's proof of the dual meaning of the Old Testament rests entirely on the first of the proofs envisaged by fragment L 274/S 305: 'Proof by Scripture itself'. Henri Gouhier reminds us that the hermeneutics of the future apology were elaborated 'in a milieu [Port-Royal] in which it seemed evident that the Bible has dual meanings'. Gouhier points to the presence of Pascal at those working sessions held at the Chateau de Vaumuriers to prepare, with Monsieur de Sacy, a new translation of the New Testament.[4] Pascal died too young to witness the ultimate fruits of these sessions. However, in *L'Ecriture et le reste* (1981) I believe I amply documented Pascal's intimate knowledge of the exegetical principles received and amended by Port-Royal.

SACY'S *PRÉFACE À LA GENÈSE*

Port-Royal's greatest legacy to the French church, the first complete Catholic translation of the Bible, commonly known as the Sacy Bible (1672–1723), contains commentaries that shed much light on Pascal's system of scriptural interpretation. This is particularly true of Le Maistre de Sacy's preface to the Book of Genesis (1682). Though published some twenty years after Pascal's death, Sacy's preface to

Genesis gathers together the sum and substance of biblical interpretation as practised at Port-Royal. Whether Pascal ever saw the
manuscript of Sacy's preface itself is of relative unimportance. The
preface, while allowing us to make sense of many of Pascal's fragments, makes it amply clear that Pascal's system of biblical interpretation is solidly anchored in the exegetical tradition of Port-Royal
and its theologians.

For Sacy, the ultimate proof of the figurative nature of the Old
Testament is to be found within the New Testament itself. Seeking to bypass scholastic exegesis and return to the principles of the
primitive church, the theologians of Port-Royal sought to follow the
example of St Augustine and to found scriptural exegesis upon models authorised by the New Testament. The whole Christian tradition,
beginning with Christ himself, has always accepted a figurative reading of the Old Testament. 'We beg those who are shocked to see us
add the spiritual to the literal meanings [of the Old Testament] to
remember that we are only following the example of all the Holy
Fathers...of St Paul...and of Jesus Christ himself who so advanta-
geously used these kinds of spiritual explications.'[5]

For both Sacy and Pascal, the single most definitive proof of the
figurative character of the Old Testament is the testimony of the
risen Christ himself on the road to Emmaus (Luke 24.27). 'And beginning at Moses and all the prophets, he expounded unto them in
all the Scriptures the things concerning himself'[6] (cf. L 253/S 285).
Those who reject an allegorical interpretation of the Old Testament,
both Sacy and Pascal insist, resemble the Jews in their rejection of
Christ.

A highly concise account of the rationale that the theologians
of Port-Royal had worked out for the existence of a figurative-level
meaning in Scripture is found in Sacy's preface to the 1702 edition
of the Sacy Bible. The Bible is incarnate in human language just as
Christ is incarnate in human flesh. Because metaphor is an essential attribute of human language, the Bible makes particular use of
figures:

The language of Scripture adapts itself to the ideas and mental apparatus of
men. Thus it speaks of God as if He had a body and resembled us. Not only
does Scripture give God eyes, a mouth and hands; it attributes to Him human
passions such as anger, compassion and rage. Thus Scripture represents God

not as He is, nor as reason makes Him known, *but as the imagination is accustomed to representing Him*, in spite of the light of reason and Faith.[7]

In neo-Augustinian theology, the imagination is the lowliest and weakest of human faculties. Pascal calls human imagination 'this mistress of error and falseness', 'this proud, powerful enemy of reason' (L 44/S 78). Yet it is to this very faculty, and not to reason, that God addresses figurative language in Scripture. Just as Christ became incarnate into the lowliest of human states, so, too, Scripture addresses its metaphors to the lowliest of human faculties.

Sacy insists that what distinguishes the Bible's use of metaphor from that of any other book is that its *figures* are organised into a completely coherent system, into an organised level of meaning known as the *sens spirituel*:

Nothing is more useful when attempting to penetrate the meaning of an author than to know what his purpose is. The purpose of the Old Testament is to represent Jesus Christ, but Jesus Christ hidden under the veil of Figures and under the obscurities of the prophets. The purpose of the New Testament is to show forth Jesus Christ plainly, and to show that he is the truth of Figures and the accomplishment of the Prophecies. Thus the two Testaments mirror and explain one another. The New Testament is hidden in the Old, and the Old is manifested in the New.[8]

FIGURES AND SACRED HISTORY

Like the 1702 preface to the Sacy Bible, Pascal calls his readers' attention to the fact that Scripture often declares itself to be speaking in enigmas. He casts his argument in terms of a practical illustration:

A cipher has two meanings. When we come upon an important letter, whose meaning is clear but in which we are told that the meaning is veiled and obscure, that it is hidden so that seeing we shall not see and hearing we shall not hear, what else are we to think but that this is a cipher with a double meaning? And all the more when we find obvious contradictions in the literal meaning. (L 260/S 291)

The prophecies might appear to be clear enough in their literal interpretation. However, the prophets clearly said that none would understand their meaning and that it was veiled (L 276/S 307). Fragment L 263/S 294 envisages a brief list of such 'contradictions'. In Genesis, Jacob predicts that 'the sceptre shall not be taken away from Judea'.[9]

Hosea, on the other hand, contains the prediction that Israel will find herself 'with neither king nor prince'.[10] Leviticus 7.34 declares the Law to be eternal. Yet Jeremiah 31.31 announces 'a new alliance'.

The Jews, practitioners of literal exegesis, would never know how to reconcile 'the end of kings and princes prophesied by Hosea with the prophecy of Jacob'. Nor can one 'reconcile all contradictory passages' by taking the Law and the sacrifices prescribed in the Old Testament as 'realities'. 'It necessarily follows that they are only figurative' (L 257/S 289).

Pascal never remotely entertains the notion that the various books of the Old Testament belong to diffent historical periods and were written by different writers. Like Le Maistre de Sacy, Pascal believes that Scripture is not a document of human origin. It hardly matters, writes Sacy, that Moses was God's 'secretary'. '*Ce sont ses pensées et ses paroles.*'[11] 'To understand the meaning of an author, one must be able to reconcile all contrary passages. Thus to understand Scripture, a meaning must be found which reconciles all contradictory passages' (L 257/S 289). Pascal never doubts that every word in Scripture – from the first of Genesis to the last of Revelation – finds its ultimate significance and meaning in Christ himself. 'En Jesus-Christ toutes les contradictions sont accordées' (L 257/S 289).

Before he can begin to advance toward the ultimate proof constituted by the Old Testament prophecies, Pascal must demonstrate the historical credibility of the Old Testament. He must draw his seeker's attention to the fact that the same book that chronicles the history of the Jewish people and contains their law also records the prophecies of the Messiah. To prove the authenticity of the Pentateuch is to establish the historicity of the prophecies.

Pascal's entire proof of the authenticity of the Pentateuch is built around the figure of Moses. 'When the creation of the world began to recede into the past, God provided a single contemporary historian and charged an entire people with the custody of this book, so that this should be the most authentic history in the world' (L 474/S 711). What distinguishes the Pentateuch from all other ancient works is the fact that its author had direct access to the events he chronicled. 'Any history that is not contemporary is suspect' (L 436/S 688).

To show that Moses was indeed a contemporary of those events he reported, not least the story of Adam's fall, Pascal makes use of an argument found also in Sacy's *Préface à la Genèse*. 'It is not the length of the years but the number of the generations which makes things obscure' (L 292/S 324). The longevity of the Patriarchs assures the accurate transmission of historical fact from Adam to Moses. The 2,000 years that separate the two in fact only amount to five generations. 'Shem, who saw Lamech, who saw Adam, also saw Jacob, who saw those who saw Moses; therefore the Flood and Creation are true' (L 296/S 327).

THE OBSCURITY OF THE HISTORICAL JESUS

Whereas modern Christian apologists focus their research on the historicity of Jesus of Nazareth, Pascal's emphasis is the reverse. Jesus' historical obscurity is a direct consequence of God's hiding himself in the incarnation. The ultimate proof of the apology, of which the chapter 'Preuves de Jésus' (xxiii/xxiv) is the final preparation, is the thesis that the 'manner' of the coming of the Messiah must be figuratively interpreted (L 255/S 287). The prophecies of a temporal Messiah had the explicit purpose of blinding those whose hearts were set on things temporal. The Messiah who actually arrived was recognised only by the pure of heart. Before proceeding to his ultimate proof, an exposition of the prophecies and their accomplishment, Pascal therefore stresses the temporal obscurity of the historical Jesus. 'Jesus is in such obscurity (according to what the world calls obscurity) that historians writing only of important political events hardly even noticed him' (L 300/S 331).

Traditionally, Christian apologists had attempted to make the best of the rare references to Jesus in Josephus and the Roman historians. Pascal departs radically from this tradition. Indeed, he makes Jesus' historical obscurity stand as the principal sign that he was truly the Messiah. What comparatively obscure historical figure, he argues, ever wrought such dramatic changes in the history of the world? Standing in inexplicable contrast to the events following Jesus' death is the story of a truly obscure life. 'For thirty of his thirty-three years, he lives without showing himself. For three years he is treated as an impostor. The priests and rulers reject him. Those who are nearest and dearest to him despise him, finally he dies betrayed by one of his disciples, denied by another and forsaken by all' (L 499/S 736). Yet after Jesus' death, 'the whole earth burned with charity, princes laid aside their rank, virgins suffered martyrdom. Whence did this force arise? The Messiah had come. These are the signs and effects of his coming' (L 301/S 331).

Jesus' historical obscurity is, of course, a corollary of the fundamental Augustinian principle of the *Deus absconditus*. His obscurity not only blinded those not predestined to recognise him; it would serve as a stumbling block to those carnal people that would follow throughout the ages. Yet Christ hidden in the incarnation was hidden only from those non-seekers whose hearts were fixed on things temporal. For those truly seeking with all their heart, Jesus was clearly not only the Messiah but also God himself in human vesture:

> Jesus without wealth or any outward show of knowledge
> dwells in his own order of holiness. He made no great discoveries.
> He did not reign, but he was humble, patient, Holy, Holy, Holy to God,
> terrible to devils,
> and without sin. With what great pomp and marvellously magnificent array
> did he come in the eyes of the heart, which perceive wisdom.
> It would have been pointless for Our Lord Jesus Christ to have come as a
> king with splendour in his reign of holiness, but he truly came in
> splendour in his own order. (L 308/S 339)

'Holy, Holy, Holy' recalls both Isaiah's vision of God enthroned in glory (Isaiah 6.1–3) and that moment in the Holy Mass when the tolling of the bell at the thrice-holy of the Sanctus heralds God's descent into the elements of bread and wine during the approaching Words of Institution and Epiclesis. Here, too, only those whose hearts are fixed on things eternal perceive Christ in 'great pomp and in marvellously magnificent array'. The carnal people, blinded by the obscurity of Christ's hidden nature in the Eucharist, perceive only the external trappings of bread and wine. 'Just as Jesus remained unknown among men, so the truth remains among popular opinions with no outward difference. Thus the Eucharist among ordinary bread' (L 225/S 258).

PROPHECIES

'The most weighty proofs of Jesus are the prophecies' (L 335/S 368). Given the key importance of its role as the definitive proof in Pascal's apology, the chapter entitled 'Prophecies' (xxiv/xxv) merits an attention that has never been accorded it by commentators on the

Pensées. This chapter is particularly inaccessible to readers. Pascal gives only limited hints as to how he planned to organise many quite enigmatic fragments and the long lists of scriptural citations that amplify the chapter in *séries* XII–VIII in Lafuma and *séries* LIV–LX in Sellier. Fortunately, the commentaries of the Sacy Bible afford enormous help in reconstructing Pascal's proofs.

Pascal insists that 'la plus grande des preuves' constituted by the prophecies originates with God himself (L 335/S 368). Sacy goes on to explain God's design in hiding such a proof in Scripture. 'Having resolved to save the world four thousand years after its creation by the death and resurrection of his Son... God wished to found this faith on proofs so convincing that they might distinguish the true religion from all the other heinous rites which Satan had already invented or might ever invent in the course of the ages.'[12] During his earthly ministry, Jesus gave clear proofs of his identity by performing an infinity of miracles. Afterwards, however, the pagans attributed these miracles to magic. Knowing that this would happen, God prepared in advance the great definitive proof constituted by the prophecies. 'God decreed that the prophecies precede the miracles [of Jesus] and that the certitude of the first bear witness to the holiness of the second.'[13]

Sacy's explanation of why the prophecies had to be obscure parallels Pascal's hypothesis that had the Jews been able to understand the spiritual meaning of their Law, 'their testimony would have had no force because they would have been on the side of the Messiah at his coming' (L 502/S 738). Like Pascal, Sacy thinks of the Jews as zealous guardians of a 'sealed book'. The Holy Spirit, speaking through the mouth of the prophets, had to adapt its words to the Jews because they only understood temporal and carnal things. The prophets promise them 'a rich abundance of all things in their cities and fields and houses' in order to ensure the conservation of the sacred texts containing the prophecies. The Jews have a special mission of bearing witness.[14]

Sacy observes that the pagans, when confronted with the Old Testament prophecies and their accomplishment in the New Testament, were so struck by the clarity of this proof that they concluded that the prophecies must be forgeries concocted after the fact. The Christians then referred the pagans to the Jews, to learn from them that the sacred texts containing the prophecies were genuine historical documents dating from long before the time of Christ. The fact that these same Jews were the mortal enemies of the Christians rendered their testimony entirely irreproachable in the minds of the pagans.[15]

For Pascal, the historicity of the prophecies is guaranteed by the historicity of the Jewish people themselves:

Prophecies. If a single man had written a book foretelling the time and manner of Jesus' coming and Jesus had come in conformity with these prophecies, this would carry infinite weight. But there is much more here. There is a succession of men over a period of 4,000 years, coming consistently and invariably one after the other, to foretell the same coming; there is an entire people proclaiming it, existing for 4000 years to testify in a body to the certainty they feel about it, from which they cannot be deflected by whatever threats and persecutions they may suffer. This is of a quite different order of importance. (L 332/S 364)

Pascal's documentation of the 4,000-year *témoignage* of this whole people certainly transcends the traditionally accepted prophetic books of the Old Testament. 'The Messiah has always been believed in...the tradition of Adam was still fresh in Noah and Moses' (L 282/S 314). 'Moses first teaches the Trinity, original sin, the Messiah' (L 315/S 346). Fragment L 609/S 504 anticipates a prophecy of the Messiah in God's words to the serpent in Genesis 3.15. Pascal's aim is to document 'Christ promised from the very beginning of the world' (L 281/S 313). God especially raised up prophets such as Daniel and Isaiah during 1,600 years. Then, during the 400 years preceding the birth of Christ, God dispersed the Jewish people, and with them the prophecies, throughout the entire world. 'Such was the preparation for the birth of Christ, and, since his Gospel had to be believed by the whole world, there not only had to be prophecies to make men believe it, but these prophecies had to be spread throughout the world so that the whole world should embrace it' (L 335/S 368).

Having explained why and how Christ's historical obscurity mandates a figurative interpretation of those prophecies related to the *manner* of the Messiah's coming, Pascal then does an about-face and focuses on the literal realisation of other aspects of the same prophecies. The documentation assembled in the chapter entitled 'Prophecies', together with its supporting dossiers (Lafuma *séries* XXI–XVIII/ Sellier *séries* LIV–LX), suggests four categories of prophecies whose literal realisation Pascal intends to demonstrate (i) the conversion of the Gentiles, (ii) the reprobation of the Jewish people, (iii) particular events in the life of Jesus, and (iv) the time of the coming of the Messiah.

The category most clearly envisaged in 'Prophecies' itself concerns those Old Testament texts predicting the conversion of the Gentiles to the God of Israel. From the time of Moses until the coming of Christ, Pascal argues, 'No pagan had worshipped the God of the Jews'. Yet at the time predicted, 'the masses of the pagans worshipped this one and only God'. 'Temples are destroyed; even kings make their submission to the Cross' (L 338/S 370). That monotheism to which Plato was able to convert only a few intellectuals remained for 2,000 years the unique possession of the Jewish people. Then, suddenly, 'a secret force made hundreds of thousands of ignorant men believe by the power of a few words. Rich men abandoned their wealth, children abandoned the luxury of their parents' home for the austerity of the desert, etc.' (L 338/S 370).

Fragment L 324/S 355, summarising Ezekiel 30.13 and Malachi 1.11, seeks to document the prophets' prediction of the ruin of paganism: 'That idolatry would be overthrown, that the Messiah would cast down all idols, and would bring men to worship the true God. That the temples of the idols would be cast down, and that amongst all the nations and in every place throughout the world, a pure sacrifice [*une hostie pure*] would be offered up to him, and not that of animals.' Pascal, of course, is thinking of the Holy Mass, the new and universal rite that would replace temple sacrifices of animals: '*Hostiam puram*, Hostiam sanctam, Hostiam immaculatam' (italics mine). In fragment L 330/S 362, a particularly obscure reference to Isaiah 19.19 notes a prophecy of 'an altar in Egypt to the true God'. Pascal offers no clue as to its meaning, but Sacy explains that it predicts the multitudes of those anchorites that would flee to the Egyptian deserts during the first centuries of Christianity: 'God made of the ancient enemies of his people a people of saints'.[16]

A second category of texts envisaged by Pascal in 'Prophecies' concerns the reprobation of the Jewish people. 'That the Jews would reject Jesus and that they would be rejected of God' (L 347/S 379). In the fragment entitled, 'Sincerity of the Jews' (L 452/S 692) Pascal points to a paradox – 'Lovingly and faithfully they hand down this book', in which it is repeatedly written that they will be deprived of their promised inheritance and of their status as God's chosen people. 'That God would strike them with blindness and that they would grope at noonday like blind men'[17] (L 493/S 736). This paradox is a sign of the supernatural character of the Old Testament prophecies. 'Sincere against their honour and dying for it; this has no example in the world nor its roots in the natural' (L 492/S 736).

A third category of prophetic texts, although not envisaged in the chapter assembled in 1658, clearly emerges in Lafuma *série* xvi/ Sellier dossier lviii. Gathered under the heading 'During the life-time of the Messiah', these texts document prophecies of literal and specific events in the life of Christ. Pascal orders these citations so as to present a more or less chronological mosaic of the life of Christ as recounted in the Gospels: Malachi 2.1 predicts that the Messiah will be heralded by a 'precursor', that is, John the Baptist. Micah 5.2 predicts that he will be born in the town of Bethlehem. A series of texts in Isaiah announce the character of his earthly ministry:

He is to blind the wise and learned... and to preach the Gospel to the poor and the meek, open the eyes of the blind, heal the sick – and lead into the light those who languish in darkness... He is to teach the way of perfection and be the teacher of the Gentiles... he is to be the victim for the sins of the world... the precious cornerstone... the stone of stumbling and the rock of offence.[18] (L 487/S 734)

In Pascal's view, Christ's crucifixion and betrayal are predicted by the prophets in particular detail. 'He is to be rejected, unrecognised, betrayed. Ps. cix.8. Zech. xi.12: spat upon, buffeted, mocked, af-flicted in countless ways, given gall to drink. Ps. lxix.21: pierced. Zech. xii.10: his feet and hands pierced, slain and lots cast for his raiment. Ps. xxii. He would rise again. Ps. xv. The third day. Hos. vi.2. He would ascend into heaven to sit on the right hand. Ps. cx' (L 487/S 734).

In assembling this collage of prophetic texts, Pascal does not have an inkling of the great textual difficulty identified by modern bib-lical scholarship. He has no clue that the writers of the Gospels made conscious use of these Messianic texts in constructing their accounts of the life of Christ. His choice of Old Testament texts is in no way original. 'Accepting with his eyes closed what the exegetes and theologians of Port-Royal had drawn from the Church Fathers',

Henri Gouhier observes, 'Pascal makes use of the methods which the practice of mathematics, the experimental method and the observation of human life had imposed on his thought: logical rigour, dialectical flexibility, and a sense of relativity.'[19]

To judge from the dossier 'Prophecies', Pascal planned to assign particular importance to a fourth category of Old Testament texts: those predicting the exact year of the arrival of the Messiah. He has already alluded to a capital distinction between the time of the arrival of the Messiah ('clearly predicted') and the manner ('predicted obscurely') (L 255/S 287). 'When the world had grown old in the carnal errors [of the Jews], Jesus Christ came at the time appointed but not in the expected blaze of glory' (L 270/S 301). In fragment L 339/S 371, Pascal spells out his argument:

Since the prophets had given various signs which were all to appear at the coming of the Messiah, all these signs had to appear at the same time. Thus the fourth kingdom had to come in when Daniel's seventy weeks were up and the sceptre had then to be removed from Judah.

And all this came to pass without any difficulty. And then the Messiah had to come, and Christ came then, calling himself the Messiah, and this again without any difficulty. This clearly proves the truth of prophecy.

In the unclassed dossier Lafuma *série* xiv/Sellier dossier lvi, Pascal copies out and translates from the Vulgate extensive passages from Daniel 2, 8, 9 and 11, which he says clearly predict the time of the arrival of the Messiah. Nowhere, however, does Pascal ever give a hint as to how he plans to explicate these passages and marshal his proof. Fortunately, the Sacy commentaries on the eighth and ninth books of Daniel greatly clarify Pascal's references. Sacy explains that the four monarchies spoken of by the archangel Daniel in his explanation of Daniel's dream (Daniel 8.20–5) are those of the Chaldeans, the Medes and the Persians, the Greeks and the Romans. The 'seventy weeks' refer to Daniel's prediction, 500 years before the fact, of the year of Christ's death (Daniel 9.24–7):

Seventy weeks are determined upon thy people and upon thy holy city, to finish the transgression, and to make an end of sins, and to make reconciliation for iniquity and to bring in everlasting righteousness, and to seal up the vision and prophecy and to anoint the Most Holy. Know therefore and understand, that from the going forth of the commandment to rebuild Jerusalem until the Christ shall be seven weeks, and threescore and two weeks...And after threescore and two weeks Christ will be put to death; and the people who must renounce him will no longer be his people...He shall confirm his alliance with many for one week: and in the midst of the week he shall cause the sacrifice and the oblation to cease.[20]

Sacy explains that the weeks in this prophecy are not ordinary weeks, but rather 'weeks of years as in Leviticus', a unit of seven years parallel to the normal week of seven days. Sacy therefore multiplies seven times seventy to arrive at the number 490. 'Thus the *seventy weeks* of which the angel speaks to Daniel add up to 490 years.' This number of years must subsequently be adjusted, since verse 27 indicates that the Christ will be put to death 'in the middle of this last week'. Sacy therefore arrives at the number 486[21] by subtracting four years from 490 years.

According to the prophecy in Daniel 9, this figure was to have been added to the date when the order went out for the rebuilding of Jerusalem. Consulting his colleague Lancelot's *Abrégé de la chronologie sainte*,[22] Sacy finds that Artaxerxes issued such an order in the 'Year of the World' 3,550, that is, 3,520 years after the creation. Counting back through the genealogies of the Old Testament, seventeenth-century chronologists had attempted to establish the year of the creation in modern notation. *La Sainte chronologie* of J. d'Auzoles presents some seventy-nine opinions, arrived at by some 122 different chronologists, varying from 3083 BC to 6984 BC.[23] For the modern reader, these differences pale into insignificance in the face of such a naïve, but universally accepted, view of the relatively recent antiquity of the world. Ancient tradition had long held that Christ was born in the 4000th year of the creation. The science of geology lay 150 years away and the abyss of deep time remained an unconsidered concept.

Adding 486 (the number derived from his explication of Daniel 9) to 3550 (Lancelot's number for the order for the rebuilding of Jerusalem), Sacy comes up with the 'Year of the World' 4036. Using 4000 BC, the traditional date for the birth of Christ, Sacy interprets Daniel 9.24–7 as predicting that Christ would be put to death in the year 36 AD.[24]

With the help of Le Maistre de Sacy, we may reconstruct the substance of Pascal's argument as follows. The prophets predicted the arrival of Christ in the fourth of four great monarchies, after the seat of power had been removed from Jerusalem, and in the fifth century following the return from exile. Christ arrived in the fourth of four successive monarchies, during the Roman occupation of Jerusalem, and in the fifth century following Daniel's prophecy.

Viewed from the perspective of divine prophecy, Pascal concludes, the whole of secular history takes on an entirely new function. 'How lovely it is to see, with the eyes of faith, Darius and Cyrus, Alexander, the Romans. Pompey and Herod, all working unwittingly for the glory of the Gospel' (L 317/S 348). Like God himself, the entire history of salvation is hidden from human reason. It is a veil that may be penetrated only by the eyes of faith. The Old Testament prophecies, however, represent a kind of extraordinary dispensation of grace. They enable 'those who seek with all their heart' to perceive the true religion hidden in secular history.

Although Pascal's proofs and the entire ancient exegetical tradition they represent would certainly fail the scrutiny of modern biblical scholarship, they nonetheless remain the key to the epistemology of his projected *Apology for the Christian Religion*. Pascal will ultimately rest his case for the truth of Christianity neither on his analysis of human nature nor on metaphysical proofs, nor on the wager. Rather, his crowning argument and what he considers his most 'weighty proofs' (L 335/S 368) will take the form of a purely empirical and mathematical calculation. Pascal's naïve, but completely comprehensible, ignorance in matters biblical and historical may come as a shock to those readers who have heard so much about his 'modernity'. How terribly finite seems the historical perspective of this greatest thinker on the infinite. But the fact remains that, for Pascal, Holy Scripture remains the only authoritative history.

NOTES

1.   Sellier, 'Avant-Propos' in Wetsel 1981, p. xi.
2.   Pascal, *Pensées*, ed. Sellier, p. 23.
3.   See ch. 4, 'The Preface to the Apology', in Wetsel 1994.
4.   Gouhier 1971, p. 206.
5.   Le Maistre de Sacy, *Les Psaumes de David* (Paris: G. Desprez, 1699), preface, pp. 5–6.

6. Sacy, *La Genèse: traduite en français avec l'explication du sens littéral et du sens spirituel* (Paris: Lambert Roullard, 1683), preface, Première partie, partie iii.

7. Sacy, *La Sainte Bible... traduite en françois... avec de courtes notes* (Liège: Broncart, 1702), preface, p. xliv (italics mine).

8. ibid., p. xlvi.

9. Genesis 49.10.

10. Hosea 3.4.

11. *La Genèse, Préface, Seconde partie*, p. i.

12. *Les douze petits prophètes* (Brussels: Fricx, 1699), preface, p. iv.

13. ibid., pp. v–vi.

14. ibid., pp. xx–xxi.

15. ibid., p. xvi.

16. *Isaïe: traduite en françois... par Le Maistre de Sacy* (Brussels: Fricx, 1699), p. 142.

17. Deuteronomy 32.21.

18. Isaiah 6.10; 8.14; 29; 61; 55.42; 39; 53.

19. Gouhier 1971, p. 226.

20. *Daniel: traduit par Le Maistre de Sacy* (Brussels: Fricx, 1700), pp. 6–7. English translation from the Authorised Version considerably amended from Sacy's French translation from the Vulgate.

21. ibid., pp. 191–4.

22. Appended to the 1702 edition of the Sacy Bible.

23. See G. Delassault, *Le Maistre de Sacy et son temps* (Paris: Nizet, 1957), pp. 210–17.

24. Whereas Sacy's calculations work out almost to the year, Pascal is more cautious. 'The seventy weeks of Daniel are ambiguous as regards their beginning, and as regards their end, because of the variations among the chronologists. But all the difference only amounts to 200 years' (L 341/S 373).

10 Pascal's *Lettres provinciales*: from flippancy to fundamentals

The *Lettres provinciales*[1] are the single polemical work of the French seventeenth century to have survived into posterity, and it is not difficult to see the reasons for their enduring appeal, by comparison both with the publications that were produced by the Society of Jesus in reply to the later pieces in the series, and with the whole unwieldy corpus of writing that was soon to bear witness to the quietist dispute.[2] There is, of course, an equivalent mass of technical theological material underpinning the *Provinciales*, but, at least in the first ten letters, it is sufficiently concealed to allow the fictional exchanges the highest possible degree of autonomy and thus accessibility. Only when we reach the later pieces do we become aware of the intertextual and contextual dimensions of the writing; and it could indeed be argued that the letters that follow the shift of perspective effected by the eleventh move progressively towards the kind of more detailed internecine dispute which in fact more typically reflects religious disagreement in the period.

The series of occasional pieces is unfinished, but demonstrates a certain symmetry of structure; and the retrospective subtitle of the composite volume, published in 1657, is *Letters written by Louis de Montalte to a provincial friend and to the Reverend Jesuit Fathers on the subject of the morals and politics of these Fathers*. The first ten letters are thus written by a figure whom we may usefully identify as Louis de Montalte (although the persona is not accorded the name until the appearance of the collection) 'to a provincial gentleman', with the additional information heading the first letter that it is 'on the subject of the present debates in the Sorbonne'. However, it is only the first three letters that address satirically the question of the recent censure of Arnauld[3] by the faculty of theology, with the fourth effecting a link to the next series, 5–10, which most memorably attack the lax penitential and spiritual practices of the Society of Jesus. Letter 11 then changes addressee, and is written, together with the pieces up to and including 16, 'by the author of the letters to a provincial to the Reverend Jesuit Fathers', bringing about thereby a change from persona to pseudonym, before the final two, 17 and 18 (and the beginning of a fragmentary nineteenth) are addressed by the same writer to the 'Reverend Father Annat, sj'. The true name of the author is, for obvious reasons, concealed throughout. The substance of the argument in the opening three and closing two letters concerns a doctrinal dispute over the roles of grace and free will as articulated in the *Augustinus* of Jansenius,[4] on which matter Arnauld, in his *Seconde lettre à un duc et pair* (Second letter to a duke and peer) (1655) had written against the papal condemnation of the 'Cinq Propositions [Five Propositions]' supposedly contained in that volume.[5] The central letters, first satirically and then directly, attack the Society of Jesus, initially for its moral and spiritual laxism, and then for its alleged calumny of the author of the *Provinciales*. Although there are apparently at least two different issues at stake, therefore, the series as a whole is linked authorially by its evolving epistoler, and thematically, as will progressively become explicit, by the fundamental relationship between doctrine and ethics.

THE OPENING LETTERS

The main effect of the opening letters is to reduce to insignificance the status of the condemnation of Arnauld, by suggesting more and more overtly that the nature of the attack is personal and not theological. The first piece thus narrows the accusation down to a purely terminological difference, agreed on by diverse parties in order to silence Arnauld, but which 'involves no question of faith' (*OC* 1, 590). The Jesuits then make their appearance in the second letter, in which they too are immediately associated with a political alliance, before the solution, once again, is revealed to be purely semantic. Two other features of the argument as it will evolve also implicitly emerge: first, that the Society of Jesus is recognised as a counter-Reformation powerhouse, and that, as a result, the label of crypto-Protestantism is likely to be attached to all those who oppose it; and secondly, that the important dialogic voice of Montalte's 'ami janséniste [Jansenist friend]', offering as he does a foretaste of the evolution in the sympathies of Montalte himself, gradually articulates the underlying world-versus-Gospel dichotomy, whereby 'worldly interests... are incompatible with the Gospel truths' (*OC* 1, 605).

The whole context of the opening, however, is one of easy sociability, reflected not only in the relationship between the fictional epistoler and the addressee, but also in the network of conveniently placed friends to whom Montalte pays visits in order to seek enlightenment, affording thereby an effortless personification of opinions by means of the extended *dramatis personae*. What we also notice straight away is how the process of assimilation of raw material has already taken place, enabling the argument to be disingenuously presented as straightforward and unproblematic in its essence: '[This] is what I am briefly going to tell you now that I am fully informed on the subject' (*OC* 1, 589). It is tightly and sharply expressed, with a strikingly readable (and strikingly untheological) degree of simplicity, even though the appearance of a word such as *temerity* alerts the more informed reader to the fact that a technical vocabulary is in play beneath the disguise of a common term. This treatment furthermore accords entirely with the recognition in the second letter of a widespread curiosity concerning matters of grace and free will: 'The faithful all ask theologians to tell them the true state of nature since its corruption' (*OC* 1, 601–2). This reinforces the impression given by the whole fiction of the attempt to convey a technical debate to a curious public in terms which it will be capable of understanding, rather than what is in fact happening, namely that a technical debate is being vulgarised in terms which minimise the burden of the theological argument, in order to propose to the public a purely political motive. Two features then afford further indications of what will ensue: first, as the pseudo-biblical allegory of the wounded man in the second letter provides, by virtue of its similarity with the parable of the Good Samaritan in Luke 10.29–37, a reminder of the scriptural context of the whole dispute as it is later to emerge; and, secondly, as Montalte is described as 'a free and private person' (*OC* 1, 603), in anticipation of the declaration of partisan independence by the still anonymous Pascal later in the series. The features of the opening pieces are, then, finely resumed in the fictive 'provincial's answer to his friend's first two letters', stressing both the idealised readership, as being 'society people' (of both sexes), and the qualities of the writing in the first letter: '[It] is most original and very well written. It narrates without being a narrative; it clears up the most complex questions imaginable; it is delicately ironic; it is instructive even for those who know little about such matters; it doubles the pleasure of those who do understand them. It offers moreover an excellent defence and, if you like, delicate and inoffensive criticism' (*OC* I, 605–6).

The third letter shows similar features of both substance and form: mention is immediately made of 'a manuscript copy of the censure' (*OC* I, 607 – the text of the censure of Arnauld had become unofficially available between the publication of the second and third pieces), but again, typically, a popularising summary takes the place of the text. The letter's opening also contains a contrastive characterisation of Montalte (the praised epistoler, seeking obscurity) and Arnauld (the denigrated theologian seeking to defend himself publicly), and further indications of a polarised theological outlook gradually and almost subliminally emerge, as the doctors of the Sorbonne are now described as 'these good Molinists' (*OC* I, 609).[6] Again, the suggestion prevails that, since theological distinctions are indiscernible to the laity ('we who do not go so deeply into [such] things'; *OC* I, 610), it will, as a result, be inclined to conclude for the innocence of Arnauld, as can be seen from the *vox populi* reaction: 'Would you believe it, Sir, but most people … have become quite annoyed and are taking issue with the censors themselves?' (*OC* I, 609). Yet again, therefore, the balance of argument is weighted in favour of simplification and presentation – spin, in modern terms – as against the examination of substantive questions of theology; and, having moved from questions of terminology to questions of semantics, it now shifts to matters of politics in such a way as to foreground the gratuity of the attack against Arnauld. As the innocence of Arnauld is progressively asserted, however, the reappearance of the Jesuits ('the Jesuits will have their way'; *OC* I, 611) points forward to the direction the series will soon take, moving from defence to attack; the shadow boxing gradually recedes as further swipes against the society ensue; and the enumeration of a whole series of schemes and tricks, euphemistically described as 'a variety of little devices which are something less than regular'

(*OC* 1, 612), makes explicit the emergent political subtext. But it is, of course, precisely because we have been persuaded to consider the account of the Arnauld affair as 'debates between theologians, not about theology' (*OC* 1, 613) that it is so readable. The flippant style of the presentation masks the substance of the doctrinal argument.

The fourth letter finally reveals the true polemical thrust of the central part of the series, beginning as it does: 'There is nothing quite like the Jesuits' (*OC* 1, 614). It goes on to accord to the Jesuit casuist Bauny (whose *Somme des péchés* (Compendium of sins) had been censured by the faculty of theology of Paris in 1641) a blasphemous status as the originator of 'a quite new form of redemption', with the rider that real blasphemy trumps false heresy. The blasphemous position that is attributed to him is founded on his assertion that a sin may be deemed not to have been committed without the awareness of its status by the sinner, and without the provision by God of a desire to avoid committing it, since 'an action cannot be imputed as sinful unless God gives us, before we commit it, knowledge of the evil contained therein and an inspiration which moves us to avoid it' (*OC* 1, 614–15), a stance whose apparent appeal to common sense is then negated in the remainder of the piece. The oppositional contrast between earth and heaven is then more lightly underscored in the exclamation 'What an excellent path to happiness in this world and the next!' (*OC* 1, 617), leading through a tonality of greater indignation to the concluding conceit of the section, 'Let us have none of these half-sinners, with some love of virtue; they will all be damned. But as for these avowed sinners, hardened sinners, unadulterated, complete and absolute sinners, hell cannot hold them; they have cheated the devil by surrendering to him' (*OC* 1, 617).

LETTERS 5–10

In the fourth letter and those that follow, a whole sequence of stylistic developments, exploiting antiphrasis and *reductio ad absurdum* for their maximum comic potential, is worked out from a simple theological starting point. Indeed the whole series of satirical letters, 5–10, is little more than an extended amplification of the primary assertions contained in the fourth, and anticipated in such phrases as 'The good Father...saw clearly enough the connection between these consequences and his principles' (*OC* 1, 617). The fictional Jesuit is thus manipulated as a kind of satirical trigger, first of all in an interplay with the 'Jansenist friend', whose arguments are predominantly scriptural (while Montalte still retains the status of the *honnête homme*, the discerning and cultivated society figure), before he is succeeded by a similar or even more gullible colleague in the direct encounters with Montalte in the subsequent letters. Scripture, too (both Old and New Testaments), plays an increasingly important role, albeit still identified by reference and paraphrase, rather than by means of lengthy quotation; and the argument gains in technicality, with the 'Jansenist friend' pitted against the first Jesuit father in a dispute whose specificity of reference is rendered plausible by the fact that 'my companion... must have studied the whole question that very morning' (*OC* 1, 620). The primary dispute is then clinched by an elegant quotation from St Augustine, introducing a distinction that has clearly been held back to permit the development of the implications of the Jesuit position, thus imparting a sense of relief as well as clarity to the end of the letter: '"[A] sin of ignorance can only be committed by the will of the person committing it, but by a will directed towards the action and not towards sin; nevertheless this does not prevent the action being a sin, because for that it is enough to have done what one was obliged not to do"' (*OC* 1, 624). The shift is then explicitly made from doctrine to ethics, as the voice of indignation is taken up by Montalte: '[W]hen I was alone with my friend, I expressed my amazement at the upheavals that such a doctrine introduced into morality' (*OC* 1, 624).

The fifth letter then inaugurates the long sequence of justly famous pieces, in which the 'morale relâchée [lax morality]' of the Jesuits is progressively exposed to an increasingly incredulous and impatient Montalte. The technique deployed resides in the second fictional Jesuit father eagerly developing to its extremes the moral guidance available to penitents from confessors in their judgment of problematic cases (and again, there is a vulgarisation here of existing material, notably Arnauld's *Théologie morale des Jésuites* (The moral theology of the Jesuits) published in 1643). The satirical device of (dis)ingenuousness brilliantly allows Pascal/Montalte to hollow out his adversaries' position, and then replace it with the simplicity of the Gospel. In this way, an utter polarisation occurs between the compromise (the 'probability') of the worldly Jesuit and the

absolutism (the 'certainty') of the Scriptures, as will be yet more
directly evident in the letters following the eleventh, and this polarisation is equally reflected in the opposition between novelty
and authority, as the flexibility of the modern manuals of direction is damningly juxtaposed with the certainty of the dictates of
the councils and fathers, dismissed by the Jesuit as 'good [only]
for the morality of their time' (OC 1, 634). Two particular features of the presentation advance this achievement: the first lies
in the manipulation of the fictional Jesuit interlocutor, who, despite his progressively more caricatural tendencies, nonetheless af-
fords a convincing exposition of the excesses that are legitimised,
not least by the tone of enthusiasm in which they are revealed.
The second depends on the (apparently) scientific accuracy with
which evidence is forwarded from the writings concerned, with as
much attention to detail of reference as would be required in an
academic journal, according a spurious objectivity thereby to the
(in fact frequently adapted) quotations.

The sixth to tenth letters deploy similar techniques, with a progressive movement towards the loss of patience and thus eventual
revelation of the true position of Montalte. In this way, the whole
series constitutes a process of education, whereby the Montalte of
the opening letter is transformed into the (still unidentified) Pascal
of the eleventh. The exploitation of ambiguity in the direction of the
penitent dominates the sixth letter, taking the insistence on flexibility of its predecessor one stage further away from 'certainty' towards 'probability', with the Jesuit father claiming again that 'we
can see better than those of old the present needs of the Church'
(OC 1, 643). What is also introduced later in this letter is the illus-
trative anecdote, here the story of one Jean d'Alba, who places the
society in an insoluble impasse by rendering it the victim of its own
flexibility. A further exemplary device is thus inaugurated in order to
point and discredit the implications of the principles advocated by
the Jesuits. The seventh letter finally introduces explicitly the practice of direction of intention with the same techniques, whereby the
enthusiastic father takes what are fundamentally pragmatic confes-
sional guidelines into those extreme case examples which render
them invalid. The whole point about casuistry, or practical penitential case ethics, is that it is designed to provide room for discretion
in the grey areas of Christian morality, as they are confronted by the

priest in the business of hearing confessions. What Pascal does so ingeniously, therefore, is progressively to apply that discretion to circumstances where it is inappropriate, to cases, in other words, where black and white are the only possible colours, and to do so to devastating effect. As Montalte acerbically puts it in the ironic cadence to the debate on the legitimacy of killing a Jansenist: 'I am not ... sure if one would not feel less regret at seeing oneself brutally killed by people in a rage, than feeling oneself conscientiously stabbed by the devout' (*OC* 1, 659). For the time being, however, the fiction holds, and still in the eighth letter it is possible to suggest that it is equal between the 'good Father', the epistoler and the 'provincial friend', although the statement by Montalte that he and his like are 'neither priests nor ecclesiastics' again anticipates Pascal's own denial of any clerical allegiance later in the series. What strongly emerges in this letter, as well, is the perversion of the concept of universality, whereby the Catholic (and catholic) ideal is achieved only by laxism: '"Nobody could ever", said the Father, "write for too many people"' (*OC* 1, 670).

The ninth letter, whilst retaining the same basic techniques and advancing the evolution in Montalte, proposes a change in the subject matter from ethics to spirituality, by exposing the practices associated with 'easy devotions' (*La dévotion aisée* was itself the title of a text by the Jesuit, Père Le Moyne, published in 1652), and culminating in an exploration of ways of hearing Mass with the least effort. Turning back to the sacrament of penance in the next letter, the political subtext is now brought to the surface, whereby the power of the Jesuits is exercised by virtue of the extent of their influence: 'You will read', Montalte promises, 'about mitigations of confession, which are surely the best means the Fathers have devised for attracting all and rebuffing none' (*OC* 1, 684). It is in this letter, however, that the pace finally quickens, the tone of indignation predominates and the true beliefs of Montalte become apparent. Phrases such as 'all this trifling ... where human wit makes such insolent sport with the love of God' (*OC* 1, 694) lead to the ironic cadence that concludes the persona's final outburst in a brilliant display of Christian paradox, as he prays 'that [God] may deign to show [the Jesuits] how false is the light that has led them to the brink of such precipices, and that He may fill with His love those who dispense men from loving Him' (*OC* 1, 696).

LETTER II

The eleventh letter is, no doubt, the single most important piece of the whole collection, even if not the most typical. It is immediately striking by the change of addressee, and by the element of reaction to the Jesuit counter-polemic that it contains (it is dated 18 August 1656; the earliest of the Jesuit replies is thought to date from May 1656). There is, however, still no sense of a detailed debate emerging at this stage; rather, the letter identifies one single and fundamental accusation and proceeds to turn it to its own advantage. The epistoler has been accused of treating Jesuit maxims irreverently: 'You repeat this constantly in everything you write, going so far as to say "that I ridiculed sacred things"' (OC 1, 697). The exact terms, from the fifth part of the *Première réponse*, deal with the accusation that the writer, in treating 'matters of theology and morality, cases of conscience and salvation, only ever does so in a scornful, jokey style, unworthy, not just of a theologian or ecclesiastic, but of a Christian, who should not treat holy things with mockery and frivolity' (OC 1, 1210). What Pascal does, therefore, is to move, by means of the obligation *topos* which is so characteristic of polemic ('Since you force me into this argument, Fathers'; OC 1, 698), to a fervent defence of his action, whereby he insists not only that it is the Jesuits who have demoted the holy, but that it would indeed be an impiety not to attack the error they represent. The intimate connection between doctrine and ethics, which has also been emerging, is finally made explicit at this point, and the whole argumentation is contained in a single vital sequence:

I would ask you to consider that, while Christian truths deserve love and respect, the contrary errors deserve contempt and hatred. This is because there are two things about the truths of our religion: a divine beauty which inspires love and a holy majesty which inspires awe; and there are similarly two things about these errors: an impiety which inspires repugnance and an impertinence which inspires derision. (OC 1, 698)

In this way, it is implied, the incorrect interpretation of Christian dogma, which arises from the perversion of Christian ethics, will militate against the credibility of Christianity itself.

The Christian therefore has a duty to combat such profanation, a position further justified by patristic evidence, with Pascal using the same citational practice as had been accorded to the Jesuit father, only now from the church fathers. Note in particular the appeal to Tertullian,[7] culminating in the memorable description of comic writing, and thus of the early letters, as 'sport before a real attack' (*OC* I, 700), with the 'real attack' now ready to occur in what will ensue; and to St Augustine, to the effect that there is no reason why those who express orthodoxy should write in a style that is 'dull enough to send their readers to sleep' (*OC* I, 701). What we again notice, however, is that even at this new and explicit stage of the dispute, the business of writing is the legitimacy or not of '*raillerie*' (ridicule) in the treatment of theological questions, rather than any detailed examination of points of doctrine *per se*, and that the degree of accessibility to the lay reader therefore remains high. What we find at the centre of this letter, and thus at the centre of the whole series, is an appeal to the criterion of discernment, a fundamental if at times implicit concern of much Christian writing in the period. Pascal insists that the means are available to discern the nature of any '*répréhensions*' (criticisms) levelled against the society, and indeed exposes these as truth and sincerity in speech, discretion and the avoidance of ridicule of the (truly) sacred. After claiming to have demonstrated all three qualities, he subsequently identifies their motive as being a charitable one, in other words, as the desire for the salvation of those who are subjected to such criticisms, manifested by the desire to 'pray to God even while we rebuke men' (*OC* I, 705). The piece ends, after the predominantly defensive tone of the first part, with an attack on what Pascal considers to be truly against the rules of discernment that he has drawn up. The attack takes the form of a poem blasphemously, because flippantly, comparing the cherubim to a blushing woman, and of an extended metaphor heretically vulgarising the dogma of the incarnation, both of Jesuit origin (but both of which will tend to strike a modern reader as relatively harmless). More seriously, and ripe for a good deal of development in the pieces that follow, is what is presented as the calumny by the society directed against Port-Royal, offending as it does the requirements of truth, discretion and charity. The letter ends with a flurry of patristic and biblical quotation, announcing the authoritative intertexts that will support the argumentation that is to follow, in contrast to the manuals whose extracts have dominated the earlier letters; there is also a postscript that endorses by its reference to other writing (the first of the *Impostures* of Arnauld's adversary, Nouet) the fact that the series has now lost its fictional autonomy and takes on from this point the status of a constituent part of a wider polemical exchange.

LETTERS 12–18

As Pascal moves into the later stages of the series so the tone becomes far more directly adversarial, confirmed in the twelfth letter by a powerful and menacingly triumphalist reiteration of the obligation *topos*: 'Just remember that it is you who compel me to clarify things, and let us see who will come off best' (*OC* 1, 711). The serious debate begins with the questions of alms-giving and simony, and antithetical constructions appealing to scriptural authority punctuate the writing. Thereafter a more general principle is adduced, whereby humankind, in the Jesuit scheme of things, is accorded the respect due to God: 'You have followed your usual method, which is to grant men their desires and fob God off with words and appearances' (*OC* 1, 715), with the speaker now adopting the characteristic tonality that will persist until the end of the series, that of the lone voice of truth pitted against the massed forces of error: 'You think you have power and impunity on your side, but I think I have truth and innocence on mine' (*OC* 1, 722). Throughout the later letters, too, the reader is made increasingly aware of the counter-polemic to which they are, at least in part, a reaction. There is not, however, an exact interlocking by either side, partly because each side is concerned to identify from the adversarial text those points with which it feels offensively or defensively most comfortable, partly because the Jesuit replies are both more diffuse and more verbose than the *Provinciales* themselves, and partly because the relative readability of even the later pieces depends on some provision of evidence from the intertext being incorporated into the countering piece. Furthermore, much of the counter-polemic was inevitably at a disadvantage by virtue of following the Pascalian texts chronologically, and of seeking to correct memorably extreme examples by an appeal to forgettably mainstream detail. Thus, one passage from the *Première imposture* appeals: 'I invite the reader to consult this treatise and to begin by looking at the first chapter' (*OC* 1, 1225), apparently little aware that the reader of polemic is temperamentally disinclined to engage in research of this nature. Where the Jesuit writing does take the initiative is in the accusation of crypto-Calvinism in the *Quatrième imposture*: the writer of the *Provinciales* is regularly referred to as 'the Calvinists' disciple', and his motivation uncovered, whereby, 'not daring to attack the Church openly, like your Calvinist brothers do, you take it out on the Jesuits, whom you have made your mind up to persecute with all your energies' (*OC* 1, 1234).[8]

Letter 13 returns to the major question of homicide and, in common with all the remaining pieces, involves detailed cross-reference. The argument now makes explicit the danger posed to doctrinal assent by ethical irregularity, and Pascal stresses the need to defend the church against what heretics may now legitimately say against it. Polarised exemplification is again a dominant feature, as is the reversal of priorities, now in the alleged readiness of the Jesuits to have regard for the laws of the state rather than the laws of God, memorably expressed in a further inversion of Christian teaching, 'You are bold before God and fearful before men' (*OC* 1, 732), and developed into a linguistic metaphor, 'We understand it, Fathers, this language of your school' (*OC* 1, 733). The conclusion reiterates the broader implications in ever more unambiguous terms: '[The] disorder in your moral teaching could spell ruin not only for your Society, but for the universal church as well' (*OC* 1, 734). It is this (for Pascal) self-evident threat to the tenability of Christian teaching that is extended in the next letter, tellingly stressing as it does that the society will show by its teaching on homicide 'how far you have departed from the sentiments of the church, and indeed of nature' (*OC* 1, 735). The perspective of the *honnête homme*, which had prevailed in the first ten letters through the persona of Montalte, is thus retained in the later series by this parallel appeal to common sense alongside orthodoxy, since the value of another human life is a truth as readily available from nature as from Scripture, and since homicide is as strongly condemned by pagan laws as by Christian ones. It is here, too, that the starkest of all expressions of polarisation is accorded a scriptural authority in the rhetorical question paraphrasing Matthew 12.30: 'All in all, Fathers, what do you want to be taken for? children of the Gospel or enemies of the Gospel? One must belong to one side or the other, there is no middle course' (*OC* 1, 746). Between the two extremes of the world and the Gospel, there is, for Pascal, not a compromise but a vacuum, a point of view that is further emphasised by an Augustinian quotation, identifying the church as the realm of God and the world as the realm of the devil,[9] asking the society to decide to which kingdom it belongs, and in conclusion taking up the linguistic metaphor, 'Which of these two languages do you understand? Which do you speak?' (*OC* 1, 746–7).

The dispute intensifies in the following letter (15), as well as becoming more personally defensive, with Jesuit calumny again accorded high relief and with the *Impostures* now replied to, in some cases compositely, in others with reference to a particular argument. What also run through this letter are the mutual accusations of heresy, from which it is clear that the word is deployed loosely as the most current, but also the most damning, inter-Christian term of abuse.[10] Yet, here again Pascal minimises the implications, according to the term no more than the status accorded by the Jesuits to those who disagree with them, and effecting thereby a further semantic revelation of the mysterious language of the society: 'It is as well, Fathers, to understand this strange language, according to which I am unquestionably a great heretic' (*OC* 1, 754). True heresy for Pascal is, rather, identified in the doctrines of his opponents, and he rejoices typically in the entrapment of the society on the strength of its own inconsistencies, whereby 'I only need yourselves to confound you … since your replies are mutually destructive' (*OC* 1, 755). Bringing the two ideas together, Pascal asserts the error of the Jesuit accusation based on Arnauld's treatise against frequent Communion[11] (that Port-Royal is thereby in line with Protestant thinking) as a further calumny, but one based on the ethical principles of the society, so allowing him to conclude that they commit calumny 'not against, but in accordance with their own precepts' (*OC* 1, 761).

More attention is then given to the specifics of the exchange in the sixteenth letter, with polemical devices shifting back and forth in a *dialogue de sourds*, so that the reader becomes progressively more aware of the futility of the argument. The centre of the Jesuit accusation is, however, now firmly identified in the conviction that the eucharistic doctrine of Port-Royal is crypto-Calvinist – a further important intertext, the *Port-Royal et Genève d'intelligence contre le Très-Saint Sacrement de l'autel* (Port-Royal and Geneva in league against the most Blessed Sacrament of the altar) by the Jesuit, Père Bernard Meynier, had appeared between the fourteenth and fifteenth letters – and it is indeed on sacramental matters that the letter concentrates. Pascal predictably (and indeed convincingly) asserts the eucharistic orthodoxy of Port-Royal and, equally typically, throws back at the society the complementary error of over-facility in the giving of Holy Communion to the unrepentant sinner. Yet again, a memorable formula resumes the essence of the argument in the form of a paradox – 'What does it matter if the holy tables of Jesus Christ are filled with abomination so long as your churches are full of people?' (*OC* 1, 768) – before a more erudite consideration is given to the status of the real presence of Christ in the Eucharist, in a tripartite formulation redolent of certain passages in the *Pensées*: 'The blessed possess Jesus Christ in reality, without figures or veils. The Jews possessed Jesus Christ only under figures and veils, like the manna and the paschal lamb. And Christians possess Jesus Christ in the Eucharist truly and really, but still covered in veils' (*OC* 1, 771). A further paradox is then directed at the society, in terms of a comparison with the Port-Royal nuns: 'You publicly cut them off from the Church while they secretly pray for you and the whole church' (*OC* 1, 776). Two further points might be made at this stage. We should first note that, whatever the efficacy of certain of Pascal's replies to such accusations, there is no doubt that the essential achievement of the letters as a whole is to inculpate the Society of Jesus, rather than to exculpate Port-Royal; and secondly that, however convincingly Pascal demonstrates the quite substantial differences between Port-Royal and Protestantism, the proximity in certain sacramental practices, in particular the opposition to the frequent reception of Holy Communion, must render such an accusation potentially the most damaging to which Port-Royal was subject.

The last two complete letters narrow down further the specificity of the quarrel. What they also allow the reader to recognise with hindsight is how the separate sections of the series have concentrated not only on a particular question at issue but also on a particular set of argumentational devices, so that a consistent didactic function is fulfilled at each stage. The burden of the dispute in the last two pieces returns to the quarrel of the outset, albeit now expressed in direct terms and involving the kind of detailed clarification (or obfuscation) of semantic issues that the lay reader may be expected to find less appealing. Further, they are written to Annat, as a single specified addressee, and, as the dispute becomes more personal, the question of identity comes increasingly to the surface. The charge of heresy is now defended by Pascal himself, who denies both heresy and membership of Port-Royal (a much commented, if technically correct assertion) and declares in reply his obedience to the church and to the Pope. Most of all in this letter, his autonomy is presented as his protection ('I am alone'; *OC* 1, 781), in distinction to the corporate nature of his adversaries. Returning finally to Arnauld and the Five Propositions, Pascal now makes an important epistemological point by insisting that an error concerning a 'question of fact' cannot be a heresy, asserts that 'your dispute barely concerns me, as it barely concerns the church' (*OC* 1, 786), and draws parallels with an early dispute between two church fathers. More church history backs up the contention that such an error can at worst only be a 'temerity', now taking up in a serious context the parodic use of a technical term at the opening of the series. In the eighteenth letter, the exact sense of the phrases in Jansenius is now examined, with Pascal concurring in the opposition to the 'sense of Calvin', and proposing a powerful paraphrase of St Augustine as a correct statement of the relationship between grace and free will. This is supported by St Paul and Trent, as against Calvin and Luther on the one hand, and Molina on the other. In this way, as in the highly technical *Ecrits sur la grâce* (Writings on grace), Pascal situates Augustinian orthodoxy as a synthesis between two erroneous understandings. Further parallels are then made with earlier disputes and the simple solution proposed of studying the texts in contention to ascertain whether or not a given phrase is exactly present. What appears to be an irenic tone thus rapidly manifests itself as an ironic one, as Pascal advises his addressee: 'Why did you not adopt the same course I used in my *Letters* to disclose the many evil precepts of your authors, which is faithfully to quote the passages from which they come?' (*OC* 1, 806). As the series comes to an end (very little can be gleaned from the fragments of the nineteenth letter), so a unilateral statement of resolution is appended, to the effect that 'your accusations are without foundation, your opponents without error and the Church without heresy' (*OC* 1, 814), and the writer signs himself off as one of those '[who] will be obliged to devote all their energies to keeping the peace' (*OC* 1, 815).

Various contemporary documents identify the qualities of the *Provinciales*. In particular, the accusation of 'ridicule' from the counter-polemical *Lettre écrite à une personne de condition* (Letter written to a person of standing) identifies (critically, of course) the comic features of the writing: 'There are subtle jokes to divert fine minds, useful ones to interest rich people, low ones to amuse valets and servant girls, impious ones to satisfy libertines, and sacrilegious ones to have sorcerers dancing at their sabbath' (*OC* 1, 1211). Most persuasive of all is the *Avertissement* to the composite volume of letters published in 1657, attributed to Nicole[12] and describing in highly sympathetic terms the achievements of the polemic. Nicole first of all draws attention to the vulgarising nature of the early part of the series, endorsing as he does so the disingenuous stance of Pascal's persona, whereby difficulties are explained 'with such clarity and simplicity that the least intelligent understood what had seemed to be reserved only for the most gifted' (*OC* 1, 580). Montalte, in the early letters, 'represents a person who is ill-informed about these disputes, as is usual for those society people into whose state of mind he enters, and has these questions clarified, without their noticing, by the doctors whom he consults' (*OC* 1, 580). He then turns to the 'lax morality' letters and describes how the Jesuits have adopted 'a politically flattering laxity in order to accommodate the disorderly passions of men' (*OC* 1, 581), and goes on to draw attention to the value of dialogues, 'which have enabled the author not only to inform us about the Jesuit maxims, but also about the subtle and skilful way in which they insinuate their teaching into society' (*OC* 1, 581).

This composite technique of the enlightenment, by means of dialogue, of an initially disingenuous interlocutor is at the heart of the success of the first ten pieces, and was to provide the model for variant uses of the same basic devices in a variety of later satirical writings. It was, furthermore, a device that the Jesuits were unable easily to combat, although there were some early and undistinguished attempts at imitation, partly because the nature of their rebuttal depended on a more serious and more nuanced argument, but also because a device of such manifest elegance and comic efficacy may not be simply transferred within a given polemical arena. Nicole also identifies the use of irony in the attitude of Montalte during the progressive (fictional) eliciting of condemnatory evidence. On the one hand, the persona of the fictional Jesuit is characterised by his enthusiastic desire to display the extent of the system he espouses: '[The father] just keeps going on, quite naturally' (*OC* 1, 580). On the other

hand, the unhindered movement into those extreme cases that accord the maximum discredit to the practices described prepares the
reader for the outburst of Montalte: 'This style is continued to the
point at which it reaches certain essentials, at which stage the author is at pains to withhold his indignation' (*OC* 1, 581). Nicole then
resumes the most fundamental argument of the entire series, to the
effect that the corrupt morality tolerated by the society is a direct
emanation from an abandonment of the basics of Christian teaching:
'They [have] changed the true rule of conduct, which is provided by
the Gospels and by tradition... We see now that this is the source
from which flow all their aberrations, and that it is capable of producing infinitely more of the same order' (*OC* 1, 581-2). He finally
turns briefly to the replies, which he criticises without entirely seeing the problem ('they laboured fruitlessly, and with so little success
that they left all their undertakings incomplete'; *OC* 1, 582), before
defending the use of ridicule by Pascal in terms which again reflect
those of the eleventh letter: '[The Jesuits] only have themselves to
blame for the derision to which they give rise' (*OC* 1, 583). He then describes the two phases of the attack, first of all 'exposing to ridicule
everything in their maxims that deserves it' and then 'postponing
to a later stage [Letters 12-16] the serious business of confounding
impiety' (*OC* 1, 583).

CONCLUSION

What is, perhaps, above all remarkable about the *Provinciales* is the
quite exceptional skill with which Pascal makes the reader side with
what, objectively, seems to be the less attractive theology. The definition of what constitutes a sin at the opening of the fourth letter
appeals by its *prima facie* logic to the non-specialist reader, who
only sees the difficulties with it when they are exposed in the body
of the letter, before the subtler Augustinian position is advanced in
preference. Over the question of the desirability of Mass being celebrated as often as possible in the sixth letter, the basic desire again
reflects sound theology, yet is rendered absurd by its overextension.
And, more globally, the pastoral (or, pejoratively, political) desire
of the Society of Jesus to be all things to all men, the weak and the
austere alike, together with the wish not to '[drive people to] despair'
(*OC* 1, 641) must also, at least in advance of its demonstrable

perversion, resonate both with the worldly and with the biblically literate reader, based indeed as it is on a Pauline precedent: 'I made myself all things to all men in order to save some at any cost' (1 Corinthians 9.22). Yet here again, the principle is subverted by the exemplification.

The key to Pascal's success thus lies in the persuasive strength of unadulterated dogma, shored up by the parody of its refinements, as he moves from worldly sophistry to biblical authority. Far from being a period piece devoted to a forgotten example of inter-Christian bickering, therefore, the *Provinciales* afford a powerfully enduring object lesson in the means and methods of efficacious dispute.

NOTES

1. The most authoritative critical edition of the *Lettres provinciales* and the related counter-polemic is in the first volume of the *Oeuvres complètes*, ed M. Le Guern (Paris: Gallimard, Bibliothèque de la Pléiade, 1998), pp. 577–816 and 1118–285. Both also contain the *Avertissement* of Nicole and substantial extracts from the Jesuit replies. English quotations from the *Lettres provinciales* are from the translation by A. J. Krailsheimer (Harmondsworth: Penguin, 1967); other translations are my own. Page references for the *Provinciales* are to Le Guern, *OC* 1. The biblical quotation is from the Jerusalem Bible.

2. This bitter dispute was to pit two prelates, Jacques-Bénigne Bossuet, Bishop of Meaux (1627–1704) and François de Salignac de la Mothe-Fénelon, Archbishop of Cambrai (1651–1715), against each other in a sequence of increasingly technical, personal and acrimonious publications during the last decade of the century. The apparent question at issue concerned the possibility of a total negation of the will and the achievement of absolute passivity in the service of God, and centred on the figure of the mystical writer Jeanne-Marie Bouvier de la Motte-Guyon (1648–1717).

3. Antoine Arnauld (1612–94), known as 'Le grand Arnauld', was both a rigorous proponent of Jansenist teaching and a distinguished grammarian.

4. Corneille Jansen (Cornelius Jansenius) (1585–1638), Bishop of Ypres, was author of the posthumously published *Augustinus* (1640), in which the teaching of Augustine on grace is asserted in opposition to the more free-will oriented position adopted, notably by the Society of Jesus, following the Council of Trent.

5. The dispute centred on the distinct questions as to whether the propositions were heretical (the *'question de droit* [question of law]') and whether they were present in the text *verbatim* (the *'question de fait* [question of fact]').

6. 'Molinists' derives from the name of the author of the strongly free-will centred *De concordia liberi arbitrii cum gratiae donis* (1588) by the Spanish Jesuit, Luis de Molina (1535–1600).

7. Tertullian (Quintus Septimus Florens) was a late second-century north African church father, second only to St Augustine in his influence on the early Latin church.

8. Jean Calvin (1509–64) was the principal architect of the French Protestant Reformation. The major superficial area of similarity between his teachings and those of Port-Royal lay in their common emphasis on the primacy of grace in the economy of salvation. Protestants were soon to be expelled from France, following the revocation of the Edict of Nantes in 1685.

9. Such a dichotomous view is indeed fundamental to Augustine's *City of God*.

10. Heresy in the early church refers, strictly speaking, to a choosing of one doctrine over another, rather than an assent to their coexistence. However, it tends by the seventeenth century to be more broadly applied to any heterodox teaching.

11. Arnauld's treatise *De la fréquente communion* [On frequent communion] was published in 1643, and sought to reinstate the rigorous practice of the primitive church.

12. Pierre Nicole (1625–95), strongly sympathetic to Port-Royal, was a scholar and moralist, whose best-known work is the *Essais de morale*.

11   Pascal and the social world

Although Pascal's social and political thought may seem at first glance to be of rather marginal interest, it is my aim in this chapter to show that elements of the sociopolitical form a fully coherent doctrine within a system where anthropology and theology meet. Pascal holds that if men are as they are and act as they do, it is because they have been both created by God and abandoned by God as a consequence of original sin. The establishment of a social and political order is necessary to curb the disorder catalysed by original sin, even if such a measure can only attenuate the effects of the Fall without addressing their root cause. I intend here to take such comments further and to suggest that Pascal's reflections on social and political order are to be related to his theory of the different orders of existence, and thus that they have consequences far beyond a limited sociopolitical sphere. If original sin deprived humankind of God, of the true and the good, nonetheless it did not destroy our capacity to attain these. From the moment that human beings judge things in relation to themselves instead of in relation to God, so Pascal argues, they embrace the false and the evil, disguising these as the truth and goodness of which they are capable and which remain in them as traces. Thus Christians are, for Pascal, faced with the need for a dual awareness. They are obliged to confess that men are abandoned to their own limited vision, unable to discern what is true and good. But they are obliged also to apply the insights of Christianity to human discourse as it confuses and blurs true and false, good and evil. In this way they can arrive at an understanding of the ultimate order and truth of this discourse.

AUGUSTINIAN ANTHROPOLOGY AND THE GENESIS
OF POLITICAL ORDER

Augustinian doctrine has much to tell us here. It teaches us that man, created by and for God, is everything to himself and places himself at the centre of everything.[1] Thus it is that disorder is born, as can be seen from several fragments of the *Pensées* that relate to the 'body of thinking members'.[2] Man is everything to himself in appropriating as his own those natural attributes that are no more essentially a part of him than the institutional attributes with which he may be clothed.[3] Man places himself at the centre of everything in claiming universal domination regardless of the proper order of things, soliciting, in the name of those natural attributes that he does have at his disposal, entitlements which would be merited only by others (and which he does not have at his disposal).[4] The 'self' that Pascal declares to be hateful because it is unjust in itself and a nuisance to others is precisely the sinning self: 'It is unjust in itself for making itself the centre of everything: it is a nuisance to others in that it tries to subjugate them, for each self is the enemy of all the others and would like to tyrannise them' (L 587/S 494). Each self is the enemy of all the others because, in making itself the centre of everything, it establishes competition and rivalry with all the others. Each self would like to act in the role of tyrant over all the others because, even at the very heart of the competition and the rivalry that together instigate a new form of equality, its goal is to be alone at the centre of everything, and thus to demolish the pretensions of its adversaries, or at the very least to obtain from its adversaries the unilateral recognition that it is indeed at the centre of everything. This aim, however, is contradictory and impossible. Apart from anything else, no self can dispense with other people. In loving himself with that infinite love which was destined only for God,[5] man does not love anybody else. '*Amour-propre*', which is nothing other than an unchecked love of self, forges links between men in spite of their mutual hostility and their propensity for tyranny. This society is a society of collective complacency that is, in reality, founded upon the concupiscence, which leads men to reap for themselves that which is due to God. This concupiscence certainly obliterates the unjust prominence of a self that would seek to impose itself upon others, but it cannot, in so doing, erase its intrinsic injustice. Such a society substitutes for a lack of charity a semblance and an image of charity.[6]

But how is it possible to extract from concupiscence such a semblance or image of charity? How is it possible to construct on such a despicable foundation that form of regulation that is inherent to citizenship? Social life depends upon rules held in common. The unquestioning acceptance of these rules depends upon their establishment by an authority. Yet if no single person possesses natural authority over others, how can the establishment of rules be envisaged in the first place? Pascal considers two separate paradigms of behaviour: firstly, that authority is granted to the wisest, and secondly, that it is granted to the strongest. He then rejects the Platonist paradigm according to which authority is granted to the wise: 'We do not choose as captain of a ship the most highly born of those aboard' (L 30/S 64).[7] We choose the most competent; in this case the most competent in the art of navigation. Should we not also, by the same token, choose the most competent of men to govern us? Pascal certainly admits that respect for wisdom is coextensive with sound thinking, but he refuses to admit that anything founded on sound thinking has a sure foundation.[8] Such a foundation is inadequate because natural wisdom does not exist, and because men have been rendered incapable of divine reason.[9] In usurping the place of God, men have substituted their individual judgment for a knowledge of what is good and true,[10] because a knowledge of what is good and true depends upon a knowledge of God, and a knowledge of God depends upon a love of God, as we read in the theological introduction to 'On the Art of Persuasion'.[11] But if authority is not granted to the wisest, it remains to be understood why it is granted to the strongest.

Two fragments in the *Pensées*, L 103/S 135 and L 88/S 668, reveal that political order depends upon force. In the first, Pascal sets up a conceptual opposition between justice and force merely to reveal that, in fact, the one could not exist without the other. His understanding of justice is that it is transmitted in and of itself and that we cannot but obey it. His understanding of force is that it is transmitted in a relationship of forces and that we obey it because we have to. But it is impossible to separate the two, because justice without force is helpless and force without justice is reprehensible. It is thus necessary to combine them, either by applying force to justice, thereby fortifying it, or by applying justice to force, thereby justifying it. But justice cannot be strengthened if it is subject to dispute in the first place. And the inherent injustice of humankind is such that justice is always going to be obscured. Therefore, and conversely, justice is applied to force, which is itself beyond dispute. But what is it that justifies force? Is it merely making might look right? Or is it, rather, conferring upon might an essential rightness? As I mentioned above, force without justice is reprehensible, and it is impossible to demand that force should be obeyed in and of itself without sanctioning tyranny. In the second fragment, Pascal's starting point is the will to dominate that characterises fallen man. All men desire to dominate, but not all men can do so. The logical consequence of this is that they fight until a dominant faction emerges, and yet no faction can assert its domination until the battle for domination has ceased. In order to achieve domination, it is necessary to prevent men from taking up arms and doing battle for it again. The measure required is the imposition of domination according to certain rules. There can be no power without the dissemination of power.

But what is it that makes men defer of their own accord to an authority that is only ever subject to force? This is the point at which, Pascal observes, imagination comes into play. It is imperative that men should believe themselves to be locating justice within force. This error is illustrated by the *First Discourse on the Condition of the Great*: taking an unknown castaway and adopting him as king, abandoned islanders worship his resemblance to the true king they have lost.[12] But this powerful example is not the only one in Pascal's œuvre to target this kind of error, which is explained and justified further in the *Pensées*:

Montaigne is wrong. The only reason for following custom is that it is custom, not that it is reasonable or just, but the people follow it solely because they think it just. Otherwise they would not follow it any more, even though it were custom, because we are only ready to submit to reason or justice. But for that, custom would be regarded as tyranny, but the rule of reason and justice is no more tyrannical than that of pleasure. These are principles natural to men. (L 525/S 454)

This exigency is, as I shall show, a throwback to man's prelapsarian state. Nobody is content to accept custom simply because it is custom; not even Montaigne, who states that he is content to accept custom because he thinks that men are naturally incapable of reason and justice. We only accept a custom because of the reason and justice we project on to it, whether because we imagine, with the people, that this custom is reasonable and just, or because we perceive, with Pascal, that there is a certain amount of reason and justice in accepting a custom that we know to be devoid of reason and justice.

Is imagination, that faculty which embellishes power with the trappings of justice, anything other than that 'mistress of error and falsehood' which reigns in the place of reason given man's fallen state (L 44/S 78)? If that which is founded on sound thinking, such as the esteem of wisdom, is ill-founded, then conversely that which is founded on irrationality, such as the acceptance of custom, is extremely well founded. It should be noted that Pascal declares in this regard that 'the power of kings is founded on the reason and the folly of the people', before adding 'but especially on their folly' (L 26/S 60). The political order is founded on the folly of the people, because the people are wrong to imagine that custom is reasonable and just. It is founded on the reason of the people, because the people are right to refuse to accept custom simply because it is custom, and right to be ready to submit only to reason and justice. So the people are both right and wrong.

It can be seen here that imagination is not universally denounced. In no sense does it stifle a natural capacity for truth and goodness; its action is rather to confuse the localisation of truth and goodness, finding truth and goodness where they do not exist instead of where they do. So the people are only wrong in that they project their demand for reason and justice, itself thoroughly reasonable and just, on to custom, which is devoid of reason and justice. What they should do is project this demand on to custom in the reasonable and just awareness that custom is devoid of reason and justice. Anything founded on the folly of the people is well founded, in the sense that this foundation is admirably sure. So the folly of the people is, in fact, a much surer foundation than the wisdom of the philosophers, which is, to Christian eyes, true folly. But it is clear that it does not fall to the people to identify their own folly and reason. This task falls to those whom Pascal calls 'true Christians' (L 14/S 48) or 'perfect Christians' (L 90/S 124).

Montaigne is reproached by Pascal for not having been able to elevate his vision to that of true or perfect Christians: the only level of vision that is capable of identifying the folly and the reason of the people. But in order to elevate one's vision to this level, Pascal thinks, one has to have recourse to the teachings of Augustinian doctrine. It is this which explains and justifies, on the basis of the dual nature of humankind, the mirage that leads fallen man to feel he finds justice in force, in the same way as the islanders in the *First Discourse* feel they have found their true king in the person of the castaway. In other words, Montaigne is deemed only to have perceived the wretchedness of humankind.

Pascal thinks that man is naturally incapable of truth and of goodness; that the political order is founded not on a knowledge of the true and the good, but on strength and imagination; that it is necessary to obey laws not because they are right but because they are laws; that the people are deluded in obeying them because they think them right; that there are only three possible standpoints, as argued in L 90/S 124: (a) that of ordinary people (the *peuple*), who obey laws because they think them right; (b) that of the half-clever ones (the *demi-habiles*), who have the potential to change the opinion of the ordinary people and to make them rebel, and who pride themselves on their capacity to judge laws and render them just; and (c) that of the clever ones (the *habiles*), who obey laws because they know that those laws will never be just, and that there is no form of justice other than that which comes from obeying laws not because they are just but simply because they are laws. Montaigne does not perceive the duality of man, his wretchedness and his greatness. As Pascal points out, it is Augustinian doctrine that teaches us man has the capacity for goodness and truth through grace, in that he is elevated to God by God; yet, at the same time, he is himself naturally incapable of attaining goodness and truth, as he is unworthy of God and abandoned by God, having claimed to be God's equal.[13] This dual capacity for truth and falsehood, for good and evil, exists in all men, with the sinner remaining receptive to the grace currently denied him and the good man remaining receptive to the sin he currently eludes. This idea is developed in Pascal's *Writings on Grace*.[14] In regarding men as naturally incapable of truth and goodness, Montaigne thus robs them of part of their nature, for they are naturally capable of truth and of goodness, although this is a result of grace and does not come from their human natures alone. Rather than defining men as incapable of attaining truth and goodness, Pascal believes that it would be better to state that their capacity for truth and for goodness is currently void, and that this leads them to locate wrongly the true and the good.

THE PROBLEM OF IDENTIFYING NATURAL LAW

This difference between the philosophical anthropology of Montaigne and the theological anthropology of Pascal has repercussions for epistemological theory. It is unsurprising that Pascal objects equally to dogmatism and to scepticism. Dogmatists are depicted as wrong in maintaining that man can know what is true and what is good of his own accord and without the aid of God. Sceptics are depicted as wrong in maintaining that man cannot ever know what is true and what is good, on account of the fact that he is incapable of such knowledge of his own accord and without the aid of God. The error of the dogmatists gives rise to man's presumption that he can build political order upon the essence of justice, as if he were capable of knowing what this means of his own accord. While natural laws no doubt exist, they cannot be identified by a corrupt reason, even one that claims to be capable of distinguishing between good and evil by itself. Through his emphasis on the fallibility of humanity, Montaigne would seem to have the upper hand in this argument.[15] However, as Pascal sees it, the error of the sceptics lies in man's presumption that he can build political order upon laws alone. Summarising the sceptical position in L 66/S 100, Pascal stresses that

It is dangerous to tell the people that laws are not just, because they obey them only because they believe them to be just. That is why they must be told at the same time that laws are to be obeyed because they are laws, just as superiors must be obeyed because they are superior. That is how to forestall any sedition, if people can be made to understand that, and that is the proper definition of justice. (L 66/S 100)

In no sense does an ignorance of natural law authorise the renunciation of all justice, even though this ignorance forces a split between law and justice. Pascal expands this last point in two directions.

First, he argues that man is incapable of knowing what is true and good because reason, or the capacity to know, is corrupted by the heart, or the capacity to love. From the moment man began to direct towards himself the infinite love due to God, his reason was no longer in a position to know the truth of things and their value, since these could only be calculated in their relation to God. The knowledge of what is true and good does bring reason into play, but this is not the same thing as reasoning. The problem here, and it is certainly only a terminological one, is that Pascal also uses the word *heart* to designate our capacity to identify first principles (L 110/S 142). According to this sense of the word, we can ascertain that the knowledge of what is good and true comes from the heart, and not from reason or from reasoning. When the good and the true are identified, they are identified as principles, without the mediating action of reasoning. But how is it possible for man to perceive falsehood and evil in the absence of goodness and truth? Falsehood and evil are only perceived through the mediation of reasoning. They can no longer be defined as the opposite of goodness and truth if goodness and truth are perceived immediately. Falsehood and evil are perceived after a process of reasoning that is denounced as wrong because it is based on erroneous principles, the consequences of which are deemed to go against what is natural. But if man is capable of knowing falsehood and evil of his own accord and without the aid of grace, can it not be objected that he should also be able to re-establish, within the same parameters, a knowledge of goodness and truth? In fact, Pascal does not deny that those people who reason sufficiently well to perceive falsehood and evil also thereby perceive goodness and truth. But it is out of the question that this is true for everyone. Given that natural law is not known immediately, it cannot be known universally. If it could be known universally, then 'true equity would have enthralled all the peoples of the world with its splendour' (L 60/S 94). Besides, nothing is more fragile than a perception that depends upon the mediation of reasoning, since one can always come to doubt what one has perceived in this way.[16] And given that natural law is not immediately known, it cannot be known permanently either. 'Merely according to reason, nothing is just in itself, everything shifts with time' (L 60/S 94). Natural law does not shine forth in all places, or at all times: this is what Pascal concedes to Montaigne. The fact that we cannot establish justice does not prevent us from denouncing injustice, and this is of extreme importance in enabling us to reconcile the *Provincial Letters* with the *Pensées*. What makes a law acceptable as such is not merely the authority of the legislator, for a law that uniformly prescribed evil would risk being accused of injustice.

Pascal's second point about natural law is that, even if men are, as I have shown, incapable of knowing of their own accord what is good and true, at least in a universal and permanent way, they still have a craving for the good and the true, a craving which demands to be satisfied. They possess within them what Pascal terms an 'idea' or an 'image' of truth and goodness, which corresponds to the capacity for truth and goodness that is present in all human beings.[17] Pascal therefore thinks, in contrast to Montaigne, that ordinary people are right not just because they obey laws, but also because they only want to obey them in the name of what is right and just. And in his view only true or perfect Christians can reassure the people, since, as Pascal states, 'true Christians are, however, obedient to these follies; not that they respect follies, but rather the divine order of God which has subjected men to follies as a punishment' (L 14/S 48).

THE THEORY OF ORDERS AND THE STRUGGLE AGAINST TYRANNY

Such analyses lead Pascal to a double undertaking: the definition of what it is to be a good king and the definition of what it is to be a good subject. If a good subject is one who obeys laws in the name of reason and justice even when he knows that these laws are not reasonable and just in themselves, a bad subject is one who promotes disobedience. This could be either because, like half-clever people (demi-habiles; L 90/S 124), he thinks that he can rise above ordinary people by not falling prey to the same myths as they do, or because, like those who are pious, he thinks he can rise above clever people (habiles) by not falling prey to the same worldly wisdom as they do. This is the logic Pascal uses to condemn the disorder that emanated from the civil unrest known as the Fronde,[18] but above all the disorder he sees represented by the Society of Jesus. Indeed, the polemic of the Provincial Letters was the logical end point of these political reflections. The Jesuits do not have the right to offer dispensations from the law either to themselves or to other people. To take the particular example of murder, it is scandalous that individual people, and religious people at that, justify murder in defiance of natural law, civil law and divine law. Motives must not be confused with causes. The concupiscence of men certainly leads them to invent all sorts of motives to justify murder, but these motives are in no sense valid causes, and only the complacency of those people who evade all forms of duty means that they grant such motives their approval. In this regard, no contradiction exists, therefore, between the *Provincial Letters* and the *Pensées*, notwithstanding those commentaries that attempt to conflate Pascal's political position with that of Montaigne.[19] Although Pascal was largely influenced by Montaigne in the formulation of his political thought, there still remains, as I have shown, a significant distance between the two.

But what makes a good king? Just as a good subject is one who knows exactly why he must obey, and in whose name, a good king knows exactly in whose name he must govern. So a good king is one who does not delude himself about what it is that makes him king. To answer the answer of what actually makes him a king, there would seem to be three main stages. First, it is the concupiscence of men, their tyrannical will to domination, which has to be curbed by the establishment of public order so that they do not harm one another. Then it is the transmission of power, the rules of succession that come into play after the initial domination acquired by force. Finally, and if it is true that concupiscence does not suppress all sense of justice, it is the imagination of men. Consequently, a good king must aim not to establish justice, but to establish public order, inasmuch as the inconstancy of all human institutions allows him to do so. A good king is one whom Pascal calls a 'king of concupiscence',[20] which is to say a king who rules within his own order, that of the body or materiality.[21] This is an order that works not through pure force or through pure justice, but through force that is constructed in the image of justice. Pascal recapitulates all the duties that come with greatness in the three *Discourses* dedicated to this condition.[22] In the *First Discourse* he exhorts those who are great to remember how they came upon their greatness, which is due not to their natural qualities but to institutional ones and to the chance that granted them possession of these. In the *Second Discourse* he urges the great not to overstep their rights in seeking to extend these beyond their own sphere of influence; in other words, not to make a claim for the respect due to natural greatness, but only for that due to institutionalised greatness. In the *Third Discourse* he exhorts them not to overstep their rights even when they do not extend these beyond their own sphere of influence; in other words, not to abuse their power, since men only submit to government in order to receive the material benefits which an aggressive stance towards others might deny them. We must not forget that men have never voluntarily surrendered to force, but, rather, they have submitted to the image of justice it is essential for force to have in order to consolidate itself. They must not, therefore, be ill-treated. A good king uses concupiscence against itself, after the fashion of Christ; more precisely, he uses it in order to satisfy those elements within it that can be satisfied. He does not convert concupiscence into charity, but moderates it to the point where it becomes a form of desire that is compatible with the desire of others. Thus, men expect of a king that he should distribute material benefits – rights, property, riches – in the same way that God distributes the blessings of charity.

According to Pascal, there are two ways to govern, as a king or as a tyrant.[23] To govern as a tyrant is to overstep one's rights, notably because one thereby abuses one's power, which is in no sense a natural force, but rather an artificial one, consolidated by institutionalisation and consequently organised in such a way as to serve the institution which consolidates it. To govern as a king is to make sure that one does not overstep one's rights, and notably to use one's force in accordance with the institution which consolidates it. It is not enough to come to be king, or to acquire the titles required to become king; it is necessary also to rule as a king and not as a tyrant. On the other hand, the injustice encompassed within the law is tolerable because it is not obvious to all (indeed, nobody can declare that it is indubitably present without the aid of grace), and because the injustice of men themselves has rendered it necessary. We should not think, simply because Pascal seeks to make us obey the law without scrutinising its content, that we should suffer a tyranny which he understands as the confusion of orders.[24] Rather, his entire œuvre goes to prove the opposite; that we should revolt and declare our revolt against tyranny, whether this is the tyranny of the Pope when he confuses material and spiritual truths in his condemnation of Galileo,[25] or the tyranny of theologians when they confuse *de facto* and *de jure* in the signing of the formulary (which those attached to Port-Royal were forced to sign, effectively condemning the very basis of their beliefs),[26] and so on. Neither the king nor the Pope can overstep his rights and rule outside the order granted to him, or even inside the order, if he is unaware of its specificity and limitations.

A good king will rule in the same way as God, without taking himself to be God. The best way of preventing such presumption is to compare the divine kingdom and the earthly kingdom, divine law and earthly law.

The Christian republic, like the Jewish republic before it, is named by Pascal as having no master but God.[27] It is governed by two laws alone – to love God and to love one's neighbour – which between them sum up all of Mosaic Law.[28] It embraces true justice and proscribes all violence.[29] It is eternal, since God's law is immoveable, entrenched in the Jewish religion, where it has always resisted, in the face of the vicissitudes of this people, both corruption from within and assaults from without. And yet it is more firmly entrenched in the Christian religion, where it remains not just stable but inviolable within the sanctuary of the heart.[30] By comparison, the republics of this world have only human masters, susceptible to illness and death and to changes of fortune. They find themselves with numerous laws in which good and evil are intertwined, which vary according to time and place and which are liable to disintegrate. If there is a uniformity and a permanence to force and its institutionalisation, there is neither uniformity nor permanence to its different institutional forms: only force is real, independent of opinion; anything else fluctuates according to collective fantasy.

CONCLUSION

There are, therefore, a number of conclusions that can be drawn from Pascal's analysis of justice. According to Pascal,

- men are carried away by the tyrannical will to domination, but are restrained by their hope for good and fear of evil
- citizenship can only mask the selfish desires of men by suppressing any inconvenience associated with citizenship, but the faith and charity offered by Christ can produce, in combination with a sense of contrition, annihilation of the self[31]
- men cannot bring themselves to endure tyranny, which is evident to them as soon as they are subjected to it, but they

can bring themselves to bear the chaotic commingling of good and evil inherent to the laws of humankind; indeed, they are condemned to endure this, considering their own injustice

- political order is destined to remedy the injustice of men but not to promote the justice of God
- nonetheless, there does exist a true form of justice, and a true satisfaction, in submitting to laws that do not themselves accord with justice, as there is also in submitting to all other practices that derive from the duality of man
- we act in vain if we congratulate ourselves on our cunning by drawing attention to the folly of men, as if we could set ourselves apart from that folly; it is healthy to be aware that we are, in fact, only human, as full of folly as all other human beings. This is what the Greek philosophers stated in their political writings and what Montaigne demonstrated so deftly. However, as Pascal argues, this can only be truly understood by those who are truly and perfectly Christian.[32]

So, while Pascal's social and political thought, fundamentally informed as it is by Christianity, could be said to refer us only to a former and now distant world, should we not say, rather, that it refers us with surprising authority to our own?

NOTES

This chapter was translated and adapted by Emma Gilby and Nicholas Hammond.

1. See L 149/S 182, L 372/S 404, L 668/S 547, L 749/S 662.
2. See notably L 360/S 392, L 368/S 401, L 370/S 402, L 371/S 403, L 372/S 404, L 374/S 406 and also L 421/S 680.
3. See L 688/S 567.
4. See L 58/S 91 and 92.
5. See the letter to M. and Mme Périer, 17.10.1651, OC II, 20.
6. See L 106/S 138, L 118/S 150, L 210/S 243, L 211/S 244.
7. See also L 977/S 786.
8. See L 26/S 60. Two fragments (L 94/S 128 and L 977/S 786) reveal that if we were to act in accordance with sound thinking, by rewarding merit for example, we would only achieve civil war, with everyone claiming to be the most meritorious.

9. See L 189/S 221: 'Quia non cognovit per sapientiam, placuit Deo per stultitiam praedicationis salvos facere' (I Cor. 1.21). There is no natural wisdom in the sense that men would only be wise and just if they were to judge things by situating them in relation to God, rather than to themselves, which would presuppose that they loved God infinitely and beyond all other things.

10. See L 919/S 571: 'Eritis sicut dii scientes bonum et malum' (Genesis 3.5). 'We all act like God in passing judgments: "This is good or evil", and in being too distressed or delighted by events.'

11. See *OC* II, 171-2.

12. See *OC* II, 194.

13. See L 149/S 182.

14. On the flexibility men possess with regard to good and evil even after original sin, see notably *OC* II, 289.

15. See L 60/S 94. This entire fragment speaks in favour of the Pyrrhonists, which does not prevent Pascal from maintaining that they are wrong, as in L 109/S 141. An erroneous use of reason makes the Pyrrhonists seem right. First principles, of morality as well as of geometry, can be sensed intuitively, but only when man is in his proper place.

16. See L 190/S 222 and L 821/S 661.

17. See L 131/S 164 and L 119/S 151, and, on this desire, L 75/S 110 and L 401/S 20.

18. See L 85/S 124.

19. Two recent works, which do not fall into the trap of such oversimplification, have relaunched the debate about Pascal's social and political thought: Ferreyrolles (1984b) and Lazzeri (1993).

20. See L 796/S 649 and the *Third Discourse on the Condition of the Great*, *OC* II, 198-9.

21. See L 308/S 339.

22. See *OC* II, 194-6 for the first *Discourse*, 196-8 for the second, 198-9 for the third.

23. See L 797/S 650.

24. This is the point at which my argument contrasts most markedly with that of Lazzeri, who does not articulate the difference between orders in the horizontal dimension and in the vertical dimension.

25. See the eighteenth *Provincial Letter*, *OC* I, 813.

26. See the seventeenth and eighteenth *Provincial Letters*, *OC* I, 780-97 and 797-815. See also *On the Signing of the Formulary*, *OC* I, 982-1000.

27. See L 369/S 401.

28. See L 376/S 408.

29. See L 85/S 119.

30. According to L 280/S 312, 'states would perish if their laws were not often stretched to meet necessity'. Neither Jewish nor Christian law has ever had to be stretched in this way.
31. See L 1006.
32. See L 412/S 31. On Plato and Aristotle, see L 533/S 457. On Montaigne's cleverness, see L 83/S 117. There is a paradoxical kind of wisdom that comes simply with wanting not to be set apart from humanity, even though only Christianity can perfect wisdom by teaching us what it is to be human.

12   Pascal and philosophical method

The idea of a philosophical method is more commonly associated with Descartes than it is with Pascal. In his *Discourse on the Method for Conducting One's Reason Well and for Seeking Truth in the Sciences*, first published in 1637, Descartes asserts that, in order to be successful, the search for philosophical and scientific truths has to obey a fixed set of guidelines. In contrast, Pascal generally uses the term *method* ironically and pejoratively. In the *Provincial Letters* the various techniques used by the Jesuits to twist the precepts of conventional morality are often referred to as a *method*.[1] In the *Pensées*, the word *method* is almost entirely absent. There exists one work, however, where Pascal uses the term in a non-pejorative way: a small, unfinished treatise written around 1655 and entitled *Mathematical Mind (De l'esprit géométrique)*. In a bold claim reminiscent of Descartes' *Discourse on Method*, Pascal presents the treatise as 'the method for mathematical [i.e., methodical and perfect] demonstrations' (*OC* II, 155). More generally, he presents mathematical reasoning as the model that one should emulate in every intellectual activity. A study of Pascal's philosophical method must thus begin with an analysis of *Mathematical Mind*.

THE EXAMPLE OF MATHEMATICS

The method presented in *Mathematical Mind* is not aimed at *discovering* scientific or philosophical truths. According to Pascal, there are 'three principal objects in the study of truth: first, to discover it when one is searching for it; second, to demonstrate it when one possesses it; third, to distinguish it from untruth when one examines it' (*OC* II, 154). Pascal goes on to say that his treatise does not

216

address the first object (the art of finding truths that were previously unknown) because the issue has been addressed extensively and excellently by others (a probable allusion to Descartes' *Discourse on Method*, or to the work of François Viète, who developed rules for the discovery of truths through *analysis*). The treatise addresses the second object (how to demonstrate truth when one possesses it) and the third by implication (because the rules one uses for demonstrating true propositions can also be applied to distinguish them from false ones). In short, the purpose of the treatise is 'to demonstrate those truths that are already known, and to shed light on them in such a way that they will be proven irrefutably' (*OC* II, 154).

The beginning of the treatise contains some sweeping claims. Pascal argues that mathematics provides the one and only method for conducting perfect demonstrations: 'Only this science', he says, 'possesses the true rules of reasoning', because 'it is based on the true method for conducting one's reason in all things'. Pascal adds that mathematics teaches this method only by example, and that 'it produces no discourse about it' (*OC* II, 154). In other words, mathematicians practise the perfect method for demonstrations, but no mathematician has ever stated what the rules of this method are. As a result, this method is 'unknown to almost everyone' (*OC* II, 155). The purpose of the treatise is, therefore, to explicate these rules in order to make them applicable beyond mathematics to the entire universe of intellectual activity. Whoever possesses this method, Pascal claims, will have an edge over his interlocutors, 'because we can see that in contests between minds that are equally strong in all other respects, the mathematical one wins' (*OC* II, 155).

For Pascal, mathematics is the only human science capable of producing flawless demonstrations, 'because it is the only one to follow the true method', while all other sciences, 'due to their very nature have some degree of confusion' (*OC* II, 155). Before sharing the rules of the true method with his reader, Pascal embarks on a digression. He mentions another method that is 'even loftier and more accomplished' (*OC* II, 155) than the method of mathematics. It is, however, out of reach for human beings, 'because what is beyond mathematics is beyond us' (*OC* II, 155). This most excellent method comprises only two rules. First, one must define every term (give a clear explanation of every term used in the demonstration). Second, one must prove every proposition (in other words, back up every

single proposition with truths that are already known). According to
Pascal, 'this would be a truly beautiful method, but it is an entirely
impossible one' (*OC* ii, 157), because the need to define all terms
would lead to infinite regress. As always in Pascal, the digression is
a way of driving home an essential point: in order to ascertain what
the perfect method is, let us assume what it would be in theory.
In theory, one should define everything and prove everything, but
anyone who tries to implement this method will keep defining terms
ad infinitum. Pascal's point is that the problem does not lie with
the method itself; it lies with the limitations of the human mind.
The fact that the perfect method leads to infinite regress proves that
'men are naturally and permanently unable to practise any science
whatsoever in an absolutely perfect order' (*OC* ii, 157).

   Nevertheless, this does not mean that no order whatsoever is possible. The order of mathematics is available. For Pascal, the virtue of
mathematics is that it is perfectly suited to both the strengths and
the limitations of the human mind:

This order, the most perfect among men, does not consist in defining or
demonstrating everything, nor does it consist in defining or demonstrating
nothing; rather it holds the middle ground: it does not define those things
that are clear and well understood by all men, and it defines everything
else; it does not prove those things that are known to all men, and it proves
everything else. (*OC* ii, 157)

   The method of mathematics is exemplary because it occupies the
middle ground between a more perfect method that is beyond the
reach of the human mind, and an absence of method that underes-
timates our intellectual capacities. One must add that, for Pascal,
the order of mathematics is inferior to the more perfect method described above 'only because it is less persuasive, not because it is
less certain' (*OC* ii, 157). Pascal makes it clear from the beginning
of *Mathematical Mind* that he does not concern himself with the
method for discovering truths that are previously unknown. In this
treatise, certainty is a given. The focus is on persuasion.

KNOWLEDGE OF FIRST PRINCIPLES

In the practice of mathematics, what saves us from infinite regress
is the fact that we arrive at 'primitive terms that can no longer be
defined, as well as principles so clear that no clearer principles are

available to prove them' (*OC* 11, 157). Mathematicians do not define such primitive terms as *space, number, movement* or *equality*. Similarly, says Pascal, physicists should not try to define terms such as *time*, and philosophers would be well advised to abstain from defining *man* and *being*. Attempting to define such terms, which are perfectly clear and understandable to all, would only bring more confusion. In that sense, the true method consists in avoiding two opposite errors: trying to define everything, and neglecting to define those things that are not self-evident.

One might be surprised that mathematics is incapable of defining its principal objects of study (*number, movement, space*), but, Pascal argues, 'the lack of definition is a perfection rather than a shortcoming; it comes not from obscurity but from complete self-evidence' (*OC* 11, 162). This self-evidence is such that, 'even though it lacks the persuasiveness of demonstration, it has the exact same degree of certainty as demonstration' (*OC* 11, 162). A primitive term cannot be defined because nothing clearer than the term itself is available to explain it. In that sense, primitive terms and first principles are 'clear and certain by the light of nature' (*OC* 11, 157). The order of mathematics is, therefore, 'perfectly true, supported as it is by nature rather than discourse' (*OC* 11, 157).

Pascal's reflection on the relationship between demonstration and first principles is in many ways consistent with the Aristotelian tradition. In the *Posterior Analytics* Aristotle argues that 'not all knowledge is demonstrative' and that 'the knowledge of first principles is not by demonstration', because 'it is necessary to know the principles from which the demonstration proceeds, and if the regress ends with the first principles, the latter must be indemonstrable'.[2] Aristotle draws a clear distinction between scientific knowledge and the knowledge of first principles. Scientific knowledge is the province of discursive reasoning. The first principles, however, 'must be apprehended by Intuition'.[3] For Aristotle, wisdom is a combination of discursive reasoning and intuition: 'The wise man therefore must not only know the conclusions that follow from his first principles, but also have a true conception of those principles themselves. Hence Wisdom must be a combination of Intuition [*nous*] and Scientific Knowledge [*episteme*]'.[4]

Pascal does not appropriate the Aristotelian tradition without submitting it to a major reinterpretation. In Aristotle, it is implied that not all minds have a sound intuition of first principles, because these principles must be reached by laborious induction: 'Induction supplies a first principle or universal, deduction works *from* universals; therefore there are first principles from which deduction starts, which cannot be proven by deduction [*syllogismos*]; therefore they are reached by induction [*epagoge*].'[5] In Pascal, on the other hand, the knowledge of first principles is given by nature and is readily available to all. Pascal also differs from Aristotle in his characterisation of the faculty that allows us to grasp first principles. The Greek term Aristotle uses to designate this faculty is *nous* (usually translated as intuition, rational intuition, or intelligence). For Pascal, the faculty that allows us to grasp the first principles is *le cœur* (the heart):

> For knowledge of first principles, like space, time, motion, number, is as solid as any derived through reason, and it is on such knowledge, coming from the heart and instinct, that reason has to depend and base all its arguments. The heart feels that there are three spatial dimensions and that there is an infinite series of numbers, and reason goes on to demonstrate that there are no two square numbers of which one is double the other. Principles are felt, propositions proved, and both with certainty though by different means. (L 110/S 142)

In Pascal's psychology the organ that allows us to experience feelings and emotions is the same organ that makes the knowledge of first principles possible. There are thus two paths towards knowing truth: one is rational knowledge, which is discursive and is located in the mind; the other is through the heart: it is intuitive and immediate. Both are equally valid and certain. One must add that these two forms of knowledge, far from being mutually exclusive, are complementary: the mind cannot reason without previous knowledge of the first principles; the heart is incapable of deducing the consequences of the first principles.

DEMONSTRATION AND PERSUASION

Mathematical Mind is a somewhat disconcerting treatise for a modern reader. It is divided in two sections. The first section is entitled 'Reflections on Mathematics in General'. The title of the second section is 'The Art of Persuasion'. These two titles (added by the early editors of the text) might lead the reader into thinking that the first section is about mathematics, while the second section is about rhetoric. For a modern reader, mathematics and rhetoric are entirely alien to each other. Mathematics is the domain of certainty and true demonstration, while rhetoric is the province of uncertainty and emotion. Most modern readers would also tend to make a broad distinction between 'scientific' discourse (which would include the more rigorous forms of philosophical reasoning) and 'non-scientific' discourse (which would involve feelings and emotions, and would consequently have less rigour). In that perspective, there is no room for rhetoric or persuasion in scientific discourse, and non-scientific discourse is entirely alien to the method of mathematics. We are therefore tempted to read the first part of Pascal's treatise as a reflection on scientific discourse, and the second section as an analysis of non-scientific discourse. In fact, as Jean Mesnard has shown, the second section is simply a later draft of the first.[6] Both sections are about mathematics *and* persuasion. As I have shown above, at the beginning of the treatise Pascal states that his purpose is to show how to communicate truths that are already known. In that sense, the purpose of the whole treatise is indeed persuasion, and the method of mathematics is chosen because it is the best way of persuading an interlocutor not only within the field of mathematics itself, but in the entire sphere of intellectual activity.

In the second section of the treatise Pascal refines and complicates the argument he has made in the first. He states that persuasion can be accomplished in two different ways:

Everyone knows that there are two paths to the acceptance of opinions by the soul: reason and will. The more natural path is reason, because one should only assent to demonstrated truths; the more ordinary one, however, is the will: men almost always form beliefs not because of proof but because of pleasure. (OC II, 171)

The crucial distinction here is between reason and the will (*la volonté*). The term *will* should not be understood in its modern sense. It does not refer to our capacity to make choices or act against our inclinations. It refers to the inclinations themselves. It is the desire, the wish, the disposition to do something. For Pascal, the mind has its first principles. The will has its own first principles too. The first principles of the mind 'are truths that are natural and known to everyone' (OC II, 172) (e.g., the whole is greater than its part). The first principles of the will 'are certain desires that are natural and common to all men like the desire to be happy, which it is impossible not to have, in addition to several specific objects that everyone pursues in order to achieve that end' (OC II, 172).

Because 'there are two paths to the acceptance of opinions by the soul' (reason and will), these paths can be combined in four different ways, depending on the nature of the things that are conveyed in the process of persuasion. In the first scenario the things one wants to convey are a direct consequence of the first principles of reason. Persuasion will be successful if the connection to the first principles is shown clearly. In the second scenario the things one wants to convey are a direct consequence of the first principles of pleasure. Persuasion will be successful 'if one shows the soul that something can lead it to what it loves the most' (OC II, 172). The third scenario is a combination of the first two. When the things one wants to convey are a direct consequence of the first principles of reason *and* pleasure, persuasion will be the most successful, human nature being what it is. The fourth scenario is problematic. When there is a conflict between the first principles of reason and the first principles of pleasure, the outcome is uncertain: 'Hence an uncertain vacillation between truth and pleasure. Knowledge of the former and experience of the latter are in a struggle without a clear outcome. To assess it would require knowing what happens in the inner recesses of man, where man himself hardly ever goes' (OC II, 173).

After examining these four scenarios Pascal draws a general conclusion that is applicable to all cases of persuasion:

Therefore, whatever the object of persuasion may be, we must pay attention to our interlocutor, we must know his mind and heart, what principles he grants, what things he likes; we must then point to the object in question in order to show its connections to the principles that have been granted or to the objects of pleasure. (OC II, 173)

Hence, says Pascal, 'the art of persuasion consists in pleasing as much as in convincing', because 'men are governed by whim more than reason' (OC II, 173). In a way, this conclusion only restates a general principle of rhetoric, known as *decorum*: the need to tailor one's speech to the needs, preferences, opinions and expectations of the audience. Pascal, however, clarifies and simplifies the concept of decorum. Here, paying attention to the interlocutor means paying attention only to the first principles of his mind and the first principles of his heart: 'what principles he grants, what things he likes'. Once this has been done adequately, persuasion is easy. It suffices to follow the two rules enunciated above: define every term (except primitive terms) and prove every proposition by showing its connection to the first principles.

These few rules and concepts form a general theory of persuasion. They are Pascal's philosophical method. What is most remarkable to a modern reader is that the model of mathematics applies to both the mind and the heart. Whether they belong to the mind or the heart, principles are still principles, and their consequences are demonstrated in the same way.

This is what leads Pascal to assert that 'the art of pleasing has rules that are just as reliable as the art of demonstrating' (OC II, 174). In addition, 'he who would have perfect knowledge of these rules would succeed in making himself loved by kings and others, just as reliably as someone would succeed in demonstrating mathematical truths' (OC II, 174).

This is only half of the truth, however. Compared to the art of demonstrating, the art of pleasing is 'more difficult, more subtle, more useful, and more wonderful' (OC II, 173). That is not because the *method* of the art of pleasing is more complicated. As above has shown, Pascal insists that it is the same in both arts. The art of pleasing is more difficult because its principles are ever-changing:

The reason for this extreme difficulty is that the principles of pleasure are neither firm nor stable. They vary from person to person, and within an individual as well, so much so that there is nothing so different from a man than this man himself over time. A man has other pleasures than a woman, a rich person and a poor person have dissimilar pleasures; a prince, a soldier, a merchant, a burgher, a peasant, the old, the young, the healthy, the sick, are all different; the slightest incidents change them. (OC II, 174)

In mathematics the number of first principles is relatively small and the principles themselves do not change. Deriving the consequences from the first principles is, therefore, not very difficult, provided that the proper method is followed. In the art of pleasing the difficulty consists in the fact that the first principles are countless and subject to change. Therefore it takes an extraordinary perceptiveness and an unusually sharp knowledge of the human heart to master the art of pleasing.

NATURE, CUSTOM AND FIRST PRINCIPLES

As I have shown above, Pascal presents the first principles of the mind as simple and easy to grasp by the light of nature. Yet he makes several remarks, both in *Mathematical Mind* and in the *Pensées*, that tend to complicate this picture: the natural knowledge of first principles is neither perfect nor universal. For instance, in *Mathematical Mind* Pascal remarks that some people 'are incapable of seeing that space can be divided *ad infinitum*' (*OC* 11, 164). The infinite divisibility of space is one of the first principles of geometry. Not being able to grasp this first principle makes one incapable of practising this science. For Pascal, this shortcoming is akin to a physical disability. Indeed, when Pascal identifies the heart as the organ that perceives the first principles, he means that there is something inherently bodily and physical about this perception. We reason with our soul, but our knowledge of first principles comes from our body: 'Our soul is cast into the body where it finds number, time, dimensions; it reasons about these things and calls them natural, or necessary, and can believe nothing else' (L 418/S 680).

Another way of expressing the same thought is to say that what makes a first principle first is nothing but the physical limitations of our intuition. In the fragment entitled 'Disproportion of Man' Pascal remarks that scientific knowledge deals with two infinities. It is clear that science studies an infinite number of *objects*, but it is also true that the number of scientific *principles* is infinite as well:

Thus we see that all the sciences are infinite in the range of their researches, for who can doubt that mathematics, for instance, has an infinity of infinities of propositions to expound? They are infinite also in the multiplicity and subtlety of their principles, for anyone can see that those which are supposed to be ultimate do not stand by themselves, but depend on others, which depend on others again, and thus never allow any finality. (L 199/S 230)

For Pascal, looking into the first principles of science is like looking into the infinitely small. However small and minute a principle might be, it can still be analysed into smaller and smaller principles. A principle is to science what an indivisible point is to a line: 'But we treat as ultimate those which seem so to our reason, as in material things we call a point indivisible when our senses can perceive nothing beyond it, although by its nature it is infinitely divisible'

(L 199/S 230). In other words, what makes a point look indivisible is the limit in the power of resolution that is natural to the human eye. Similarly, first principles look like first principles to us only because our minds are not sharp enough. From this, Pascal concludes that writing a book about the first principles of science is just as presumptuous as writing a book about *everything*:

> Of these two infinites of science, that of greatness is much more obvious, and that is why it has occurred to few people to claim that they know everything. 'I am going to speak about everything', Democritus used to say.
>
> But the infinitely small is much harder to see. The philosophers have much more readily claimed to have reached it, and that is where they have all tripped up. This is the origin of such familiar titles as *Of the Principles of Things, Of the Principles of Philosophy*, and the like, which are really as pretentious, though they do not look it, as this blatant one: *Of All That Can Be Known*. (L 199/S 230)

Pascal does not only argue that our knowledge of first principles is defined by the natural limitations of our bodies. He also takes into account the fact that our bodies themselves are shaped by custom. Societal norms and beliefs determine the way we feel and perceive things in the most basic and profound fashion (i.e., before any rational or explicit understanding of these matters). All these norms and beliefs are registered, as it were, in our bodies, in ways that we cannot see, let alone change. In that sense, says Pascal, 'custom is our nature' (L 419/S 680). Therefore, for Pascal, the critique of custom (a familiar theme borrowed from Montaigne) applies not only to societal norms and beliefs, but also to the first principles of mathematics:

> Custom is our nature. Anyone who grows accustomed to faith believes it, and can no longer help fearing hell, and believes nothing else.
>
> Anyone accustomed to believe that the king is to be feared . . .
>
> Who then can doubt that our soul, being accustomed to see number, space, movement, believes in this and nothing else? (L 419/S 680)

Let me summarise Pascal's reasoning. Knowledge of the first principles comes from the body. The body is shaped by custom. Custom is, by definition, variable. Our knowledge is, therefore, based on the shakiest foundations. Pascal gives several examples of this fact. For instance, the force of custom makes us unwilling to give up familiar explanations of natural phenomena, even after these explanations have been discredited by new discoveries. Hence the resistance to the new theories regarding blood circulation: 'When we are accustomed to use the wrong reasons to prove natural phenomena, we are no longer ready to accept the right ones when they are discovered. The example given concerned the circulation of the blood, to explain why the vein swells below the ligature' (L 736/S 617). From a slightly different point of view, Pascal also argues that, because our grasp of first principles is determined by habit and custom, it is influenced by the company we keep:

Our minds [esprit] and feelings [sentiments] are trained by the company we keep, and perverted by the company we keep. Thus good or bad company trains and perverts respectively. It is therefore very important to be able to make the right choice so that we train rather than pervert. And we cannot make this choice unless it is already trained and not perverted. This is thus a vicious circle from which anyone is lucky to escape. (L 814/S 658)

In addition, Pascal remarks, there is a constant interaction between 'feeling' [sentiment] and reason: 'Memory and joy are feelings [sentiments], and even mathematical propositions can become feelings, for reason makes feelings natural and natural feelings are eradicated by reason' (L 646/S 531). In other words, habitual reasoning can turn some propositions into principles that have the same status as the first principles we know by the light of nature. Conversely, critical reasoning can demote some first principles and make them appear conventional or artificial, instead of obvious and natural.

Fundamentally, the difficulty comes from the fact that, in Pascal's psychology, the heart, which allows us to grasp the first principles, is also the organ of whim, fancy and passion. Because reason depends upon the heart for knowledge of first principles, it is fair to say that 'all our reasoning comes down to surrendering to feeling (sentiment)' (L 530/S 455). By the word sentiment, Pascal means a highly personal, yet non-relativistic, perception of the first principles.[7] However, because sentiment is located in the heart, it is very hard to distinguish from individual fantasy: 'One person says that my feeling is mere fancy, another that his fancy is feeling' (L 530/S 455). How does one distinguish fancy from feeling? 'Reason is available', Pascal replies, 'but can be bent in any direction. And so there is no rule' (L 530/S 455).

ORDER OF THE MIND VS. ORDER OF THE HEART

In the *Pensées* a significant number of fragments discuss the possible structure and presentation of the apology of the Christian religion that Pascal intends to write. The word Pascal uses to refer to this issue is *order*, and the question that nags him is: what is the proper order? For instance, he asks: 'Order. Why should I choose to divide my ethics into four rather than six? Why should I define virtue as four, or two, or one?' (L 683/S 562). To a modern reader, the question of order will probably seem important but not essential. It has to do with form rather than content. For Pascal, on the contrary, the question of order is an essential one. This will appear quite clearly if we look back at the work discussed at the beginning of this chapter, *Mathematical Mind*. In this treatise Pascal discusses mathematics as the 'true method' for performing demonstrations of things that are already known. After a digression stating that 'men are naturally and permanently unable to practise any science in an absolutely perfect order', Pascal claims that 'the order of mathematics is available' (OC 11, 157). The order of mathematics is imperfect with respect to an absolute standard. It is perfect with respect to human standards. In that sense it is the 'true method'. In this treatise, Pascal uses the words *method* and *order* as synonyms. In that sense inquiring about Pascal's philosophical method is the same as inquiring about his reflections on *order*. As above has shown, in *Mathematical Mind*, Pascal's reflections on mathematics cannot be separated from his reflections on rhetoric and persuasion. Mathematics provides the order, or method, that will make persuasion possible. In other words, the central question for Pascal is: in what order should I put my thoughts and arguments, given the fact that my goal is to persuade my interlocutor?

Because of a spontaneous tendency we have to separate form from content, we may have difficulty grasping how essential the question of *order* or *method* is for Pascal. For us, considerations of method are preliminary or formal in nature. For Pascal, following the proper method is essential, because only the proper method can persuade an interlocutor, and the only purpose in discussing truths is to share them with an interlocutor.

Pascal's praise for the method of mathematics has paradoxical implications. It is necessary to understand the method of mathematics in order to understand how persuasion works. Yet at the same time one must realise that the method of mathematics is rhetorically ineffective. Mathematics shows us what the perfect method is, but this method is inapplicable beyond the field of mathematics itself:

> *Order.* I could easily have treated this discourse in this kind of order: show the vanity of all kinds of conditions, show the vanity of ordinary lives, then the vanity of philosophers' lives, whether sceptical or Stoic, but the order would not have been kept. I know something about it and how few people understand it. No human science can keep it. St Thomas did not keep it. Mathematics keeps it, but it goes so far as to be useless. (L 694/S 573)

This order that 'few people understand' is the demonstrative order of mathematics. For Pascal, the central question of philosophy is the understanding of human nature. The countless number of principles involved in the study of human nature makes it impossible to explain with the method of mathematics. And mathematics itself is useless because its object is not human nature.

According to Pascal, the method of mathematics is doubly inadequate. On the one hand, an author who tries to mirror the nature of the thing he discusses will not be able to follow the method of mathematics. On the other hand, an author who tries to follow a demonstrative order will soon lose his reader:

> Discuss those who have dealt with self-knowledge; Charron's depressing and tedious divisions; Montaigne's muddle; the fact that he certainly felt the defects of a rigid method; that he avoided them by jumping from one subject to another; that he wanted to cut a good figure. (L 780/S 644)

For a persuasive description of human nature, Montaigne's disorder is preferable to the order of his disciple, Charron, who tried to present Montaigne's philosophy in neatly arranged but ultimately boring chapters and subchapters. In that sense, Montaigne's 'muddle' is a genuine literary model.[8] This disorder is an order of a different kind, which can also be found in Pascal's ultimate literary model, the Bible:

> *Order.* Against the objection that there is no order in Scripture.
> The heart has its order, the mind has its own, which uses principles and demonstrations. The heart has a different one. We do not prove that we ought to be loved by setting out in order the causes of love; that would be absurd.

Jesus Christ and St Paul possess the order of charity, not of the mind, for they wished to fire up, not to teach.

The same with St Augustine. This order consists mainly in digressions upon each point which relates to the end, so that this shall be kept always in sight. (L 298/S 329)

As I have shown, in *Mathematical Mind* 'there are two paths to the acceptance of opinions by the soul: reason and the will' (*OC* 11, 171). In the *Pensées* Pascal explains that

The will is one of the chief organs of belief, not because it creates belief, but because things are true or false according to the aspect by which we judge them. When the will likes one aspect more than another, it deflects the mind from considering the qualities of the one it does not care to see. Thus the mind, keeping in step with the will, remains looking at the aspect preferred by the will and so judges by what it sees there. (L 539/S 458)

The perfect rhetoric, or the true method, must speak to the heart and the mind at the same time. It must satisfy the mind by following the two rules mentioned in *Mathematical Mind*: define all terms (except primitive terms) and connect all propositions to the first principles. However, connecting a proposition to a first principle can be done in two different ways. It can be done step by step, in accordance with the mathematical method. It can also be done directly, when the desire to enjoy a truth leads the mind to contemplate one aspect of the object at hand that is directly connected to the first principles. That is St Augustine's (and Pascal's) digressive method: showing in a few words how a point that had apparently nothing to do with it is related to charity or the salvation of the soul. For instance, in the fragment entitled 'Disproportion of Man', after a long, step-by-step analysis of the double infinity of the universe, Pascal asks abruptly: 'Who can follow these astonishing processes?' He replies: 'The author of these wonders understands them: no one else can' (L 199/S 230). The allusion to God is out of step with the logic of the demonstration. Yet it is perfectly consistent with the 'order of the heart' and with the overall purpose of the fragment, which is to fill the reader with awe and confusion in order to kindle a desire for a more profound knowledge of causes. This 'order of the heart' is possible only because it is driven by 'certain desires that are natural and common to all men, like the desire to be happy' (*OC* 11, 172).

SCEPTICISM AND BEYOND

The first part of *Mathematical Mind*, as shown above, deals extensively with our ability (or inability) to comprehend the infinitely small. It ends with the following remark, suggesting that the real purpose of the treatise may be moral rather than epistemological:

> But those who will see these truths clearly will also marvel at the greatness and power of nature in this double infinity that surrounds us; thanks to this wonderful contemplation they will learn to know themselves; they will see themselves as placed between infinite extension and zero extension, between an infinite number and zero, between infinite movement and zero movement, between infinite time and zero time. This will allow us to evaluate ourselves correctly, and to produce reflections that are worth more than everything else in mathematics. (*OC* II, 170)

This passage contains the essence of the argument that Pascal developed several years later in the fragment of the *Pensées* entitled 'Disproportion of Man'. Knowing man's true place in the universe is a humbling thought. An epistemological reflection on infinity turns into a reflection on self-knowledge.

Similarly, Pascal's seemingly inconclusive discussion of our knowledge of first principles has a purpose beyond the discussion itself. Pascal argues in some places that we have a natural, immediate and true perception of first principles. In other places he seems to argue the opposite, by showing that nature is shaped by custom and so forth. His discussion of our knowledge of first principles follows the method of sceptical philosophy: an argument is always followed by a counter-argument.

This sceptical approach is especially visible in Pascal's discussion of our knowledge of time and space. In *Mathematical Mind* Pascal argues on the one hand that it is not necessary to define the word *time* because when I utter this word, everybody knows what I am talking about. On the other hand, he says, this does not necessarily mean that we all have the same idea of what time is:

> There are many differences of opinion regarding the nature of time. Some say it is the movement of created things; others that it is the measure of movement, etc. Thus I am not saying that there is common knowledge of the nature of these things; only the relationship between word and thing; so that when the word *time* is uttered, all direct their minds towards the same object. This suffices to make it unnecessary to define the term, even though

the differences of opinion regarding the nature of time will emerge once our minds are applied to it. (*OC* II, 159)

The word *time* points to an object that everyone recognises, but whose nature remains unknown. In the *Pensées* Pascal carries these reflections further in fragment L 109/S 141, entitled 'Against Scepticism'. The fragment starts with the familiar claim that it is unnecessary to define primitive terms, 'because we cannot define these things without making them obscure'. Pascal goes on to say that 'we have no proof' that everyone has the same conception or mental image of such primitive terms as *time*, *space* or *movement*. The only thing we know is that 'we apply these words on the same occasions; every time two men see a body change its position they both use the same word to express what they have seen, each of them saying that the body has moved'. In other words, the meaning of a word resides entirely in its usage. But precisely, Pascal adds, the regularity in the usage of the word makes one suspect that there is perhaps a conception of *movement* that we all share: 'Such conformity of application provides a strong presumption of conformity of thought.' However, 'it lacks the absolute force of total conviction, although the odds are that it is so, because we know that the same conclusions are often drawn from different assumptions'. The conclusion is awkwardly sceptical and anti-sceptical at the same time:

That is enough to cloud the issue, to say the least, though it does not completely extinguish the natural light which provides us with certainty in such matters. The Academics would have wagered on it, but that makes the light dimmer and upsets the dogmatist, to the glory of the sceptical clique which stands for ambiguous ambiguity, and a certain dubious obscurity from which our doubts cannot remove every bit of light any more than our natural light can dispel all the darkness. (L 109/S 141)

This 'ambiguous ambiguity' is exactly where Pascal wants to bring his reader. A thoroughly sceptical discussion of our knowledge of first principles ends with the conviction that there is something to the idea that we all have a natural and true intuition of those principles. That is why the fragment is entitled 'Against Scepticism'.

On one side, the 'dogmatists' (Plato, Descartes) believe in our natural ability to grasp the nature of things. On the other hand, the sceptics (Pyrrho, Montaigne) use reason to question this natural ability. The conflict remains unresolved: 'We have an incapacity for proving anything which no amount of dogmatism can overcome. We have an idea of truth which no amount of scepticism can overcome' (L 406/ S 25).

The whole purpose of the discussion is to bring the reader into a state of confusion and anxiety, to make him feel that man is 'a monster that passes all understanding' (L 130/S 163). This anxiety, however, is meant to yield positive results. Even though the discussion is inconclusive on a cognitive level, it does have results from a moral point of view. Or rather, it is the very inconclusiveness of the discussion that makes it useful from a moral point of view:

Know then, proud man, what a paradox you are to yourself. Be humble, impotent reason! Be silent, feeble nature! Learn that man infinitely transcends man, hear from your master your true condition, which is unknown to you.
     Listen to God. (L 131/S 164)

At this point there is a shift in Pascal's argument. The sceptical examination of our cognitive abilities gives way to dogmatic discourse. Pascal proposes the original sin narrative as the key to the enigma of human nature: 'We perceive an image of the truth, and possess nothing but falsehood, being equally incapable of absolute ignorance and certain knowledge; so obvious it is that we once enjoyed a degree of perfection from which we have unhappily fallen' (L 131/S 164).

This aspect of Pascal's argument is well known. What may be less well known is that Pascal suggests some practical ways of overcoming the limitations of our natural intuition of first principles. For instance, for those who have no natural intuition of infinite division, Pascal proposes to use a telescope to observe a point in the sky that looks very small to the naked eye. They will discover that this apparently indivisible point is in fact a huge chunk of space. It is thus conceivable that with an even better telescope this small point would seem as large as the firmament does to the naked eye, and so on (OC II, 165–6). What Pascal proposes here is an *exercise*, based on the assumption that our grasp of first principles resides in the body, not in the mind. It is therefore essential to *experience* something similar to infinite divisibility in order to have an intuition of it. The fragment entitled 'Disproportion of Man' is a textual equivalent of this exercise. Pascal appeals to his reader's imagination, his emotions, his senses, in order to help him have an intuition of the double infinity of the universe. This is also why, after expounding the wager argument (which is flawlessly demonstrative but fails to cause a change in the reader's behaviour) and instead of elaborating further on the demonstration, he proposes some practical steps that will alter the reader's fundamental preferences: 'taking holy water, having masses said, and so on' (L 418/S 680). The goal here is to help the reader put God rather than the objects of his passions as the first principle of his pleasure. This is why Pascal calls the wager argument 'le discours de la machine' (L 11/S 45). As he puts it elsewhere, 'we are as much automaton as mind' (L 812/S 660). Persuasion must therefore work on both the automaton and the mind:

> Demonstration is not the only instrument for convincing us. How few things can be demonstrated! Proofs only convince the mind; habit provides the strongest proofs and those that are most believed... Who ever proved that it will dawn tomorrow, and that we shall die? And what is more widely believed? It is then habit that convinces us and makes so many Christians... In short, we must resort to habit once the mind has seen where the truth lies, in order to steep and stain ourselves in that belief which constantly eludes us, for it is too much trouble to have the proofs always present before us. We must acquire an easier belief, which is that of habit.
>
> Reason works slowly, looking so often at so many principles, which must always be present... Feeling does not work like that, but works instantly, and is always ready. We must then put our faith in feeling, or it will always be vacillating. (L 814/S 658)

In the business of persuasion, demonstration is the easy part. The hard part consists in altering the interlocutor's perception of first principles. It can be done, however, because, as the sceptics have noticed, our perception of first principles is shaped by habit and custom. Ultimately, Pascal wants his interlocutor to adopt the habits and customs that will gradually change his perception of first principles. Pascal's philosophical method is a method for changing one's way of life.

NOTES

1. See, for instance, letter VII in *Provincial Letters*, translated by A. J. Krailsheimer (Harmondsworth: Penguin, 1967), p. 109.
2. Aristotle, *Posterior Analytics*, 1.iii, 75b20 (Cambridge, MA: Harvard University Press, 1960; translation modified).

3. Aristotle, *Nicomachean Ethics*, vi.vi, 2 (Cambridge, MA : Harvard University Press, 1934; translation modified).
4. *Nicomachean Ethics*, vi.vii, 3 (translation modified).
5. *Nicomachean Ethics*, vi.iii, 3.
6. Mesnard, *Oeuvres complètes*, iii, 360–89.
7. On Pascal's *sentiment* in the sciences, see Jones 2001.
8. On the issue of order in Pascal and Montaigne, see Thirouin 1994.

13 Pascal's *Pensées* and the art of persuasion

The term 'art of persuasion' is one used by Pascal himself in a section of his *De l'esprit géométrique*.[1] Although he is careful to stress that it is not within his remit to speak of divine truths (*OC* 11, 171), many of the questions he poses in *De l'esprit géométrique* about how people are most effectively convinced by particular arguments form a fundamental part of the persuasive design of his *Pensées*. At every juncture Pascal seems to refuse oversimplification, constantly attempting to view issues from many different angles. Therein lies the great originality of the *Pensées*. Far from being a traditional apologia of the Christian religion, it not only confronts but also assumes many of the ideas held by those sceptics and non-believers at whom the work is generally thought to be targeted.

Much critical attention has been paid to Pascal's use of persuasive language.[2] Indeed, the way in which he both has recourse to rhetorical techniques and reacts against traditional rhetoric exemplifies the difficulties of his persuasive task. Arnauld and Nicole write in their *Logique* of 'the late M. Pascal who knew as much about true rhetoric as anybody has ever known',[3] and this is indicative of their belief that much of the rhetoric which was taught at the (primarily Jesuit) schools in France was false. Far from being anti-rhetoric *per se*, those at Port-Royal were opposed to what they deemed to be the abuse of rhetoric. It is this abuse that Pascal himself contrasts with the notion of true eloquence in his statement in the *Pensées* that 'la vraie éloquence se moque de l'éloquence [true eloquence has no time for eloquence]' (L 513/ S 671).

EDUCATION

The question of the teaching of rhetoric leads to an examination of the wider role of education in France at the time, which may be seen to be crucial to persuasive strategies in Pascal's work, and which has remained largely unexplored in this regard. Some shorter works by Pascal, such as his *Discours sur la condition des grands* and his *Eléments de la géométrie*, are explicitly pedagogical. But it is my contention that the art of persuasion in many of his other works can be better understood if considered from an educational perspective.

Between 1637 and 1660 a number of schools (known as *petites écoles*) had been founded by Port-Royal, largely in reaction against what was deemed to be the ineffectual teaching methods of the Jesuits, who had a monopoly of teaching establishments in France at the time. It would seem that the Jesuits felt threatened in this battle of persuasion over the hearts and minds of children, and periodically the Port-Royal schools had to be moved or disbanded, culminating in their definitive closure in 1660, just at the time that Pascal was working on the *Pensées*. If one famous former pupil of the Port-Royal schools, the dramatist Jean Racine, is to be believed, 'this instruction of young people was one of the main reasons which led the Jesuits to the destruction of Port-Royal'.[4]

The Port-Royal schools based much of their pedagogical methods on small-group teaching, relying largely on active discussion and conversation rather than memorising long passages by rote. This notion of conversation is crucial in many ways to Pascal's own ideas on persuasion. Indeed, the section devoted to the art of persuasion in *De l'esprit géométrique* was itself largely inspired by Montaigne's *De l'art de conférer* (art of conversing). Moreover, in one intriguing fragment from the *Pensées*, where Pascal refers to himself as Salomon de Tultie (an anagram of his pseudonym Louis de Montalte from the *Lettres provinciales*), he names himself, Montaigne and Epictetus as examples of particularly effective writers, because their style is based on 'ordinary conversations' (L 745/S 618).

In 1655, the very time that he is believed to have formulated his ideas on persuasion in *De l'esprit géométrique*, Pascal became more actively involved at Port-Royal. His famous discussion with Sacy, his spiritual director, published by Sacy's secretary Fontaine (himself a teacher at the Port-Royal schools) as *Conversation with M. de*

Sacy, took place at Port-Royal des Champs in all probability at the beginning of 1655. The principal topic of the conversation, namely the choice of which authors to read, was one which was actively debated by educationalists at Port-Royal, as can be seen in treatises on education published by teachers who were based there, such as Pierre Nicole and Pierre Coustel.[5] In the *Conversation* Pascal views the reading of the same two secular writers whose writing he praises in the *Pensées*, Montaigne and Epictetus, as potentially useful, as long as such readings are 'carefully regulated' (*OC* 11, 98), because of the self-knowledge that can be gained from their divergent views on human strength and weakness. Similarly, the Port-Royal teachers counselled the reading and memorisation of carefully selected extracts from secular writers (notably authors such as Cicero and Quintilian, who wrote on rhetoric). That same year Pascal devised a new method for learning how to read, to be used by pupils at the schools, which is discussed in a letter written to Pascal by his sister Jacqueline, who at that time was mistress of novices at Port-Royal.[6] He makes one direct reference to the children at the Port-Royal schools in the *Pensées*, where he expresses the worry that they should not 'fall into a state of nonchalance' (L 63/S 97). Moreover, after the closure of the schools, where his eldest nephew, Etienne Périer, had been a pupil, Pascal took on the education of his two elder nephews, Etienne and Louis.

SPEAKERS AND READERS

It is perhaps unsurprising, therefore, that the two major works he wrote in his remaining years during and in the immediate aftermath of the Port-Royal schools' closure, the *Provincial Letters* and the *Pensées*, should be so concerned with questions of education and, concomitantly, of persuasion.

The first ten *Provincial Letters* revolve around the fictional education of the innocent narrator, Louis de Montalte, as he listens to the advice of, amongst others, a Jesuit priest and a Jansenist friend, and as he reports the conversations to a 'provincial friend', who is not only a fictional recipient but also in many ways an idealised reader.[7] Apart from the short response the provincial friend gives after the first two letters, his function is no more than as a sounding board as Montalte progresses through the different stages towards autonomy of thought.

Over the course of these letters, the gradually more enlightened pupil gains intellectual autonomy, as he challenges the inconsistencies in the teaching of the Jesuit, culminating in the abandonment of the fictional exchange in the eleventh letter. Some of the issues that were debated in Port-Royal educational treatises are taken up in the letters, most notably the comparison between recent and ancient textual authorities. However, there are a number of other axes of persuasion in the letters, which lie beyond the fictional exchanges. Perhaps the most significant feature of the text at the time was that it opened up a narrowly theological debate between Jansenists and Jesuits to a much wider lay audience. The general interest with which the successive publication of each letter was greeted is eloquent proof of their persuasive success on this level.[8] Moreover, Pascal's own persuasive task in writing the text changed over the course of the letters. Starting as an attempt to defend Antoine Arnauld, the letters became an attack on the Jesuits as a result of Arnauld's censure by the Sorbonne, thereafter changing, in reaction to the publication of various pieces of counter-polemic, to a mixture of attack and self-defence.

Whereas the *Provincial Letters* are dominated by the attempts of the Jesuit priest and the Jansenist friend to educate the naïve narrator (bringing into play a mostly non-responding reader in the form of the provincial friend), the *Pensées* place at the heart of the persuasive process a variety of imagined speakers and readers, who engage in debate with each other. It is clear that Pascal conceived the *Pensées* as being made up of a variety of formats, including dialogues (L 2/S 38) and letters (L 4/S 38 and L 5/S 39), in many ways replicating the exchange of views that was so central to Port-Royal teaching methods. Indeed, there are many imagined conversations between a variety of speakers in the *Pensées*. These speakers are sometimes clearly defined but often they remain unnamed, leaving the reader with the task of decoding their identity. Although this lack of identified speakers can lead to notorious misreadings, where sceptical interlocutors are assumed to be Pascal himself,[9] the multiplicity of voices gives to the text an energy and fluidity that allows for different viewpoints to be expressed without them being entrenched in rigid opposition to each other. The long passage known as the Wager (L 418/S 680), for instance, which is discussed at greater length elsewhere in this book, is peppered with exclamations and questions posed by a sceptical interlocutor, lending the arguments a vivacity and sense of progression that a single voice would not achieve.

Similarly, the reader is never assigned a fixed role. Many possible readers are evoked in the fragments, ranging from hardened atheists to seeking agnostics, to fully committed believers. Pascal's own division of three types of people can act as an instructive tool in this regard:

> There are only three sorts of people: those who have found God and serve Him; those who are busy seeking Him and have not found Him; those who live without either seeking or finding Him. The first are reasonable and happy, the last are foolish and unhappy, those in the middle are unhappy and reasonable. (L 160/S 192)

The first two categories mentioned here are clearly catered for within the *Pensées*. Both types are lauded and encouraged. As far as those who have found God are concerned, 'no one is so happy as a true Christian, or so reasonable, virtuous and worthy of love' (L 357/S 389). For those seekers who have not found God, Pascal reserves special praise: 'I can feel nothing but compassion for those who sincerely lament their doubt, who regard it as the ultimate misfortune, and who, sparing no effort to escape from it, make their search their principal and most serious business' (L 427/S 681). It might be all too easy, then, to assume that the final category of people, the hardened unbelievers who do not even deign to search, would be excluded from the persuasive remit of the *Pensées*. Yet Pascal's repeated insistence that it is impossible to be indifferent or neutral must surely be aimed at shaking such a reader out of his or her indifference. In L 427/S 681, for example, he stresses that 'the immortality of the soul is something of such importance to us, affecting us so deeply, that one must have lost all feelings not to care about knowing the facts of the matter'. Again, in L 428/S 682 he writes that 'I find it necessary to point out how wrong are those men who live their lives indifferent to seeking the truth about something of such importance to them, and affecting them so closely'. Moreover, those who claim neither to believe nor not to believe are dismissed as epitomising scepticism, because not knowing is the essence of the sceptical doctrine: 'anyone who imagines he can stay neutral is a sceptic *par excellence*' (L 131/S 164).

The very direct way in which Pascal engages with these different kinds of reader brings to the fore the reader's role in the persuasive framework of the *Pensées*. Just as the existence of different speakers in the text achieves a more flexible and less dogmatic form of argumentation, so too does each individual reader seem to have greater autonomy in making sense of the text for him or herself. However carefully crafted each argument may be, the coexistence of different viewpoints allows the reader to come to his or her own conclusions. And this, I would argue, is the major trump card of Pascal's persuasive strategy. Rather than regarding the *Pensées* as a conventional religious apology, it is perhaps more helpful to view the text as a self-help or self-education manual. Self-persuasion is ultimately far more effective than any other form of coercion, because change is effected from within oneself: 'We are usually more easily persuaded by the reasons which we ourselves have discovered than by those reasons which have occurred in the minds of others' (S 617/L 737).

STYLES AND DIVERSIONS

Pascal's words in the section of *De l'esprit géométrique* devoted to 'the art of persuasion' provide useful pointers to aspects that are developed more fully in the *Pensées*. His initial statement, for example, that 'the art of persuasion is necessarily linked to the way in which men agree to what is suggested to them, and to the types of things we want them to believe' (*OC* II, 171) is significant for his acknowledgement that style can often be more persuasive than content. Although, as I shall show, such reliance on style is viewed by Pascal as evidence of our corruption, this does not prevent him from playing a subtle game, both drawing his readers into the text and reminding them of their fallen state. Indeed, the wide array of styles Pascal uses in the *Pensées*, ranging from gnomic utterances (e.g., 'He has four lackeys'; L 19/S 53) to maxims ('The heart has its reasons that reason can never know'; L 423/S 680), to prose poems (such as the fragment devoted to the three orders, L 308/S 339), to longer discursive passages (such as the fragment known as 'Disproportion of Man'; L 199/S 230), provide compelling evidence of the seductive manipulations of the text.

Moreover, within the *Pensées* themselves repeated references are made to the persuasive impact of '*manière* [way/manner]', almost always as a way of demonstrating the absurdity of how easily human beings are swayed by appearances. In a long fragment devoted to imagination, for example, a magistrate is envisaged entering a church to listen to a sermon, only to have his serious demeanour destroyed by the possibility that the preacher has 'a hoarse voice or strange expression on his face, or his barber has shaved him badly' (L 44/S 78). Similarly, even the act of reading – a figure which (as I shall show) recurs in the course of the *Pensées* – can be obscured by external factors: 'When one reads too quickly or too softly, one hears nothing' (L 41/S 75). In another fragment related to imagination, which is worth quoting at greater length, he shows how seemingly insignificant factors, such as tone of voice or facial expression, can ultimately be more convincing than the inherent truth of a statement:

How difficult it is to propose something for someone else to judge without affecting his judgment by the way we do it. If you say: 'I think it is excellent', 'I think it is obscure', or something like that, you either persuade his imagination to agree with you or irritate it, in the opposite sense. It is better to say nothing, and then he can judge according to what it really is, that is what it is then, and according to the way in which other circumstances over which we have no control have affected the issue. But at least we shall have added nothing, unless our silence also produces an effect, according to the twist or interpretation he may feel like giving to it, or according to what he may surmise from our gestures and expression, or tone of voice, depending on how skilful he is at reading faces. It is so difficult not to dislodge judgment from its natural basis, or rather this is so seldom firm and stable. (L 529/S 454)

As can be seen from the above examples, such a need to be entertained is considered by Pascal to be an inevitable part of human imperfection. In 'De l'art de persuader' he perceives it as indicative of human beings' basest postlapsarian state. Although we should all be convinced by rational argument alone, he acknowledges that there are other more effective means:

No one is unaware that there are two ways by which opinions are received into the soul, which are its two principal powers: understanding and will. The most natural is by the understanding, for we ought never to consent to anything other than demonstrated truths; but the most usual, although against nature, is by the will. For every man is almost always led to believe not through proof, but through what is most attractive. This way is base, unworthy and alien, and so everyone refuses to acknowledge it. Everyone professes to believe and even to like only that which they know to merit it. (*OC* ii, 171)

It is this reliance on our will (*volonté*) that leads to Pascal's later assertion, in the same text, that 'we believe almost only what pleases us'. Pascal makes this dictum an essential part of his persuasive strategy in the *Pensées*, not only by continually warning the reader of the dangers of '*divertissements* [diversions]' but also by making use of these very diversions to retain the attention of his envisaged reader. In one seemingly minor fragment, just such a double game is played: 'When our passions impel us to do something, we forget our duty. For example, if we like a book, we read it when we ought to be doing something else' (L 937/S 763). We are warned here of the dangers of being diverted from our, presumably spiritual, duty when enticed by various diversions. The example of reading a book is given, which is precisely what we as readers are engaged in as we consider the import of the text before us. It would seem that at the very moment the words on the page are diverting the reader, that same reader is being alerted to the potential dangers which accompany such an act. This kind of reflexivity recurs at various points of the *Pensées*, making the reader an active participant in the persuasive process.[10] In another fragment a similar reflexivity can be found, where what may seem at first to be general musing on human vanity becomes a more urgent and direct inclusion of both writer and reader, emphasised by the succession of conjunctions (polysyndeton) which only serves to add reader and writer to the clutter of examples of vain humanity:

Vanity is so firmly anchored in man's heart that a soldier, a boor, a cook or a porter will vaunt himself and expect admirers, and even philosophers want them; and those who write against them want to enjoy the prestige of having written well, and those who read them want the prestige of having read them, and perhaps I who write this want the same thing, and perhaps my readers... (L 627/S 520)

There are other ways also in which diversions are used in the *Pensées*. Many of the independently minded seventeenth-century readers (known as *libertins*) for whom it is likely that Pascal was writing would recognise the frequent reference to imagery of gambling, hunting, dancing, billiards and even tennis, reflecting the leisure pursuits of the aristocracy of the time. To a large extent these images are evoked precisely to accentuate their futility when compared to the quest for spiritual truth, such as in the long fragment devoted to diversion, L 136/S 168. Yet, even where diversions appear to be unequivocally condemned, a subtle counter-assertion is often implied. In L 136/S 168, for example, although man's albeit misdirected search for repose through diversions is seen to be indicative of human corruption, the fact that man is searching at all reveals an implicit acceptance of the innermost ennui of the human condition in a world without God: men 'sincerely believe they are searching for peace but in fact are only seeking restlessness'. Even more strikingly, Pascal often supports his arguments with examples drawn from precisely such aristocratic pursuits. The most famous instance is surely that of the wager (L 418/S 680), where gambling imagery becomes the focal point of a debate on the existence of God. Images that might be familiar to the educated reader occur sometimes in unexpected places and are often aimed to stir the reader from complacency: the ordering of the apologist's (or persuader's) material is compared to a tennis ball being placed with differing success by two players ('When we play tennis, each player uses the same ball, but one places it better'; L 696/S 575); a man whose only son has just died is pictured being diverted from thoughts of his son by a wild boar pursued by hunting hounds (L 136/S 168); the life-span of humans is compared to prisoners on death row awaiting their fate (L 434/S 686).

SELF-INTEREST

As can be seen from these examples, Pascal is not afraid to confront the readers with their own experiences, or what he calls their own 'condition' (L 24/S 58). The task confronted by the apologist is a delicate one, for, on the one hand he needs to appeal to readers' self-interest in order to capture and then hold their attention, and on the other hand he must make use of the very examples that attract the reader in the first place, in order to show the inner wretchedness of the human condition without religion. In a long passage such as that known as 'Disproportion of Man' (L 199/S 230), Pascal appeals to the scientific curiosity of his worldly reader by making use of recent scientific research, namely the discovery of distant planets (as a consequence of the invention of the telescope) and the existence of minute organisms invisible to the human eye (resulting from the invention of the microscope), to comment upon the contradictions of humanity. Such contrasts, he argues, can only lead to self-contemplation, moving on to the more general question: what is man's place in nature? The only answer is that man is 'a nothing compared to the infinite, a whole compared to the nothing, a middle point between all and nothing, infinitely removed from an understanding of the extremes'. Such 'extremes' can only be resolved 'in God, and in God alone'. At several junctures in the *Pensées* where human nature is evoked, the term '*contrariétés* [contradictions]' appears. Not only do we find elaborate developments of the theme, as in the passage on the 'Disproportion of Man', but some of the shortest fragments reiterate the same idea, no more so than in the poetically pithy 'L'homme est naturellement crédule, incrédule, timide, téméraire [man is naturally credulous, incredulous, timid, foolhardy]' (L 124/S 157).

Self-interest (*amour-propre*) is indeed central to Pascal's Augustinian vision of humanity, and one long passage is devoted to precisely this subject. Unlike his contemporary La Rochefoucauld, who writes also at length on the subject but who deliberately removes spiritual significance from his interpretation of *amour-propre*, Pascal overtly opposes self-love (*amor sui*) to love of God (*amor Dei*); *amour-propre* is seen as the direct consequence of humankind's fall from grace. Starting with an almost neutral definition of the term – 'The nature of *amour-propre* and of this human self is to love only oneself and to consider only oneself' (L 978/S 743) – the passage then takes up the theme of '*contrariétés*'. There exists a discrepancy between man's desires and his true self-perception (as brought out by the alliterative repetition of the verbs *vouloir* and *se voir*):

> But what is it to do? It cannot prevent the object of its love from being full of faults and wretchedness; it wants to be great and sees that it is small; it wants to be happy and sees that it is wretched; it wants to be perfect and sees that it is full of imperfections; it wants to be the object of men's love and esteem and sees that its faults deserve only their dislike and contempt. (L 978/S 743)

For Pascal, this self-love is inextricably linked to an 'aversion to the truth' and forms such a part 'of everyone to a certain degree' that we force others to put on a performance directed entirely by ourselves in order to fulfil the picture that we would like to have of ourselves:

'We are treated as we want to be treated: we hate the truth, so it is hidden from us; we want to be flattered, so we are flattered; we want to be deceived, so we are deceived' (L 978/S 743).

One of Pascal's concluding comments in L 978/S 743, that 'human life is nothing but a perpetual illusion', in which 'there is nothing but mutual deception and flattery', finds its counterpart in another seemingly more personal passage where the themes of self-love and persuasion appear together.[11] As can be seen from some of the other fragments quoted thus far, the possible pitfalls as well as the effectiveness of human means of persuasion are signalled here. In keeping with the rigorous Augustinianism of his thought, Pascal directs persuasion away from love of the self and towards love of God:

It is unjust that anyone should become attached to me even though they do so gladly and of their own accord. I should be deceiving those in whom I aroused such a desire, for I am no one's goal nor do I have the means of satisfying anyone. Am I not ready to die? Then the object of their attachment will die. Thus, just as I should be culpable if I made someone believe a falsehood, even though I used gentle means of persuasion, and it gave them pleasure to believe it and me pleasure that they should; in the same way I am culpable if I make anyone love me. And, if I attract people to become attached to me, I must warn those who might be ready to consent to the lie that they must not believe it, whatever benefit I might derive from it; and likewise that they must not become attached to me, because they must devote their lives and efforts to pleasing God or seeking Him. (L 396/S 15)

ORDER AND ORDERS

There is much debate about what form the *Pensées* would have taken had Pascal lived to complete his task. Although Pascal had arranged about one-third of the fragments into various bundles (*liasses*), the task undertaken by some scholars to place all the fragments into a more rigorous order is ultimately a fruitless one, as any categorisation can only be conjectural.[12] Pascal himself writes in *De l'esprit géométrique* that, although he would like to attempt 'an explanation of true order, which consists of defining and proving everything', such an ideal order is ultimately 'absolutely impossible', because 'men are naturally and immoveably powerless to treat any knowledge in an absolutely accomplished order' (*OC* II, 157). Moreover, there are many indications that Pascal was considering a radical new way of arranging his material in the *Pensées*. He claims that his ordering ('disposition') will be 'new' (L 696/S 575) and that he will be compiling a carefully constructed 'disorder', which is different from the random 'confusion' of the sceptics (L 532/S 457).[13]

Whatever final ordering Pascal may have undertaken for his *Pensées*, throughout his writing we find a propensity to divide human experience into different categories. In one of a number of fragments that are entitled 'Raison des effets', for example, he considers the various attitudes of different groups towards the appearance of 'people of high birth' (L 90/S 124), showing how each set veers between respect and scorn, each having a different reason for such an opinion. Although what he terms 'the people', 'the crafty [*habiles*]' and 'perfect Christians' may be in agreement over the need to show respect for those of noble birth, the reasons behind such a choice are very different from each other, just as the 'semi-crafty' and 'zealots' have different reasons for showing scorn. As he states in another related fragment, 'It is necessary to have a hidden thought [*pensée de derrière*] and to judge everything from this perspective' (L 91/S 125). This sense of a *'pensée de derrière'* is crucial to Pascal's persuasive methods in the *Pensées*, for, as seen in *De l'esprit géométrique*, rational argument alone is not going to persuade others.

It is, therefore, important for the persuader/apologist to acknowledge and make use of other means. In the *Pensées* this is most compellingly introduced by Pascal's use of the terms *'esprit de géométrie* [mathematical mind]' and *'esprit de finesse* [intuitive mind]'. He goes to great lengths to distinguish between these two 'minds', both of which are related to reasoning but in very different ways. Whereas the geometrical mind is deemed to deal with principles that are *'palpables* [obvious]', but 'removed from ordinary usage', relying largely on the need for 'all things to be explained by definitions and principles', the *'esprit de finesse'* is more concerned with principles that are 'in ordinary usage and before the eyes of everybody', where all that is required is to have 'good sight' (L 512/S 670). In another fragment Pascal elaborates on the difference between these two minds: 'For judgment is what goes with instinct [*sentiment*], just as knowledge goes with mind. Intuition [*finesse*] falls to the lot of judgment, mathematics to that of mind' (L 513/S 671). *Finesse*, which is associated here with judgment, is clearly perceived to be more effective than pure reason in the realm of persuasion. In this case, 'sentiment' (which is a notoriously complex term in the *Pensées*) can most use-fully be linked to intuition, although it is worth bearing in mind that in the course of the *Pensées* it is variously evoked as an operation that involves the reception of sensual, intellectual and even divine impressions, while at the same time forming opinions about them.[14] The reader is being scrupulously prepared to accept the need not to view larger questions, such as the nature of religious belief, from single or narrow perspectives.

The clear distinction between these two minds is essential to Pascal's wider apologetic project, for much of his discourse consists of a strong opposition to the attempt by rationalist philosophers, most notably Descartes (who is witheringly dismissed by Pascal as 'useless and uncertain'; L 887/S 445), to prove the existence of God through purely rational means. By relying exclusively on the dominance of reason, so Pascal argues, such philosophers place too much emphasis on human strength, thereby raising the human to quasi-divine status. Instead, Pascal tries to prove the inherent flaws of reason (which, he states elsewhere, 'is always deceived by the inconstancy of appear-ances'; L 199/S 230) and its ultimate inadequacy when considering questions such as religious faith. After all, so he argues, 'if we submit everything to reason, our religion will have nothing mysterious and supernatural about it' (L 173/S 204). It is in this context that Pascal gives priority to the role of the heart (*'cœur'*), which has nothing to do with sentimental feelings but rather is closely tied to intuition. As he states: 'We know the truth not only through our reason but also through our heart' (L 110/S 142). Aspects such as 'space, time, movement, numbers' are what he calls 'first principles', which can far more easily be sensed intuitively than explained at length in a logical manner. His aim, he tells us, is to 'humiliate reason, which would like to judge everything' (L 110/S 142), so that we may recog-nise the fallibility of rational discourse. When it comes to religion, it is the heart which is the principal receptacle for faith, even though Pascal acknowledges that reason can play an important part too:

That is why those to whom God has given religious faith through the intu-ition of their heart are truly happy and legitimately persuaded. But to those who do not have it we can only give such faith through reasoning, until God gives it through the intuition of their heart, without which faith is only human and useless for salvation. (L 110/S 142)

It is surely no coincidence that Pascal's choice of the adjective *inutile* (useless) to define faith based on reason alone is the same word used to describe Descartes (L 887/S 445).

The distinction Pascal makes between heart and mind is taken up and developed in a number of fragments devoted to what are generally known as the Three Orders. Two major passages, L 308/S 339 and L 933/S 761, explore the three orders at greater length, establishing a clear hierarchy between the categories. The lowest order, termed variously as '*chair* [flesh]', '*corps* [body]' and '*charnels* [carnal]', concerns those people who take advantage of worldly wealth, such as 'the rich', 'captains' and even 'kings'. The second order, that of the mind (called '*esprit*' or '*esprits*'), is comprised of the 'curious', 'scientists' and 'great geniuses', people who rely on the supremacy of reason. Archimedes is given as an example of this second order (L 308/S 339), and he is clearly placed above those who value material goods. But the highest order of all is deemed to be that of 'will' ('*volonté*', used in a different sense from the '*volonté*' that is described in 'On the art of persuasion' as part of the need to be entertained) or 'charity', the domain of true 'justice' and 'wisdom', where the heart plays a significant role. Christ, who 'without worldly goods or any outward show of knowledge has his own order of holiness' (L 308/S 339), is offered as the supreme example of this order of charity. These different hierarchies are progressively distanced from each other. As Pascal emphasises, 'The infinite distance between body and mind figures the infinitely more infinite distance between mind and charity, for charity is supernatural' (L 308/S 339).

It is clear, then, that Pascal considers this hierarchy of orders to be crucial for the reader to reach a state of self-knowledge. As much as one might admire the exploits of kings or the thought of philosophers, there is always a higher sphere towards which one should aspire.

This movement between different orders features prominently, not only thematically but also linguistically. Throughout the *Pensées* certain key terms, such as 'justice', 'happiness' and 'truth', are used in very different ways. On the lowest level, what one might call the equivalent of the bodily or worldly order, we find inauthentic manifestations of these absolute concepts. These concepts are often governed by deceptive powers (*puissances trompeuses*), which manage to create their own spurious 'second nature'. One of these powers is a term we have already met, *imagination*. In the major passage devoted to the subject, Pascal calls the imagination 'this mistress of error and falsity, all the more deceptive for not being invariably so, for it would be an infallible criterion of truth if it were infallibly that of lies' (L 44/S 78). In other words, on this level truth becomes almost interchangeable with falsity. Moreover, 'Imagination orders everything; it creates beauty, justice and happiness, which amounts to everything in the world' (L 44/S 78). The emphasis on the world in this extract is significant, for it coincides with the material order, where those, like kings and wealthy people, hold temporal, and temporary, power. Imagination influences also the field of the second order, that of the mind or reason, for it is not only dubbed 'enemy of reason' but also has the strength to make us 'believe, doubt, deny reason' (L 44/S 164).

The linguistic equivalent of the second order, that of the mind, incorporates this corruption of reason through imagination, as it is less concerned with the example of scientists or philosophers that Pascal gives in the fragments on the three orders than with the state towards which fallen human beings think themselves to be aspiring. I have shown already, with respect to the long fragment on diversion (L 136/S 168), how this search, albeit misdirected, reflects a positive impetus on the part of the searcher, because of its implicit acceptance of the need to search at all. If we take the example of happiness from another fragment, L 131/S 164, the persuader argues that it is the corruption of all humans after the Fall which explains why 'we have an idea of happiness but cannot attain it'. The elusiveness of this concept of happiness shows that it is neither completely spurious (as on the first material order) nor complete (as on the third spiritual order).

Perfect happiness, consistent with the third order of charity, is posited in the same fragment, for it is explicitly likened to the notion of how human beings in a state of perfection, unblemished by the Fall, might be: 'if man had never been corrupted, he would, in his innocence, confidently enjoy both truth and happiness' (L 131/S 164).

The solution, for the searching reader in the *Pensées*, lies not only in the importance of accepting the need for spiritual happiness, but also in recognising the complexity of the notion of happiness as a *point de départ* for that search. Two fragments that were originally written on the same piece of paper (and which were therefore in all probability written at the same time as each other) underline this complexity.[15] In the one, L 407/S 26, examples are given of people (such as the Stoics, who try to find happiness in themselves alone, or others who try to seek it through diversions) whose hopes of finding happiness are too narrowly focused:

> The Stoics say: 'Withdraw into yourself, that is where you will find peace.' And that is not true.
> Others say: 'Go outside and seek happiness in some diversion.' And that is not true, because illness may ensue.
> Happiness is neither outside nor within us: it is in God, both outside and within us.

In the other fragment, L 399/S 18, two apparently contradictory questions are posed: 'If man was not made for God, why is he only happy in God? If man was made for God, why is he so opposed to God?' The seeming paradox of these two questions can only be solved through the recognition of all human beings' postlapsarian state and their original perfect nature, because, although we may be obliged to search for happiness, our fallen condition cannot guarantee that we will find it.

Pascal's famous discussion of the hidden God is in this respect closely linked to human corruption. Moreover, the reading of the *Pensées* as a tool for self-instruction can further be supported by the pedagogical language used in a passage that brings together all these issues:

> It is true then that everything teaches [*instruit*] man his condition, but there must be no misunderstanding, for it is not true that everything reveals God, and it is not true that everything conceals God. But it is true when put together that He hides from those who tempt Him and that He reveals himself to those who seek Him, because men are at once unworthy and capable of God; unworthy through their corruption, capable through their original nature. (L 444/S 690)

CONCLUSION

Persuasion works, then, in the *Pensées* through the recognition of difference and complexity. Although purely human means of persuasion are necessarily flawed and corrupt, these means can both remain effective for fallen readers and, in their imperfection, point towards a 'rhetoric' which is perfect, that of God and Christ.

Christ as described in the Bible acts as the persuasive *exemplum*: 'Jesus said things so simply that he seems not to have thought about them, and yet so clearly that it is obvious what he thought about them. Such clarity together with such simplicity is admirable' (L 309/S 340). Similarly, God's words, as found in the Bible, are the best way to direct readers in their search for God: *'Dieu parle bien de Dieu'* – God speaks well of God (L 303/S 334). Whereas human language remains imperfect because of the 'mutual deception' (L 978/S 743) that Pascal perceives to characterise all human interaction, God's word is unblemished: 'In God word and intention do not differ, for He is truthful, nor do word and effect, for he is mighty, nor do means and effect, for he is wise' (L 968/S 416).

By recognising that true persuasion lies finally with God, the reader has reached the ultimate stage of self-persuasion: 'We must keep silence as far as we can and only talk to ourselves about God, whom we know to be true, and thus persuade ourselves that He is' (L 99/S 132).

NOTES

1. All references to Pascal's works will be from the two-volume Le Guern edition. All references to the *Pensées* will be from the Lafuma and Sellier editions. Translations are my own, except for some fragments from the *Pensées*, which are adapted from Krailsheimer's Penguin translation. Where the sound of the original French words is particularly important, I give both the French and English versions.

2. See, for example, Topliss 1966; Le Guern 1969; Kim 1992; Koch 1997.

3. A. Arnauld and P. Nicole, *La Logique, ou l'art de penser* (Paris: Vrin, 1981), p. 267.

4. J. Racine, *Abrégé de l'histoire de Port-Royal* (Paris: La Table Ronde, 1994), p. 90.

5. P. Coustel, *Lés Règles de l'éducation des enfants* (2 vols., Paris: Estienne Michallet, 1687); P. Nicole, *De l'éducation d'un prince* (Paris: veuve Charles Savreux, 1670).

6. See the Mesnard edition of Pascal, III, 439.

7. See Parish 1989, pp. 50–1.

8. Mme de Sévigné, for example, who makes frequent references to the letters in her correspondence, writes on the 12 September 1656 of her enjoyment upon reading the eleventh letter, which only recently had appeared.

9. The poet Paul Valéry, for example, misreads many of the fragments by stating that 'one sees too much the hand of Pascal at work'. See Parish 1989, p. 135.

10. For a subtle analysis of reflexivity in the *Pensées*, see Gilby 2001.

11. Pascal is believed to have carried this passage with him at all times. Its content is in keeping with his sister Gilberte's assertion that he did not wish other people to have any attachment to him.

12. The two most prominent scholars to attempt to place all the fragments into such a putative order are Ernst 1970 and Pugh 1984. Ernst's subsequent work, *Géologie et stratigraphie des Pensées de Pascal* (1996), is far less conjectural, as it explores the chronological composition of the fragments through an analysis of such aspects as the watermarks of the paper on which the *Pensées* were written and the way in which the sheets of paper were cut up.

13. For a more sustained discussion of order in the *Pensées*, see Hammond 1994, pp. 50–78.

14. See Norman 1988, pp. 3–17 for useful analysis of the different meanings of *sentiment* in the *Pensées*.

15. See Ernst 1996 for a reconfiguration of many of the original sheets on which Pascal wrote fragments.

14 The reception of Pascal's *Pensées* in the seventeenth and eighteenth centuries

The first commentary on the *Pensées*, before the Port-Royal edition was even published, is to be found in the *Logique de Port-Royal* (1662), the manual of logic edited by the theologians of Port-Royal, Arnauld and Nicole, who sought to establish a synthesis between Augustine, Descartes and Pascal. This attempt was significant because of the very nature of Pascal's thought and of the philosophy he attributes to his unbelieving interlocutor in the *Pensées*: that philosophy is inspired by Gassendi, particularly by Gassendi's *Objections* to Descartes' *Meditations* (French translation by Clerselier, 1647). Not that Gassendi was himself an unbeliever: despite R. Pintard's efforts to read irony and hypocrisy between the lines,[1] most modern interpreters accept that Gassendi was an orthodox believer, but his philosophy inspired a number of notorious unbelievers, among whom Cyrano de Bergerac is the most prominent. Not that Pascal could have read Cyrano: the chronology of their writing and publication made that impossible. But Pascal did perceive, in the alliance between the philosophy of sociability – *honnêteté* – theorised by Méré and the sceptical philosophy inherited from Montaigne and modernised by Gassendi, a major threat to Christian doctrine, and he deliberately elaborated his apologetic arguments in order to resist that threat. The very structure of the apologetic argument in the *Pensées* requires that the unbeliever be led from principles he recognises and adopts to acceptance of the Christina doctrine which he initially refuses. Pascal thus attributes Gassendist principles to his unbeliever and builds his apology on those foundations. The attempt to harness Pascal to a Cartesian logic, and to reconcile Descartes with Augustinian thought, an attempt which is characteristic of the 'second Port-Royal' (in the vocabulary of

Henri Gouhier),[2] could only lead, at best, to an ambiguous, makeshift doctrine.

The attempt is nevertheless significant because Pascal's editors, his friends from Port-Royal and above all the theologians Arnauld and Nicole, whose commentaries and emendations are to be found in the manuscript copy of Pascal's work established immediately after his death, were convinced and ardent disciples of Descartes. Thus, the *Logique* seeks to establish the legitimacy of metaphysical proofs of God's existence, and those proofs are held to be self-evident and demonstrative: only the bad faith of the unbeliever could allow him to escape the logic of Christian doctrine. The fact that such a conception of metaphysical proof is radically opposed to Pascal's own thought was concealed by a subtle play on words. Whereas Pascalian *sentiment* designated a function of the *heart*, and thus founded a Gassendist psychology opposed to the intellectual intuition of Descartes' *cogito*, the Port-Royal theologians suggest that Pascal's *sentiment* is no more than a *sentiment d'évidence*: Pascal's most vehement opposition to Cartesian psychology and epistemology is thus disguised as a Christian philosophy perfectly compatible with Cartesian metaphysics. Cartesian proofs and Pascalian testimony are called on to prove the truth of Christian doctrine. Ultimately, it may be said that the Port-Royal theologians proposed a confused alliance between the *Dieu des Philosophes* and the *Dieu d'Abraham, d'Isaac et de Jacob*, the rational God of philosophy and the hidden God of Scripture.

THE PORT-ROYAL EDITION

That such was the effect of the first interpretation of the manuscript *Pensées* is confirmed by subsequent publications. Throughout the 1670s, Port-Royal theologians developed the concept of *foi humaine*, faith legitimately founded on human testimony: this conception of faith is strongly developed in Arnauld's and Nicole's anti-protestant publications on the theme of *perpétuité*; the same theme is to be found in Filleau de La Chaise's *Discours* on Pascal's *Pensées* (originally written as a preface to the *Pensées*, published separately in 1672 and included in the Port-Royal editions of the *Pensées* from 1678), and can be led back to the final chapters of the *Logique de Port-Royal* dealing with the status of historical testimony. But at the same time

Nicole published in 1670, the same year as the *Pensées*, an essay on 'natural proofs' of God's existence and declared that such proofs were eminently compatible with the apologetic stance of Pascal. The Port-Royal edition of the *Pensées* thus seeks a synthesis – or at least a compromise – between two radically different philosophies of religion: a conception of faith founded on demonstration and rational conviction and a conception of faith founded on historical testimony, on uncertainty, on revelation and on mystery. In this sense, it may be said that the Port-Royal edition of the *Pensées* constituted another episode in the conflict that had opposed, half a century earlier, Garasse and Saint-Cyran: Garasse (1623) requiring demonstration and refusing philosophical scepticism, Saint-Cyran (1626) defending the orthodoxy of Pierre Charron (and therefore of Montaigne) and the compatibility of that scepticism with the Augustinian analysis of the human condition.

Such is also the lesson to be drawn from the upheaval of the argumentative structure in the Port-Royal edition (1670, 1678) and from the many emendations of the Pascalian text in the Port-Royal edition. A Gassendist text edited by Cartesians necessarily appeared incoherent. The reversal of the order of the chapters – introduced by an enumeration of the proofs of Christian truth, concluded by a portrait of human nature and a number of chapters devoted to *miscellanea*: the seventeenth- and eighteenth-century reader could not grasp a coherent apologetic argument, but had to be content to treasure a homage to Pascal's memory. By the disruption of the order, Pascal's arguments are transformed into reflections and pseudo-confessions.

This is nowhere more apparent than in chapter 7 of the Port-Royal edition, devoted to the wager argument. The very grounds for the wager – uncertainty as to God's existence – have been ruined by the affirmed existence of demonstrative proofs of God's existence, in the *Logique* and in Nicole's *essai de morale*. The wager thus appears as a strange contradiction in terms. The very first refutation of the *Pensées* – by the abbot Montfaucon de Villars in 1671 – laboured this point: the wager reduces faith to a superficial, flippant declaration of self-interest, whereas the real question is that of the truth. It was quite impossible, in the context created by the Port-Royal editors, to grasp the coherence of Pascal's scepticism, its relation to Montaigne, its role in the conversion of the egoism of the libertine interlocutor into a desire to discover the truth of Christian doctrine. Indeed, the presentation of the wager in the Port-Royal edition underlines its peculiarity and the text is modified to make doubt in God's existence appear as a momentary concession to the libertine adversary, an *ad hominem* argument of purely tactical value. Subsequent readers generally adopted the position defined by the abbé de Villars: Montesquieu, Voltaire and the clandestine philosophers pointed out that the wager argument is valid for any religion; it is not specifically Christian. Following the abbé de Saint-Pierre (1730), Diderot (1796) was to transform the argument into a wager on social virtue.

MALEBRANCHE

The status of reason and rational demonstration was also at the heart of another work that played a decisive role in defining the interpretation of Pascal's *Pensées* in the seventeenth and eighteenth century: Malebranche's first treatise, *De la Recherche de la vérité* (1674–5), contained a violent attack on Port-Royal theologians – among whom we can count Pascal – disguised under the label *personnes de piété*. Paradoxically, Malebranche chose to ignore the declared allegiance of Port-Royal to Cartesian demonstration and to underline those texts in which they made manifest their Augustinian reservations on the status of human reason and on the ambitions of natural science. Nuances are important here, of course, insofar as Malebranche was himself an Augustinian and also proposed a synthesis between Cartesian rationalism and Augustinian anthropology. The conflict between Port-Royal and Malebranche is a token of the violent conflict within the Catholic Church – as well as in controversy with the Protestants – between the different currents of thought that contributed to the counter-Reform.

In 1677 Malebranche was to build his apologetics in the *Conversations chrétiennes* on Pascal's historical arguments, relayed and reformulated by Filleau de La Chaise. But this was, in Malebranche's own eyes, no more than a momentary concession to small and vulgar minds: all his main works present a dogmatic version of Christian rationalism, doing away with Cartesian reticence (and in particular with Descartes' doctrine of the creation of eternal truths). God's existence can be demonstrated. It is blasphemy to question the capacity of human reason to attain certainty on such a question:

'The certainty of faith depends on the knowledge that reason gives us of the existence of God.'³ God's existence is thus not 'hidden', but manifest. Reason is the legitimate instrument whereby man discovers truth: 'The Reason I speak of is infallible, immutable, incorruptible. It should always be our guide; God Himself follows it.'⁴ It is therefore impossible that the truth discovered by reason should contradict the truth of revelation: the truth of revelation necessarily conforms to rational truth: 'Without doubt, nothing conforms so closely to reason as the substance of our faith.'⁵ This is a crucial aspect of Malebranche's rationalism: God cannot change the nature of things; he simply recognises the nature of things as they are. Human reason can therefore perceive things as they are, independently of God's will. Rational truth – the nature of things discovered by man by the exercise of his reason – is thus a necessary truth, independent of God's will, a truth that weighs – as Pierre Bayle was to declare – like a *fatum* on the will of God (*Continuation des pensées diverses*, section 114). This was to have crucial consequences for anti-Christian philosophy in the eighteenth century.

The second field in which Malebranche was to play a decisive role was the anthropology of human passions. The Port-Royal version of Augustinian anthropology – strongly expressed in Pascal's *Pensées*, in the *Maximes* of La Rochefoucauld (1665) and in the *Essais de morale* of Pierre Nicole (1670) – condemned the passions as corrupt emanations of self-love (*amour-propre*). Pascal's condemnation of *le moi haïssable* left no room for human virtue without a radical conversion of the will, which could be operated only by divine grace. Malebranche rejected this absolute condemnation of self-love, since, in his eyes, self-love was the first movement of the will: without self-love there could be no love, and therefore no love of God. Self-love needs to be guided by reason, informed and redirected – converted – towards an appreciation of God as the source of all good. In this sense, self-love – corrected and conducted by reason – can be the source of virtue: we need only to reason coherently – and that is within our power – to redirect self-love to a love of God and to convert selfish actions into acts of virtue. Passions themselves, by this same reasoning, can become virtuous, if only their goal be transformed by reason.

Fénelon's pedagogical exploitation of self-love in *Télémaque* (1699) was to be one of the first results of this rehabilitation of self-love and of human nature, and the same doctrine was soon to be found in the moral essays of the abbé de Saint-Pierre (1730). Through his influence in the *club de l'Entresol*, the *philosophes* were soon to declare passions innocent, provided they contributed to the common good. Self-love thus became the foundation of morality based on social utility: After Montesquieu (1721) and Marivaux (1721–4), Voltaire gave eloquent expression to this violent rejection of Augustinian anthropology: 'self-love supports our love of others; it is by our mutual needs that we are useful to the community; it is the foundation of all commerce; it is the eternal link between men ... Let us not blame the instinct that God has given us and let us apply it according to His commandments.'[6]

These two aspects of Malebranche's philosophy thus constituted strong rebuttals of Pascalian thought and doctrine: reason was the legitimate instrument of man's search for truth and the authority of revelation was thus subjected to the scrutiny of human reason; self-love was the legitimate source of human action; informed and redirected by reason, it could be the source of virtue. The influence of Malebranche was to weigh heavily on clandestine philosophy of the early eighteenth century. The danger was obvious, and Pascal had made it clear: reason gives access only to the God of philosophers, and not to the God of Abraham, Isaac and Jacob. In other words, deism is a far reach from Christianity. Indeed, if, as Malebranche had declared, human reason was a sure guide to truth, what need, then, of divine revelation? The *philosophes* were quick to seize the logic of this rationalism: God necessarily conforms to our conception of His qualities. The contradictions between our conception of the qualities of an infinitely perfect being and the God of the Bible thus argue strongly in favour of a rejection of the Old Testament as an imposture:

> Je ne suis pas Chrétien, mais c'est pour t'aimer mieux.
>
> I am not a Christian, but I love you [God] all the better.
> (Voltaire, *Epître à Uranie*)

Meanwhile, eighteenth-century apologetics confirms the confusion between the God of philosophers and the God of the Bible; indeed, following Pierre-Sylvain Regis' example (1704), the apologists refuse to recognise any contradiction between the God of the Christian and the God of the Deist.

BAYLE

The role of Malebranche in the evolution of Christian and anti-Christian rationalism at the turn of the century is closely linked to the attention paid to his Christian philosophy by Pierre Bayle. Bayle wove into his commentaries on contemporary philosophy a series of allusions to Pascal's philosophical scepticism. His attitude to Pascal and his interpretation of the *Pensées* is complex and fascinating, because of the coded style of the refugee philosopher. He is a disciple of the *libertins érudits*.

He devotes a short catalogue article in the *Nouvelles de la République des Lettres* (December 1684) to the *Vie de M. Pascal* composed by Gilberte Périer and published in the 1684 edition of the *Pensées*. The main theme here is the maxim of Pascal to 'renounce all pleasure': Bayle quotes the maxim with astonishment and goes on to compare Pascal with Epicurus – a surprising comparison, of which the key is given some twelve years later in the article 'Epicure' of the *Dictionnaire historique et critique* (1697). It is there revealed that Bayle's irony in the 1684 article bore on the polemic between Malebranche and Arnauld concerning the nature of pleasure: Bayle was taking a firm position in favour of Malebranche and, in the *Dictionnaire*, he goes so far as to suggest doubt that Pascal, claiming to renounce all pleasure, could be 'born of woman'. The key to this new enigmatic expression is the analysis by Malebranche himself of the psychology of Adam before the Fall (*De la recherche de la vérité*, 1674, 1.5): before the Fall, Adam could renounce all pleasure and follow reason unhindered by his passions; after the Fall such rational control over the passions was no longer in his power. Pascal's ambitious maxim therefore likens him to Adam before the Fall – according to Malebranche's analysis – and allows Bayle to conclude that we are here dealing, in the *Vie de M. Pascal*, with devout reflections devoid of any philosophical foundation.

Another expression in the *Nouvelles* article is worthy of commentary. Bayle there concludes by applying the term '*Philosophe Chrétien*' to Pascal. This is noteworthy simply because the expression is habitually used by Malebranche to designate his own brand of Christian rationalism, which is radically opposed to Pascal's religious philosophy and psychology of faith. One is thus led to seek an explanation by Bayle as to what he understands by 'Christian

Philosophy', and that explanation is to be found much later in a letter to his cousin, Jean Bruguière de Naudis:

The *Christian Philosophers* who speak sincerely declare bluntly that they are Christians either by education or by the grace of the faith that God has given them, but that philosophical and demonstrative arguments could only make them sceptics for the rest of their lives. (Bayle to Naudis, 8 September 1698)

Bayle's conception of religious philosophy is thus radically opposed to Malebranchist rationalism: faith is, as Montaigne had established, an effect of grace or of education – and the two are indistinguishable. Thus, from the standpoint of 1698, Bayle's defence of Malebranche throughout the early years (1684–5) may appear as a bygone conviction or as a bluff: Malebranche's Christian rationalism was then constantly put forward as the only coherent Christian philosophy, but Bayle seems to hold in 1698 that there are insoluble objections to that rationalism. In the *Dictionnaire*, it could be argued, Bayle adopts the philosophical scepticism of Pyrrho and had intended to suggest in the 1684 article that Pascal's pyrrhonism was indeed a coherent religious philosophy.

It is an important step towards the Christian religion that we should receive from God the knowledge of what we should believe and of what we should do: that religion commands that we harness our understanding to faithful obedience. (*Dictionnaire*, art. 'Pyrrhon', rem. C)[7]

Indeed, the *Eclaircissement sur les pyrrhoniens* seems to confirm this interpretation: philosophy and faith appear incompatible.

We have necessarily to choose between Philosophy and the Bible: if you want to believe nothing that is not self-evident and in conformity with common notions, take Philosophy and abandon Christianity; if you want to believe the incomprehensible mysteries of Religion, take Christianity and abandon Philosophy, for it is quite impossible to hold both self-evidence and incomprehensibility... You must choose... (*Eclaircissement sur les pyrrhoniens*, 1702)

Bayle might thus be regarded as a disciple of Pascal, ready to submit reason to divine mystery.

But let us not blindly follow the path that Bayle points out to us. Another article in the *NRL* must be compared with these bald statements of submission. In Bayle's review of Wissowatius' *Religio rationalis* (September 1684, art. IX), he immediately suggests a comparison of Socinian principles with Pascal's *soumission et usage de la raison*, and he goes on to denounce the Socinian position as an impossible compromise: there are no articles of religious faith that are compatible with reason. We might thus be tempted to interpret this article as another declaration of fideism, blind faith in the mysteries of religious doctrine, and to understand that Bayle attributes this brand of faith to Pascal. But in the article 'Socin, Fauste' in the *Dictionnaire*, he lifts the veil as to his real intention. He first evokes the status of religious mystery:

It is supposed that, without entertaining doubt as to the truth of [Christian] mysteries, [the Socinians] pretended to criticise them in order to attract more people to their sect. It is a heavy yoke for Reason to bear, to bend reason to faith in the three persons of the Divine Being and in a Man-God; it is therefore an infinite relief to Christians, if you deliver them from that yoke, and it is feasible that you will be followed by throngs of people, if you deliver them of that burden. That is why these Italian refugees, transplanted into Poland, denied the Trinity, hypostatic union, original sin, absolute predestination, etc. ('Socin', rem. H)

But Bayle rejects this supposition: mysteries do not make a religion more difficult for the people to believe, on the contrary . . .

But it can be replied that they would have been very silly, and unworthy of their Italian education, had they taken that wily path. The speculative mysteries of religion do not bother the people; they do indeed trouble a Professor in Theology, who contemplates them with attention and tries to explain them and to resist heretical objections. Some other studious persons, who examine them with curiosity, may also be fatigued by the resistance of their reason; but all the rest of humankind enjoy, in this respect, perfect tranquillity: *they believe, or think they believe* any commentary [on mysteries] that you care to offer, and they are perfectly at ease in that persuasion . . . They are much happier with a mysterious, incomprehensible doctrine, raised above reason; all men admire much more what they cannot understand; they have a more sublime idea of such beliefs, and even find more consolation in them. All the aims of religion are better satisfied by things we cannot understand: they inspire more admiration, more respect, more fear, more confidence . . . In a word, it must be admitted that, in certain fields, incomprehensibility is a positive quality. ('Socin', rem. H; my italics)

Mystery is here designated as a characteristic trait of popular religion and the laconic expression: *'they believe, or think they believe'* implicitly calls into doubt our capacity to believe in something that we cannot conceive nor express in clear, unambiguous terms. In other words, the very Pascalian expressions that Bayle uses to suggest his submission to mystery are, in fact, intended to denounce faith in incomprehensible articles of doctrine. Such articles can only be repeated parrot fashion. Bayle's expression here suggests a blunt refusal to submit reason to mystery, since the logical contradictions of religious mystery are indistinguishable from the absurdities of popular superstition. Far from being a disciple of Pascal, Bayle is thus revealed as one of his most radical critics.

CONCLUSION

The stage was thus set for the violent rejection of Pascalian religious philosophy, which was to be a characteristic trait of the eighteenth-century *philosophes*. Fontenelle follows Bayle's example and builds his Spinozistic 'Chinese' philosophy on a critique of Pascal's wager argument (1743, 1768), on the rejection of miracles, on the definition of happiness without faith and without hope of life after death (1714). Voltaire had only to gather up the various threads of this *anti-Pascal* in his attempt to gain Jesuit support for his *Lettres philosophiques* (1734). Against the Pascalian and Augustinian conception of human 'misery', Voltaire invokes the order of the world which is 'as it should be', reflecting the infinite qualities of the creator: we can read here the triumph of Malebranchist rationalism called on to justify Pope's 'optimism' (*Essay on Man*, 1733). At the same time, following Bayle and Fontenelle, the clandestine manuscript *La Nouvelle Moysade* (1734) denounced the contradictions between our conception of God's qualities and the very human, choleric and fallible God of the Old Testament. Whereas the conservative Houtteville (1722) relied on Pascalian proofs of the historical truth of the Bible, history was rejected by the philosophical disciples of Malebranche: they demanded demonstration. Robert Challe (composed *c.* 1720, published 1768) thus refuses to submit to any 'factual' religion, since facts depend on unreliable human testimony: he does not 'believe' in God, he 'knows' Him. Diderot follows suit: 'A single demonstration convinces me more than fifty facts.'[8]

Pascal's rejection of metaphysical demonstrations of God's existence is thus interpreted by his philosophical enemies as an admission of uncertainty: D'Alembert (1772–6) opposes Pascal's 'Christian thoughts' to his 'philosophical principles', and Condorcet (1776, 1778) adopts the same principle, confirming the triumph of Malebranchist rationalism and the defeat of Pascalian apologetics.

The very hostile reception of Pascal's work in the eighteenth century can thus be read as the direct consequence of the confusion which reigned in the original edition of the *Pensées* and of the criticism of Pascal's apology in the works of two attentive readers, Malebranche and Bayle.

NOTES

1. See Pintard 1983.
2. Gouhier 1978.
3. N. Malebranche, *Oeuvres completes*, ed. A. Robinet (Paris: Vrin, 1958–69), II, 52. All references will be to this edition.
4. ibid., XII, 33–4.
5. ibid., XII, 220.
6. Voltaire, *Lettres philosophiques* (1734), XXV, *remarque* 11.
7. P. Bayle, *Dictionnaire historique et critique* (Rotterdam, 1697, 1702).
8. Diderot, *Pensées philosophiques* (1746), no. 50.

BIBLIOGRAPHY

TEXTS AND EDITIONS: PASCAL

Brunschwicg, L., Boutroux, P. and Gazier, F. (eds.), *Oeuvres complètes*, 14 vols. (Paris: Hachette, 1904–25)

Ferreyrolles, G. and Sellier, P. (ed.), *Pensées* (Paris: Livre de Poche, 2000)

Krailsheimer, A. J. (trans.), *Lettres provinciales* (Harmondsworth: Penguin, 1967)

Krailsheimer, A. J. (trans.), *Pensées* (Harmondsworth: Penguin, 1966)

Lafuma, L. (ed.), *Oeuvres complètes* (Paris: Seuil, 1963)

Le Guern, M. (ed.), *Oeuvres complètes*, 2 vols. (Paris: Gallimard, 1998–2000)

Levi, H. (trans.), *Pensées and other writings* (Oxford: Oxford University Press, 1995)

Mesnard, J. (ed.), *Oeuvres complètes*, 4 vols. (Paris: Desclée de Brouwer, 1964–92)

Pascal, B., *Pensées sur la religion et sur quelques autres sujets* (Paris: G. Desprez, 1670, 1678; Amsterdam: Wolfgang, 1684: designated as the 'Port-Royal edition')

TEXTS AND EDITIONS: OTHER PRE-TWENTIETH-CENTURY WRITERS

Alembert, J., Le Rond d', *Eloge de l'abbé Houtteville* (composed between 1772 and 1776), published in *Oeuvres complètes*, vol. III (Paris, 1821)

Arnauld, A., *Oeuvres*, ed. G. Du Pac de Bellegarde and J. Hautefage, 42 vols. (Paris: Sigismond d'Arnay, 1775–81)

Arnauld, A., Nicole, P., *La Logique, ou l'art de penser*, Paris, 1662, ed. P. Clair and F. Girbal (Paris: Vrin, 1981)

Arnauld, A. and Nicole, P., *Logic, or the Art of Thinking*, trans. and ed. J. V. Buroker (Cambridge: Cambridge University Press, 1996)

Arnauld, A. and Nicole, P., *La Perpétuité de la foi de l'église catholique touchant l'eucharistie*, 3 vols. (Paris, 1669–74)

Bayle, P., *Continuation des pensées diverses* (Rotterdam: Reinier Leers, 1705)

Bayle, P., *Dictionnaire historique et critique* (Rotterdam: Reinier Leers, 1697, 1702)

Bayle, P., *Nouvelles de la République des Lettres* (Rotterdam, 1684–7)

Berkeley, G., *The Works of George Berkeley, Bishop of Cloyne*, 4 vols. (Edinburgh and London: Nelson, 1949)

Boyle, R., *The Works of Robert Boyle*, ed. M. Hunter and E. B. Davis (London: Pickering and Chatto, 1999)

Calvin, J., *Institution de la religion chrétienne*, ed. J.-D. Benoît, 5 vols. (Paris: Vrin, 1957–63)

Challe, R., *Difficultés sur la religion proposées au Père Malebranche* (composed between 1711 and 1720), (published 'London' [Amsterdam: Marc-Michel Rey], 1768)

Cicero, *The Nature of the Gods*, trans. H. C. P. McGregor (Harmondsworth: Penguin, 1972)

Condorcet, J.-A.-N. de Caritat, marquis de, *Eloge et pensées de Pascal* (Paris, 1776), (in collaboration with Voltaire, 1778)

Cousin, V. M., *Fragments de philosophie cartésienne* (Paris: Didier, 1856)

Coustel, P., *Les Règles de l'éducation des enfants*, 2 vols. (Paris: Estienne Michallet, 1687)

Cyrano de Bergerac, S. de, *Oeuvres diverses* (Paris, 1654, 1661–2)

Descartes, R., *Discourse on Method and the Meditations*, trans. F. E. Sutcliffe (Harmondsworth: Penguin, 1971)

Descartes, R., *Méditations métaphysiques* (French translation with Gassendi's *Objections*, 1647)

Descartes, R., *Oeuvres*, ed. C. Adam and P. Tannery, 12 vols. (Paris: Vrin/ CNRS, 1964–76)

Descartes, R., *Oeuvres et lettres*, ed. A. Bridoux (Paris: Gallimard, 1953)

Descartes, R., *The Philosophical Writings of Descartes*, ed. and trans. J. G. Cottingham, R. Stoothof and D. Murdoch, 2 vols. (Cambridge: Cambridge University Press, 1985)

Diderot, D., 'Entretien d'un philosophe avec la maréchale de***', in Suard et Bourlet de Vauxcelles, *Opuscules philosophiques et littéraires* (Paris, 1796)

Diderot, D., *Pensées philosophiques* (n.p., 1746)

Filleau de La Chaise, Nicolas, *Discours sur les Pensées de M. Pascal* (Paris: G. Desprez, 1672)

Fontenelle, B., Le Bouyer de, *La République des philosophes, ou l'histoire des Ajaoiens* (Geneva, 1768) (composé vers 1684)

Fontenelle, B., Le Bouyer de, *Du Bonheur* (n.p., 1714; Paris, 1724)

Fontenelle, B., Le Bouyer de, *Réflexions sur l'argument de M. Pascal et de M. Locke concernant la possibilité d'une autre vie à venir*, Arsenal MS 2557, published in *Nouvelles libertés de penser* (Amsterdam, 1743) (attribution unknown)

Garasse, François, *La Doctrine curieuse des Beaux esprits de ce temps ou prétendus tels, contenant plusieurs maximes pernicieuses à la religion, à l'estat et aux bonnes mœurs, combattue et renversée par le Père François Garassus* (Paris, 1623–4)

Houtteville, abbé C.-F., *La Religion chrétienne prouvée par les faits* (Paris, 1722)

Jansenius, C., *Augustinus* (Rouen: Jean Berthelin, 1643)

La Bruyere, *Oeuvres complètes*, ed. J. Benda (Paris: Pléiade, 1957)

Leibniz, G. W. L., *Mathematische Schriften*, ed. C. I. Gerhardt (Berlin, 1849–63)

Locke, J., *An Essay Concerning Human Understanding*, ed. P. H. Nidditch (Oxford: Clarendon Press, 1970)

Luther, M., *Luthers Werke in Auswahl*, ed. O. Clemen, 4 vols. (Berlin: De Gruyter, 1966–7)

Malebranche, N., *Conversations chrétiennes* (Mons, 1677)

Malebranche, N., *De la recherche de la vérité* (Paris, 1674–5)

Malebranche, N., *Oeuvres complètes*, ed. André Robinet (Paris: Vrin, 1958–69).

Malebranche, N., *Traité de morale* (Rotterdam, 1684)

Méré, Antoine Gombaud, chevalier de, *Les Agrémens* (Paris, 1677)

Méré, Antoine Gombaud, chevalier de, *Les Conversations* (Paris, 1668, 1671)

Méré, Antoine Gombaud, chevalier de, *De la conversation* (Paris, 1677)

Mersenne, M., *Correspondance du P. Marin Mersenne*, ed. C. de Waard and A. Beaulieu (Paris: CNRS, 1969–88)

Molina, L. de, *Liberi arbitrii concordia cum gratiae donis, divina praescientia, providentia, praedestinatione et reprobatione*, 1588, 3rd edn (Antwerp: Joachim Trognaesius, 1609)

Montaigne, M. de, *Essais*, Bordeaux, 1580, 3 vols., ed. A. Micha (Paris: Garnier Flammarion, 1969)

Montaigne, M. de, *The Complete Essays*, trans. M. A. Screech (Harmondsworth: Penguin, 1991)

Nicole, P., *De l'éducation d'un prince* (Paris: veuve Charles Savreux, 1670)

Nicole, P., *De la foi humaine* (Paris, 1664)

Nicole, P., *Essais de morale* (Paris, 1671) and years following)

La Nouvelle Moysade, Aix-en-Provence, Méjanes, MS 10 (703) (composed 1734?, published 'London', 1765, 1775)

Pope, A., *Essay on Man* (London, 1733–4)

Racine, J., *Abrégé de l'histoire de Port-Royal*, ed. A. Couprie (Paris: La Table Ronde, 1994)

Saint-Cyran, Jean-Ambroise Onvergier de Hauranne, abbé de, *La Somme des fautes et faussetés capitales contenues en la Somme théologique du P. fr. Garasse* (Paris, 1626)

Saint-Pierre, C.-I. Castel de, *Oeuvres diverses* (Paris, 1730)

Suárez, F., *Disputationes metaphysicae*, 1585, in *Disputaciones metafísicas*, ed. and trans. S. Rábade Romeo, S. Caballero Sánchez and A. Puigcerver (Madrid: Gredos, 1960)

Todhunter, I., *A History of the Mathematical Theory of Probability* (London: Macmillan, 1865)

Voltaire, *Lettres philosophiques* ([Rouen], 1734)

Zanón, *Biblioteca hispánica de filosofía*, 7 vols. (Madrid: Gredos, 1960)

BOOKS AND ARTICLES PUBLISHED AFTER 1900

Ainslie, G., 1992. *Picoeconomics*. Cambridge: Cambridge University Press

Akagi, S., 1964. 'Les Pensées fondamentales de la physique pascalienne et leur originalité'. *Etudes de Langue et Littérature Françaises* 4: 20–36

Akagi, S., 1967, 1968, 1969. 'Pascal et le problème du vide'. *Osaka Daigaku Kyoyobu. Kenkyn Shoroku: Gaikokug Gaikoku Bungaku* 3, 4, 5: 185–202, 170–84, 109–49

Attali, Jacques. 2000. *Blaise Pascal on le génie français*. Paris: Fayard

Auger, L., 1962. *Un savant méconnu: Gilles Personne de Roberval (1602–1675)*. Paris: Librairie Scientifique, A. Blanchard

Baird, W. S., 1964. 'La Méthode de Pascal en physique'. In R. Taton (ed.), *The Beginnings of Modern Science: from 1450–1800*, trans. A. J. Pomerans. London: Thomes & Hudson

Bergler, E., 1957. *The Psychology of Gambling*. n.p.: International Universities Press

Birault, H., 1964. 'Science et métaphysique chez Descartes et chez Pascal'. *Archives de Philosophie* 27: 483–526

Blanchet, L., 1919. 'L'Attitude religieuse des Jésuites et les sources du pari de Pascal'. *Revue de Métaphysique et de Morale* 26: 477–516 & 617–47

Bloch, O. R., 1971. *La Philosophie de Gassendi*. The Hague: Martinus Nijhoff

Bold, S. C., 1996. *Pascal Geometer. Discovery and Invention in Seventeenth-Century France*. Geneva: Droz

Bostrom, N., 2001. 'Existential Risks: Analyzing Human Extinction Scenarios and Related Hazards'. www.nickbostrom.com/existential/risks.html

Briggs, R., 1977. *Early Modern France, 1560–1715*. Oxford: Oxford University Press

Briggs, R., 1978. 'The Catholic Puritans: Jansenists and Rigorists in France'. In D. Pennington and K. Thomas (eds.), *Puritans and Revolutionaries in France*. Oxford: Oxford University Press

Carraud, V., 1992. *Pascal et Descartes*. Paris: Presses Universitaires de France

Cognet, Louis 1961. *Le Jansénism*. Paris: Presses Universitaires de France

Conant, J. B., 1957. 'Robert Boyle's Experiments in Pneumatics'. *Harvard Case Studies in Experimental Science* 1: 1–63

Croquette, B., 1974. *Pascal et Montaigne: étude des réminiscences des essais dans l'œuvre de Pascal*. Geneva: Droz

Daston, L., 1988. *Classical Probability in the Enlightenment*. Princeton: Princeton University Press

David, F. N., 1962. *Gods, Games and Gambling*. London: Griffin

Davidson, H. M., 1979. *The Origins of Certainty: Means and Meanings in Pascal's 'Pensées'*. Chicago: University of Chicago Press

Davidson, H. M., 1993. *Pascal and the Arts of the Mind*. Cambridge: Cambridge University Press

Dear, P., 1988. *Mersenne and the Learning of the Schools*. Ithaca, NY: Cornell University Press

Dear, P., 1995. *Discipline and Experience: The Mathematical Way in the Scientific Revolution*. Chicago: University of Chicago Press

Denzinger, H. and Schönmetzer, A. 1973. *Enchiridion symbolorum, definitionum et declarationum de rebus fidei et morum*. 35th edn, Barcelona, Freiburg-in-Breisgau, Rome, New York: Herder

Descotes, D., 1993. *L'Argumentation chez Pascal*. Paris: Presses Universitaires de France

De Waard, C., 1936. *L'Expérience barométrique*. Thouars: Deux-Sèvres

Duchêne, R., 1985. *L'Imposture littéraire dans les* Lettres provinciales *de Pascal*. Aix-Marseilles: Université de Provence

Dugas, R., 1958. *Mechanics in the Seventeenth Century*, trans. F. Jacquot. Neuchatel: Editions du Griffon

Duhem, P., 1905. 'Le Principe de Pascal'. *Revue Générale des Sciences Pures et Appliquées* 16: 599–610

Duhem, P., 1906. 'Le P. Marin Mersenne et la pesanteur de l'air'. *Revue Générale des Sciences* 17: 769–82, 809–17

Edwards, A. W. F., 1982. 'Pascal and the Problem of Points'. *International Statistical Review* 50: 259–66

Edwards, A. W. F., 1983. 'Pascal's Problem: The "Gambler's Ruin"'. *International Statistical Review* 51: 73–9

Edwards, A. W. F., 1987/2002. *Pascal's Arithmetical Triangle*. London: Griffin; Oxford: Oxford University Press; Baltimore, MD: Johns Hopkins University Press

Elster, J., 1975. *Leibniz et la formation de l'esprit capitaliste*. Paris: Aubier-Montaigne

Elster, J., 1982. *Sour Grapes*. Cambridge: Cambridge University Press

Elster, J., 1989. *The Cement of Society*. Cambridge: Cambridge University Press

Elster, J., 1999. 'Gambling and Addiction'. In J. Elster and O.-J. Skog (eds.), *Getting Hooked: Rationality and Addiction*. Cambridge: Cambridge University Press

Elster, J. (forthcoming), 'Emotions and Rationality'. In A. S. R. Manstead, N. H. Frijda and A. H. Fischer (eds.), *Feelings and Emotions: The Amsterdam Symposium*. Cambridge: Cambridge University Press

Ernst, P., 1970. *Approches pascaliennes*. Gembloux: Ducolot

Ernst, P., 1996. *Les Pensées de Pascal: géologie et stratigraphie*. Paris: Voltaire Foundation

Fanton d'Andon, J.-P., 1978. *L'Horreur du vide: expérience et raison dans la physique pascalienne*. Paris: Editions du Centre National de la Recherche Scientifique

Ferreyrolles, G., 1984a. *Blaise Pascal: les provinciales*. Paris: Presses Universitaires de France

Ferreyrolles, G., 1984b. *Pascal et la raison du politique*. Paris: Presses Universitaires de France

Ferreyrolles, G., 1995. *Les Reines du monde. L'imagination et la coutume chez Pascal*. Paris: Champion

Force, P., 1989. *Le Problème herméneutique chez Pascal*. Paris: Vrin

Franklin, J., 2001. *The Science of Conjecture: Evidence and Probability Before Pascal*. Baltimore, MD: Johns Hopkins University Press

Fraser, G. S., 1952 (trans). *Pascal, His Life and Works*. London: Harvill

Garber, D., 1992. *Descartes' Metaphysical Physics*. Chicago: University of Chicago Press

Gilby, E., 2001. 'Reflexivity in the *Pensées:* Pascal's Discaire on Discourse'. *French Studies* 55.3: 315–26

Gouhier, H., 1971. *Pascal: Commentaries*. Paris: Vrin

Gouhier, H., 1974. *Pascal et les humanistes chrétiens: l'affaire Saint-Ange*. Paris: Vrin

Gouhier, H., 1978. *Cartésianisme et augustinisme au XVIIe siècle*. Paris: Vrin

Gouhier, H., 1986. *Blaise Pascal: conversion et apologétique*. Paris: Vrin

Grant, E., 1981. *Much Ado About Nothing: Theories of Space and Vacuum from the Middle Ages to the Scientific Revolution*. Cambridge: Cambridge University Press

Guenancia, P., 1976. *Du vide à dieu: essai sur la physique de Pascal*. Paris: F. Maspero.

Guenancia, P., 1979. 'Pascal et la "méthode expérimentale"'. In *Méthodes chez Pascal*: 121–8.

Hacking, I., 1975. *The Emergence of Probability*. Cambridge: Cambridge University Press.

Hald, A., 1990. *A History of Probability and Statistics and their Applications Before 1750*. New York: Wiley

Hammond, N., 1994. *Playing with Truth: Language and the Human Condition in Pascal's* Pensées. Oxford: Clarendon Press

Hammond, N., 2002. 'L'Illusion de la parole chez Pascal'. *Littératures Classiques* 44: 305–11

Harrington, T. M., 1982. *Pascal philosophe: une étude unitaire de la pensée de Pascal*. Paris: SEDES

Humbert, P., 1947. *Cet effrayant génie. L'œuvre scientifique de Blaise Pascal*. Paris: Albin Michel

Jones, M., 2001. 'Writing and *Sentiment*: Blaise Pascal, the Vacuum, and the *Pensées*'. *Studies in History and Philosophy of Science* 32.1: 139–81

Keynes, J. M., 1921. *A Treatise on Probability*. New York: Harper & Row

Kim, H.-K., 1992. *De l'art de persuader dans les pensées de Pascal*. Paris: Nizet

Koch, E., 1997. *Pascal and Rhetoric*. Charlottesville, VA: Rookwood Press

Kolakowski, L., 1995. *God Owes Us Nothing*. Chicago: University of Chicago Press

Koyré, M. A., 1956. 'Pascal savant'. In *Cahiers de Royaumont, No. 1, Blaise Pascal; l'homme et l'œuvre*. Paris: Editions de Minuit

Koyré, M. A., 1968. *Metaphysics and Measurement*. Cambridge, MA: Harvard University Press

Lafond, J., 1977. *La Rochefoucauld: augustinisme et littérature*. Paris: Klincksieck

Laporte, J., 1950. *Le Cœur et la raison selon Pascal*. Paris: Elsevir

Lazzeri, C., 1993. *Force et justice dans la politique de Pascal*. Paris: Presses Universitaires de France

Le Guern, M., 1969. *L'Image dans l'œuvre de Pascal*. Paris: Armand Colin

Le Guern, M., 1971. *Pascal et Descartes*. Paris: Nizet

Lenoble, R., 1971. *Mersenne ou la naissance du mécanisme*. Paris: Vrin

Loeffel, H., 1987. *Blaise Pascal 1623–1662*. Basel: Birkhäuser

Manson, N., 1999. 'The Precautionary Principle, the Catastrophic Argument, and Pascal's Wager'. In *Ends and Means*: 412–16

Marin, L., 1975. *La Critique du discours. Sur la 'Logique de Port-Royal' et les 'Pensées' de Pascal*. Paris: Minuit

Martin, M., 1983. 'Pascal's Wager as an Argument for not Believing in God'. *Religious Studies* 19: 57–64

McFarlane, I. D. and McLean, I. (eds.) 1982. *Montaigne: Essays in Memory of Richard Sayce*. Oxford: Clarendon Press

McKenna, A., 1990. 'De Pascal à Voltaire: le rôle des *Pensées* de Pascal dans l'histoire des idées entre 1670 et 1734'. In *Studies on Voltaire and the Eighteenth Century*. Oxford: Voltaire Foundation.

Mesnard, J., 1951. *Pascal, l'homme et l'œuvre*. Paris: Boivin. Rev. 5th edn, Paris: Hatier, 1967

Mesnard, J., 1976. *Les Pensées de Pascal*. Paris: CDU-SEDES

Méthodes chez Pascal. 1979. Paris: Presses Universitaires de France

Middleton, W. E. K., 1964. *The History of the Barometer*. Baltimore, MA: Johns Hopkins University Press

Miel, J., 1969. *Pascal and Theology*. Baltimore, MD: Johns Hopkins University Press

Morel, J., 1986. *Littérature française: de Montaigne à Corneille*. Paris: Arthaud

Morris, T., 1986. 'Pascalian Wagering'. *Canadian Journal of Philosophy* 16: 437–54

Neveu, B., 1994. 'Le Statut théologique de saint Augustin au XVIIe siècle'. In *Erudition et religion aux XVIIe et XVIIIe siècles*. Paris: Albin Michel

Norman, B., 1988. *Portraits of Thought: Knowledge, Methods and Styles in Pascal*. Columbus: Ohio State University Press

O'Connell, M. R., 1997. *Blaise Pascal: Reasons of the Heart*. Grand Rapids, MI: Eedermans

Ore, O., 1960. 'Pascal and the Invention of Probability Theory'. *American Mathematical Monthly* 67: 409–19

Parish, R., 1989. *Pascal's* Lettres provinciales: *a Study in Polemic*. Oxford: Clarendon Press

Pasqua, H., 2000. *Blaise Pascal, penseur de la grâce*. Paris: Téqui

Pintard, R., 1983 (1943). *Le Libertinage érudit dans la première moitié du XVIIe siècle*. Geneva: Droz

Poulet, G., 1950–68. *Etudes sur le temps humain*. 4 vols. Paris: Plon

Pugh, A. R., 1984. *The Composition of Pascal's Apologia*. Toronto: University of Toronto Press

Quattrone, G. and Tversky, A. 1986. 'Self-Deception and the Voter's Illusion'. In J. Elster (ed.), *The Multiple Self*. Cambridge: Cambridge University Press

Quine, W. V. O., 1953 (1980). *From a Logical Point of View*. Cambridge, MA: Harvard University Press

Robinson, A., 1966. *Non-Standard Analysis*. Amsterdam: North Holland

Rochot, B., 1964. 'Comment Gassendi interprétait l'expérience du puy de Dôme'. In R. Taton (ed.), *L'Oeuvre scientifique de Pascal*, Paris: Presses Universitaires de France

Saka, P., 2001. 'Pascal's Wager and the Many Gods Objection'. *Religious Studies* 37: 321–41

Sayce, R. A. and Maskell, D. 1983. *A Descriptive Bibliography of Montaigne's Essais 1580–1700*. Oxford: Alden Press

Scriven, N., 1966. *Primary Philosophy*. New York: McGraw Hill

Sedgwick, A., 1977. *Jansenism in Seventeenth-Century France*. Charlottesville: University Press of Virginia

Sellier, P., 1966. *Pascal et la liturgie*. Paris: Presses Universitaires de France

Sellier, P., 1970. *Pascal et saint Augustin*. Paris: Armand Colin

Shapin, S. and Schaffer, S. 1985. *Leviathan and the Air-Pump: Hobbes, Boyle, and the Experimental Life*. Princeton, NJ: Princeton University Press

Smith, G. V., 1986. 'Prophecy, False'. *International Standard Bible Encyclopedia*. Grand Rapids, MI: Eerdmans

Strotz, R. H., 1955–6. 'Myopia and Inconsistency in Dynamic Utility Maximization'. *Review of Economic Studies* 23: 165–80

Strowski, F., 1921–2. *Pascal et son temps*. Paris: Plon-Nourrit

Tanner, M., 1976–7. 'Sentimentality'. *Proceedings of the Aristotelian Society* 77: 127–47

Tapié, V. L., 1952/1984. *La France de Louis XIII et de Richelieu*. Paris: Flammarion. Trans D. M. Lockie, *France in the Age of Louis XIII and Richelieu*. Cambridge: Cambridge University Press

Thirion, J., 1907, 1908, 1909. 'Pascal, L'horreur du vide et la pression atmosphérique'. *Revue des Questions Scientifiques* 12: 383–450; 13: 149–251; 15: 149–201

Thirouin, L., 1991. *Le Hasard et les règles. Le modèle du jeu dans la pensée de Pascal*. Paris: Vrin

Thirouin, L., 1994. 'Le Défaut d'une droite méthode'. *Littératures Classiques* 20: 7–21

Topliss, P., 1966. *The Rhetoric of Pascal*. Leicester: Leicester University Press

Weber, M., 1958. *The Protestant Ethic and the Spirit of Capitalism*. New York: Scribner

Wetsel, D., 1981. *L'Ecriture et le reste: the* Pensées *of Pascal in the Exegetical Tradition of Port-Royal*. Columbus: Ohio State University Press

Wetsel, D., 1994. *Pascal and Disbelief*. Washington, DC: Catholic University of America Press

Williams, B. A. O., 1973. 'Deciding to Believe'. In *Problems of the Self*. Cambridge: Cambridge University Press

INDEX

273

For EU product safety concerns, contact us at Calle de José Abascal, 56–1°, 28003 Madrid, Spain or eugpsr@cambridge.org.

www.ingramcontent.com/pod-product-compliance
Ingram Content Group UK Ltd.
Pitfield, Milton Keynes, MK11 3LW, UK
UKHW020337140625
459647UK00018B/2197